AUTOCAD® CIVIL 3D® 2013

ESSENTIALS

Eric Chappell

WILEY

John Wiley & Sons, Inc.

Senior Acquisitions Editor: Willem Knibbe
Development Editor: Kelly Talbot
Technical Editor: Joshua Modglin
Production Editor: Rebecca Anderson
Copy Editor: Linda Recktenwald
Editorial Manager: Pete Gaughan
Production Manager: Tim Tate
Vice President and Executive Group Publisher: Richard Swadley
Vice President and Publisher: Neil Edde
Book Designer: Happenstance Type-O-Rama
Compositor: Craig W. Johnson, Happenstance Type-O-Rama
Proofreader: Jen Larsen, Word One New York
Indexer: Ted Laux
Project Coordinator, Cover: Katherine Crocker
Cover Designer: Ryan Sneed
Cover Image: © Tony Marinella

Dear Reader,

Thank you for choosing *AutoCAD® Civil 3D® 2013 Essentials*. This book is part of a family of premium-quality Sybex books, all of which are written by outstanding authors who combine practical experience with a gift for teaching.

Sybex was founded in 1976. More than 30 years later, we're still committed to producing consistently exceptional books. With each of our titles, we're working hard to set a new standard for the industry. From the paper we print on, to the authors we work with, our goal is to bring you the best books available.

I hope you see all that reflected in these pages. I'd be very interested to hear your comments and get your feedback on how we're doing. Feel free to let me know what you think about this or any other Sybex book by sending me an email at nedde@wiley.com. If you think you've found a technical error in this book, please visit http://sybex.custhelp.com. Customer feedback is critical to our efforts at Sybex.

Best regards,

NEIL EDDE
Vice President and Publisher
Sybex, an Imprint of Wiley

To my parents, Red and Verna Chappell

ACKNOWLEDGMENTS

It is the second year for this book and I feel honored and privileged to be able to put it out there yet another time. Of course, this was a team effort, and I would like to thank the great folks at Wiley/Sybex for making it so much better than I could have made it by myself. To Willem Knibbe, thanks for being my sounding board, go-to person, and filling many other roles that were so vital in keeping things moving and keeping the communication going between the editing team and me. To Kelly Talbot, Becca Anderson, and Linda Recktenwald, thanks for putting up with me and providing top-notch editing to make the book great. To Joshua Modglin, thanks for serving as technical editor and for providing the peace of mind of knowing that the technical aspects of the book were in capable hands.

In last year's book, I acknowledged people from long ago who helped me along the way so that I could get where I needed to go. This time around, I wanted to acknowledge the people who keep me going in the present, the amazing Civil 3D community that is so generous and helpful, every day. There are too many to mention all of you, but the ones who stand out in my mind are Matt Anderson, Cyndy Davenport, Angel Espinoza, John Evans, David Garrigues, Donnie Gladfelter, Jason Hickey, Louisa Holland, Alan Jones, Kati Mercier, Curt Moreno, Melanie Perry, Lisa Pohlmeyer, Dana Probert, Mark Scacco, Ishka Voiculescu, James Wedding, and Edward Winter. There are many more. It's great to know that help is always a tweet away.

And of course, without the love, encouragement, understanding, help, and support of my wonderful wife Dixie, none of this, and a whole lot of other stuff, would be possible for me. Dixie, thank you. I love you.

ABOUT THE AUTHOR

*Eric Chappell has been* working, teaching, writing, and consulting in the world of civil engineering software for over 20 years and is a recognized expert in the world of AutoCAD® Civil 3D® software. Over the past 11 years, he has written training materials and performed training for end users, trainers, and Autodesk employees around the globe. He is the author of the AutoCAD Civil 3D Assessment, Certified Associate, and Certified Professional exams.

He is also the design systems manager for Timmons Group, a civil engineering and surveying firm based in Richmond, Virginia, where he manages software, standards, and training for over 200 users. In addition, Eric is a consultant for Engineered Efficiency, where he has authored and edited a myriad of Civil 3D tutorials and training materials. Among these materials are training manuals for Engineered Efficiency clients, Autodesk official training publications, and internal training manuals for Autodesk staff. Eric is also a highly rated instructor at Autodesk University, where he has taught for the past eight years.

Prior to writing and consulting, Eric spent nearly 10 years in the civil engineering and surveying fields while working for the H.F. Lenz Company in Johnstown, Pennsylvania. During his time at H.F. Lenz, he gained considerable practical experience as a survey crewman, designer, engineer, and CAD supervisor. Eric also holds a B.S. degree in civil engineering technology from the University of Pittsburgh at Johnstown and is certified in Pennsylvania as an EIT.

Eric is originally from southwestern Pennsylvania but has lived in the Richmond, Virginia, area for the past 11 years with his wife and four children. He enjoys playing music, being outdoors, and spending time with his family.

If you would like to contact the author regarding comments or suggestions, please email CivilEssentials@gmail.com. You are also welcome to visit Eric's blog at http://ericchappell.blogspot.com.

Contents at a Glance

CONTENTS

CHAPTER 14   Designing Pipe Networks   251

CHAPTER 15   Displaying and Annotating Pipe Networks   287

INTRODUCTION

When the first version of this book was born just over a year ago, my hope was for it to be one book in a long and successful series that will educate, inspire, and even excite many people about the use of AutoCAD® Civil 3D®. In order to do all this, I decided that each book in the series has to meet the following criteria:

- ▶ It should be basic enough to enable *anyone* to learn Civil 3D.

- ▶ It should be in-depth enough to enable a person to be productive using Civil 3D for basic tasks.

- ▶ It should foster understanding by associating the things you do in Civil 3D with familiar things that you see every day.

- ▶ The examples and exercises should be based on the real world.

- ▶ The book should not simply demonstrate random software features but should teach the process of project completion using Civil 3D.

Since last year's version was released, I have received tons of great feedback about how well this book functions in many learning environments. I have also used the book myself to teach classes in a corporate environment, and I am very pleased with how it performs. I am confident that the goals listed above have been met, and for that reason I have held to the same writing style, format, and delivery that proved to be so successful in last year's version.

As you work your way through the book, either as a teacher, student, or end user, you will find that the first two chapters, although very important, are more general and introductory. After that, you are going to take a journey through the completion of a residential land development project—start to finish. In fact, the example project is based on a residential development that was built about 10 years ago, not far from my home. The topics are presented as though you have never touched a CAD program before, and wherever possible, there are sidebars and other forms of augmentation that relate what you're doing to the real world.

You will also find that as I wrote this book, I tried to sympathize with future readers by thinking back to my college days when I was learning about surveying and civil engineering for the first time. There were many times when I felt frustrated and lost because I was learning many new and foreign concepts and did not see how they related to the real world. I can remember being out in the field during my surveying class—looking through the survey instrument, writing down measurements, and having no idea why. That was not an enjoyable feeling and not one that I want you to experience as you learn the new and foreign concepts in this book. Eventually, I learned all about surveying and now have an in-depth understanding of how those measurements relate to designing and building roads, buildings, and other things—but it took many years. It is my sincerest hope that this book gives you a head start on some of those types of concepts, while at the same time relating them to Civil 3D in ways that hit home for you.

What's New In This Book?

If you already own *AutoCAD Civil 3D 2012 Essentials*, you'll be happy to know that *AutoCAD Civil 3D 2013 Essentials* has been updated to address the major new features in AutoCAD Civil 3D 2013. The most prominent new features are pressure pipe design and some changes to the workflow of corridor design, both of which are addressed in detail in this book. In addition, the entire book has been reviewed and updated to be consistent with any changes to the 2013 user interface or command structure.

Another exciting change is that videos have been made available that show the author completing the exercises in "The Essentials and Beyond" sections at the end of each chapter. You can access these videos at www.sybex.com/go/civil2013essentials and use them to compare your results with the author's and gain some additional insight about alternate ways to apply what you've learned.

Who Should Read This Book

This book should be read by anyone who needs or wants to begin learning AutoCAD Civil 3D. It is appropriate for ages ranging from high school to retirement, and although it is intended for those who have no experience or skills with Civil 3D, it can also serve as a great resource for refreshing one's knowledge base or for filling in any gaps. This book can also be used as a resource for preparing to take the AutoCAD Civil 3D 2013 Certified Professional exam. See www.autodesk.com/certification for more certification information and resources.

In addition to those pursuing a certification, here are some specific examples of individuals who would benefit from this book:

- ▶ High-school students following a design-related educational track
- ▶ College students learning to be designers or engineers
- ▶ Employees who have recently joined a company that utilizes Civil 3D
- ▶ Employees who work for companies that have recently implemented Civil 3D
- ▶ Experienced Civil 3D users who are self-taught and want to fill in gaps in their knowledge base

What You Will Learn

This book covers the basic skills and concepts needed to begin using Civil 3D to design land development projects. The concepts include those related to Civil 3D as well as those related to civil engineering and surveying in general. It does not cover all topics or all Civil 3D features, but it provides a solid foundation that you can use to perform basic tasks and work toward an in-depth understanding of Civil 3D.

The first two chapters will give you a basic understanding of Civil 3D and help you to understand and appreciate how it "thinks." The remaining 16 chapters will teach you how to use the tools that Civil 3D provides to complete a typical land development design project.

What You Need

Specific hardware requirements for running AutoCAD Civil 3D 2013 had not been released as this book went to press. See the Autodesk website (www.autodesk.com) for current requirements.

To perform the exercises in this book, you must have AutoCAD Civil 3D 2013 installed on your computer. It is recommended that you use the default software setup with two exceptions: Change your drawing screen color to white and dock the command line at the bottom of the screen. This book contains many screen captures of Civil 3D drawings, which were all produced with these distinctive changes to the user interface. Also, at times the exercises refer to drawing entities by color, which is sometimes dependent on the background color.

To complete the exercises, you will need to download the necessary files from www.sybex.com/go/civil2013essentials. Here you will find a list of ZIP files, one for each chapter, which you should unzip to the local C: drive of your computer. This will create a folder named Civil 3D 2013 Essentials with the chapter folder inside it. As you unzip additional chapter files, simply merge the new Civil 3D 2013 folder into the old one. The resulting files and folders will appear similar to the following image:

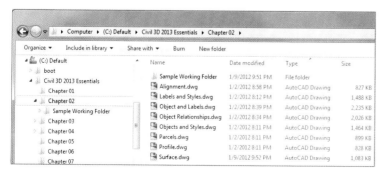

ZIP files are available in imperial and metric units. As you complete the exercises, metric values will be shown in parentheses. The imperial and metric values for a given item are usually *not* equivalent to avoid using irregular values for the design. For example, the value for the width of a sidewalk would be shown as 3′ (1m) even though 3′ does not exactly equal 1m.

Each chapter ends with a section titled "The Essentials and Beyond," which contains an additional exercise. You can find the answers to the additional exercises and completed versions of the exercise drawings by visiting www.sybex.com/go/civil2013essentials. And new for this version of the book, you can visit the same location to view videos of the author completing these exercises.

Finally, be sure to check the book's website for any updates to this book should the need arise. You can also contact the author directly by email at CivilEssentials@gmail.com or visit the author's blog at http://ericchappell.blogspot.com to read even more about the book and Civil 3D in general.

Attention: Instructors

As you know, the best classes start with good preparation, and we've done most of the work for you by providing instructor materials to accompany this book. Please visit www.sybex.com/go/civil2013essentials to download the instructor materials, which contain suggested syllabi, PowerPoint files, additional exercises, and quiz questions that you can use to assist you in making your class a success.

What Is Covered in This Book

AutoCAD Civil 3D 2013 Essentials is organized to provide you with the knowledge needed to master the basics of AutoCAD Civil 3D 2013.

Chapter 1: Navigating the AutoCAD Civil 3D User Interface   Familiarizes you with the Civil 3D environment so that you can navigate more easily within the software.

Chapter 2: Leveraging a Dynamic Environment   Demonstrates the dynamic Civil 3D environment to establish its importance and encourage you to take full advantage of it whenever possible. This chapter focuses on important relationships between different components of a typical design model.

Chapter 3: Establishing Existing Conditions Using Survey Data   Demonstrates how to convert survey field measurements into a Civil 3D drawing while focusing on the *survey* functions of Civil 3D. This chapter covers creating a survey database, importing data, and processing the data to create a map of the project.

Chapter 4: Modeling the Existing Terrain Using Surfaces Demonstrates how to create a model of the existing terrain of the project while focusing on the *surface* functions of Civil 3D. This chapter covers creating a new surface and adding data to it to form a 3D model of the before-construction condition of the project.

Chapter 5: Designing in 2D Using Alignments Demonstrates how to perform basic 2D layout while focusing on the *alignment* functions of Civil 3D. This chapter covers creating alignments, applying design criteria, and editing alignments.

Chapter 6: Displaying and Annotating Alignments Demonstrates how to control the appearance of alignments and provide annotation while focusing on Civil 3D *alignment styles* and *alignment labels*. This chapter covers applying alignment styles, creating alignment labels, and creating alignment tables.

Chapter 7: Designing Vertically Using Profiles Demonstrates how to design the vertical aspect of a linear feature while focusing on the *profile* functions of Civil 3D. This chapter covers creating profiles, applying design criteria, editing profiles, and displaying profiles in profile views.

Chapter 8: Displaying and Annotating Profiles Demonstrates how to control the appearance of profiles and provide annotation while focusing on Civil 3D *profile styles* and *profile labels*. This chapter covers applying profile styles, creating profile labels, and object projection.

Chapter 9: Designing in 3D Using Corridors Demonstrates how to design a 3D model of a linear feature while focusing on the *corridor* functions of Civil 3D. This chapter covers creating assemblies, creating and editing corridors, and creating corridor surfaces.

Chapter 10: Creating Cross Sections of the Design Demonstrates how to generate and display cross sections of your design while focusing on the *sample line* and *section* functions of Civil 3D. This chapter covers creating sample lines, sampling various sources, and creating section views.

Chapter 11: Displaying and Annotating Sections Demonstrates how to control the appearance of sections and provide annotation while focusing on Civil 3D *section styles* and *section labels*. This chapter covers applying section styles, creating section labels, and object projection.

Chapter 12: Designing and Analyzing Boundaries Using Parcels Demonstrates how to design a lot layout for a residential land development project while focusing on the *parcel* functions of Civil 3D. This chapter covers creating and editing parcels.

Chapter 13: Displaying and Annotating Parcels   Demonstrates how to control the appearance of parcels and provide annotation while focusing on Civil 3D *parcel styles* and *parcel labels*. This chapter covers applying parcel styles, creating parcel labels, and creating parcel tables.

Chapter 14: Designing Pipe Networks   Demonstrates how to design underground gravity and pressure pipe systems for a residential land development project while focusing on the *pipe network* and *pressure network* functions of Civil 3D. This chapter covers creating and editing pipe networks and pressure networks.

Chapter 15: Displaying and Annotating Pipe Networks   Demonstrates how to control the appearance of pipe networks and provide annotation while focusing on Civil 3D *pipe styles*, *structure styles*, and *pipe network labels*. This chapter covers displaying pipe networks in profile view, creating pipe network labels, and creating pipe network tables.

Chapter 16: Designing New Terrain   Demonstrates how to design a proposed ground model for a residential land development project while focusing on the *feature line* and *grading* functions of Civil 3D. This chapter covers creating and editing feature lines and grading objects.

Chapter 17: Analyzing, Displaying, and Annotating Surfaces   Demonstrates how to perform surface analysis and display the results as well as annotating design surfaces. This chapter covers managing multiple surfaces, labeling surfaces, and analyzing surfaces.

Chapter 18: From Design to Construction   Demonstrates how to perform quantity analysis while focusing on *QTO* (quantity takeoff) functions and how to create construction documents while focusing on *Plan Production* functions. This chapter covers calculating quantities, creating individual sheets, and creating multiple sheets.

Appendix: AutoCAD Civil 3D 2013 Certification   Provides information about AutoCAD Civil 3D Certification as well as how this book will help you to prepare for the certification exams. This appendix includes specific certification objectives along with where they appear in the book.

Answers to Additional Exercises   Provides instructions on how to complete the additional exercises as well as information on how to locate completed example drawings and online videos that show the author completing the exercises. This appendix is available online at www.sybex.com/go/civil2013essentials.

The Essentials Series

The Essentials series from Sybex provides outstanding instruction for readers who are just beginning to develop their professional skills. Every Essentials book includes these features:

▶ Skill-based instruction with chapters organized around projects rather than abstract concepts or subjects

▶ Suggestions for additional exercises at the end of each chapter, where you can practice and extend your skills

▶ Digital files (via download) so you can work through the project tutorials yourself. Please check the book's web page at www.sybex.com/go/civil2013essentials for these companion downloads.

The certification margin icon will alert you to sections that are especially relevant to AutoCAD Civil 3D 2013 certification. See the certification appendix and www.autodesk.com/certification for more information and resources.

**Certification
Objective**

CHAPTER 1

Navigating the AutoCAD Civil 3D User Interface

If you're new to the AutoCAD® Civil 3D® software environment, then your first experience has probably been a lot like staring at the instrument panel of a 747. Civil 3D can be quite intimidating, with lots of buttons, strange shapes, and strange icons—all packed into a relatively small area. In addition, you may be even more intimidated by the feeling that there is a lot of power under the hood. This leads us to our main objective for this chapter, which is to alleviate that feeling of intimidation and make you feel much more at ease within the Civil 3D environment. Let me start you down that path by saying that there's a big difference between a 747 and Civil 3D. In Civil 3D, if you really mess up, you can simply close the drawing file without saving. When piloting a 747, it's a little more difficult to undo your mistakes.

After completing this chapter, you will have achieved a greater comfort level within the Civil 3D environment by being able to identify main user interface components and utilize them for basic functions. You will also be able to use two specific features that will serve you well throughout the program: the Transparent Commands toolbar and the Inquiry Tool.

▶ **Getting to know the Civil 3D user interface**

▶ **Using the application menu**

▶ **Using the ribbon**

▶ **Using the Toolspace**

▶ **Using the drawing area**

▶ **Using the command line**

▶ **Using Panorama**

▶ **Using the Transparent Commands toolbar**

▶ **Using the Inquiry Tool**

Getting to Know the Civil 3D User Interface

Certification
Objective

To begin learning about the Civil 3D environment, let's take our 747 analogy down a notch and think about this as learning to drive an automobile. When your parents first sat you down at the wheel and talked about the car's controls, they probably didn't mention the air conditioning or the radio. Those, of course, are important parts of the driving experience, but I'm betting they started with the most important parts, such as the steering wheel, the gas pedal, and most important, the brake pedal. We're going to approach your first experience with "driving" Civil 3D in much the same manner.

There are many, many parts to the Civil 3D user interface. For the purposes of this book, I'll cover just the ones that will be most important in enabling you to navigate the software effectively. Figure 1.1 shows the major components of the user interface.

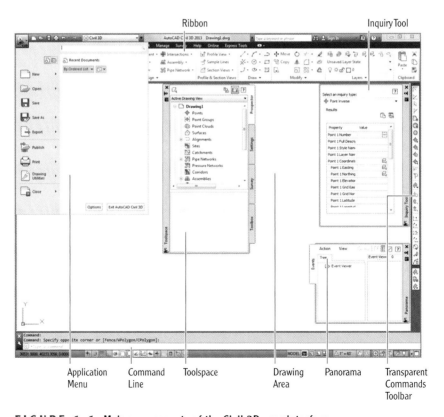

FIGURE 1.1 Major components of the Civil 3D user interface

Application Menu   The place where everyday file handling commands can be found that enable you to do things like open, save, and print your drawings

Ribbon   The place where most Civil 3D commands are launched

Toolspace   The Civil 3D "command center" where all of the data and settings are laid out in an organized fashion

Drawing Area   The place where the drawing is created

Command Line   The chat window where you and Civil 3D talk to one another

Panorama   A multipurpose window where you can view and/or edit drawing information and properties

Inquiry Tool   A tool with many smaller tools within it that enable you to get information about your design

Transparent Commands Toolbar   Special commands that allow drafting and geometric construction to be done the way that civil engineers and surveyors do it

Using the Application Menu

The application menu (Figure 1.2) expands out from the square AutoCAD Civil 3D icon located at the top left of your screen. In previous versions of Civil 3D, this icon was often referred to as "the big red C" but due to its new look, that name will now be "the big purple A." Here you'll find commands for creating, opening, saving, and printing your drawing files.

The Quick Access Toolbar just to the right of the big purple A is a handy subset of your most commonly used general-purpose tools. It can be customized to add more tools if you like.

FIGURE 1.2 Part of the Civil 3D application menu

To use the application menu to open a file, follow these steps:

1. Launch Civil 3D by double-clicking the Civil 3D 2013 Imperial (Metric) icon on the desktop of your computer.

2. Click the application menu icon (the big purple A). Click Open, and then click Drawing.

3. Browse to the Chapter 01 class data folder and open User Interface.dwg.

4. Open the application menu once more and investigate the commands that are listed there. You'll notice that most of them have to do with creating, opening, saving, and printing drawing files.

5. Keep this drawing open for the next exercise.

Using the Ribbon

The ribbon is located at the top of your screen and is the launching pad for most of your Civil 3D commands. The commands that it contains are organized into groups through the use of *tabs and panels*. The ribbon itself is divided into a series of tabs that include Home, Insert, Annotate, and so on, as illustrated in Figure 1.3.

FIGURE 1.3 Tabs arrange large numbers of similar Civil 3D commands into groups.

Each tab is divided into *panels*. For instance, the Home tab shown in Figure 1.4 includes the Palettes, Create Ground Data, Create Design, and Profile & Section Views panels.

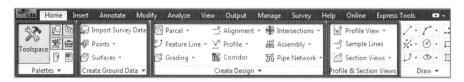

FIGURE 1.4 Panels provide another level of grouping within a ribbon tab.

Because Civil 3D groups the commands in this way, you never have to choose from more than a handful of commands once you've taken your best guess at the correct tab and panel. Also, you'll find that the more you use Civil 3D, the better you will be at knowing where the commands are. It's not so much memorizing their locations as it is learning how Civil 3D "thinks"—that is, the way in which it relates commands to one another and categorizes them into tabs and panels.

One other thing you should know is that most panels expand downward to show you the less frequently used commands in that particular category. You'll know they expand when you see a downward-pointing black triangle next to their name. For example, Figure 1.5 shows the Home tab's Create Design panel expanded with more commands. Don't forget to look on these hidden panels when searching for commands.

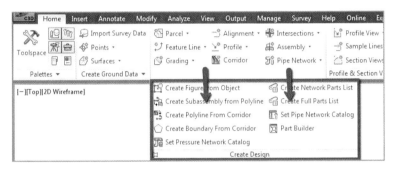

FIGURE 1.5 Most panels expand downward to reveal more commands, as is the case with the Create Design panel on the Home tab of the ribbon.

One of the best features of the ribbon is its ability to respond to what you select in the drawing area. For example, if you click a Civil 3D alignment, the ribbon changes and serves up alignment-related commands on a special tab. The same is true for surfaces, parcels, and so on. These special tabs are referred to as *contextual* ribbon tabs. They are a huge help when you're first learning Civil 3D and a huge time-saver even after you've become a master.

Follow these steps to familiarize yourself with the ribbon's tabs and panels (User Interface.dwg should still be open from the previous exercise):

1. Click the Home tab of the ribbon to bring it to the forefront (it may be already). Notice that there is a mixed assortment of commands here. The Home tab is designed to contain your most heavily used commands. Since you don't yet know what most of the commands mean, the selection of commands could seem kind of random.

2. Click the gray strip at the bottom of the Create Design panel and note how it expands out, as shown in Figure 1.5.

3. Click the Insert tab of the ribbon. Here, you see words like *insert*, *import*, and *attach*—all ways of bringing information into the drawing. The commands here are much more specific to a certain purpose as compared to the randomness of the Home tab.

4. Click the other tabs of the ribbon and see whether you can relate some of the words you see in the commands to the title of each ribbon tab.

5. Place your cursor in the drawing area, and roll the mouse wheel forward to zoom in to the drawing. Keep zooming in until you can clearly see the road centerlines labeled with stationing numbers (these are Civil 3D alignments). Click one of the road centerlines, and note that the ribbon displays a contextual tab to make alignment commands accessible (Figure 1.6).

6. Keep this drawing open for the next exercise.

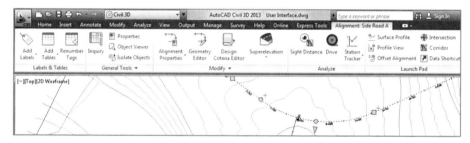

FIGURE 1.6 The ribbon displays the contextual Alignment: Side Road A tab, because an alignment has been selected in the drawing.

Using the Toolspace

Think of the Toolspace as the Civil 3D "command center" where all Civil 3D data and settings are laid out in a nice, orderly arrangement. It has several main functions that are represented by the different tabs it can contain. Altogether, the Toolspace can house four tabs: Prospector, Settings, Survey, and Toolbox.

Prospector Tab

Certification
Objective

Prospector is arguably the most important part of the Civil 3D user interface. As you build your design, Prospector arranges the different components of your design in a tree structure (Figure 1.7). Why a tree structure and not just a list of items? Later in this book, you'll study how Civil 3D creates relationships between different parts of your design. In some ways, this tree structure helps represent some of those relationships as a hierarchy. Another, more practical reason for a tree structure is that it's an efficient way to show a long list of items in a relatively small area—the branches of the tree can be collapsed to make room to expand other branches.

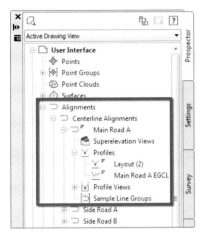

FIGURE 1.7 The Prospector tab with a portion of the tree structure highlighted in red.

Another way to think about Prospector is that it arranges your design categorically rather than spatially. In other words, in your drawing area, you see road centerlines crossing through parcels, which cross through contours, which cross through survey points. Everything is in the right place spatially, but from an organizational standpoint, it's kind of a mess. Prospector sorts out this mess and puts all the points in one place, all the parcels in one place, and so on. Prospector also knows exactly where those objects are in the drawing. You can right-click an object in Prospector and use the Select command or Zoom To command to locate that object within the drawing.

To explore the Prospector tab, follow these steps (you should still have User Interface.dwg open):

1. If the Toolspace is not already open, click Toolspace on the Home tab of the ribbon.

2. Click the Prospector tab of Toolspace to bring it to the forefront.

3. Explore the tree structure of Prospector by clicking the plus signs to expand the different branches.

If the Prospector tab is not visible, click the Home tab of the ribbon, and then click the Prospector icon on the Palettes panel.

4. Expand Alignments ➤ Centerline Alignments ➤ Main Road A ➤ Profiles. This hierarchical arrangement provides effective organization and suggests a relationship between the alignment and its profiles (as described later in the chapter).

5. Right-click Side Road B and select Zoom To. Notice how Prospector knows where the alignment named Side Road B is, even if you don't.

6. Keep this drawing open for the next exercise.

It's important to point out that Prospector isn't just a place for viewing your design; it's also a place where you can change the appearance of your design, create new components for your design, edit your design, and so on. These types of functions are accessed through contextual menus such as the one used in step 5 of the previous exercise. A good rule of thumb when using Prospector is, "When in doubt, right-click it."

Settings Tab

Civil 3D has a lot of settings that control nearly every aspect of how the software behaves. In fact, one of the things that make Civil 3D so powerful is that you can customize its settings to accommodate nearly any type of design, company standard, or any other factor that defines the environment within which you use it. The Settings tab is where these settings are managed; however, you won't be spending much time here for the early part of your Civil 3D career. This area is more often the territory of a CAD manager or Civil 3D guru.

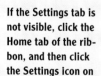

If the Settings tab is not visible, click the Home tab of the ribbon, and then click the Settings icon on the Palettes panel.

To explore the Settings tab, follow these steps (you should still have User Interface.dwg open from the previous exercise):

1. Click the Settings tab of the Toolspace.

2. Expand Surface ➤ Surface Styles and take note of the list of styles shown there. These styles control the appearance of models that represent the shape of the ground.

3. Expand Surface ➤ Label Styles ➤ Contour and take note of the list of styles shown there. These styles control a certain type of label that is used to annotate surface models.

4. Keep this drawing open for the next exercise.

Survey Tab

The Survey tab is specifically for working with survey data. You could call it "Prospector for surveyors," because it serves the same functions and works in much the same way as the Prospector tab. It displays survey data in a tree structure, and it allows you to launch commands through contextual menus.

Toolbox Tab

As if Civil 3D didn't have enough stuff packed into it already, the Toolbox is a place where other add-ons can be plugged in. Your company may have some custom programming that is designed to run in Civil 3D or some add-on modules provided by Autodesk®. This is the place where you can load and run these additional enhancements to Civil 3D.

Using the Drawing Area

The drawing area is where you can actually see and "touch" the design model you are creating. The design model is most often viewed from above, referred to as *plan view*, but it can be viewed from any perspective. For example, because Civil 3D specializes in representing designs as 3D models, you may want to display your model using 3D view. Figure 1.8 shows a model in both plan and 3D views.

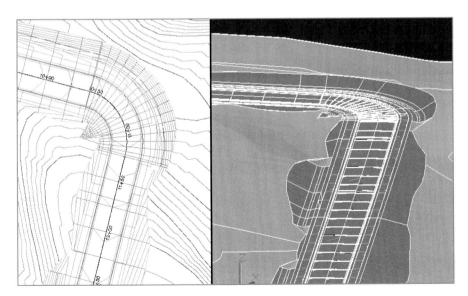

FIGURE 1.8 The drawing area showing the same model in plan view on the left and 3D view on the right

Using the Command Line

Think of the command line (Figure 1.9) as a chat window where you talk with Civil 3D. Nearly everything you do is reported on the command line along with Civil 3D's response to it. A response can be a request for more information, reporting of a result, or notification of a problem. It's good to get into the habit of always watching the command line, because it often tells you what to do next. You can also launch commands from the command line, but you will likely find it much easier to use the visual interface provided by the ribbon and other tools.

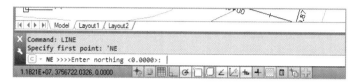

FIGURE 1.9 A view of the command line while using a transparent command (covered later in this chapter) to draw a line. Notice how the command line reports that the LINE command has been started and then prompts for the first piece of information: the "first point."

Using Panorama

Panorama is a multipurpose window that is used to show and/or modify many different types of information. It works by displaying a tab for the information that you or the program has called for. For example, the Events tab (also known as the Event Viewer) will show up when Civil 3D needs to tell you something about the drawing. In another example, if you launch the command to edit the geometric details of an alignment, the Alignment Entities tab will appear. As shown in Figure 1.10, while Panorama displays information for one task, it also displays tabs for other tasks that you can access with a single click. This enables you to multitask within the same window.

No.	Type	Tangency Constraint	Parameter Constrai...	Parameter C...	Length
1	Line	Not Constrained (Fixed)	🔒	Two points	169.723m
2	Curve	Constrained on Both Sides (Free)	🔒	Radius	16.753m
3	Line	Not Constrained (Fixed)	🔒	Two points	122.922m
4	Curve	Constrained on Both Sides (Free)	🔒	Radius	95.756m
5	Line	Not Constrained (Fixed)	🔒	Two points	107.912m
6	Curve	Constrained on Both Sides (Free)	🔒	Radius	42.712m
7	Line	Not Constrained (Fixed)	🔒	Two points	165.035m

FIGURE 1.10 Panorama showing the Events and Alignment Entities tabs

To get a feel for the Panorama window, follow these steps (you should still have User Interface.dwg open from the previous exercise):

1. On the Home tab of the ribbon, expand the Palettes panel and click the icon for Event Viewer.

2. Experiment with resizing, auto-hiding, and docking the Panorama window. You'll find that it behaves much like other dockable windows in Civil 3D.

3. Press Esc to clear any selections in the drawing. Click one of the contour lines in the drawing to display the Tin Surface: Existing Ground ribbon tab, and then click Volumes Dashboard on the Analyze panel. Notice the Volumes Dashboard tab that shows up next to the Events tab in Panorama.

4. Keep this drawing open for the next exercise.

Using the Transparent Commands Toolbar

As you may already know, civil engineers and surveyors draw things a little differently than architects or mechanical engineers. They use things such as bearings, curve deltas, northings, and eastings to define geometry. The Transparent Commands toolbar enables Civil 3D users to draw things based on the special geometric concepts that are unique to civil engineers and surveyors.

For example, when drawing a line, you can use the Northing Easting transparent command to specify the first point and the Bearing Distance transparent command to specify the end point (Figure 1.11).

Certification Objective

Bearing
Distance

Northing
Easting

FIGURE 1.11 The Transparent Commands toolbar with red lines pointing to the Bearing Distance and Northing Easting transparent commands

You can dock and undock the Transparent Command toolbar by dragging the double line at the end of the toolbar to the appropriate location.

To practice using the Transparent Commands toolbar, follow these steps (you should have User Interface.dwg open from the previous exercise):

1. Type **LINE** at the Command: prompt, and press Enter.

2. When prompted to specify the first point, click any point within the drawing.

3. When prompted to specify the next point, click Bearing Distance on the Transparent Commands toolbar. Refer to Figure 1.11 for the location of this command.

4. When prompted for a quadrant, either enter 1 or click in the upper-right quadrant created by the crosshairs on the screen.

5. When prompted for the bearing, type 45 and press Enter.

6. When prompted for the distance, type 500 (150) and press Enter. Press Esc twice to exit the command. You have just drawn a line that is 500 feet (150 meters) long at a bearing of N 45° E.

USING SPECIALIZED LINE AND CURVE COMMANDS

Another Civil 3D feature that enables you to draw like a surveyor or civil engineer is a set of specialized line and curve commands. These commands are mixed in with basic AutoCAD line and curve commands on the Draw panel of the ribbon. You can find specialized line commands by expanding the Line icon to reveal commands like Create Line By Bearing, Create Line By Point # Range, and so on. There is also a Curves icon that expands to reveal commands like Create Curve Through Point and Create Multiple Curves. Finally, there is also a Best Fit icon that expands to include commands for best fit lines and curves. The following image shows the expanded form of the Line, Curve, and Best Fit icons.

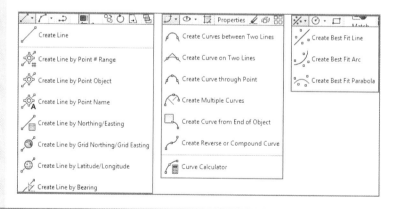

Using the Inquiry Tool

Most of the time, you'll be the one providing the information for a drawing, but sometimes, you need your drawing to tell *you* something. That's where the Inquiry Tool comes in. The Inquiry Tool is a separate window whose sole purpose is to give you information about things in the drawing. There is a long list of drawing items to choose from, and beneath each item is a list of things that you can ask about (Figure 1.12).

Certification Objective

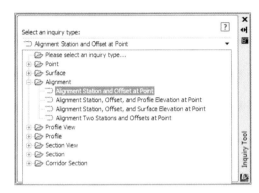

F I G U R E   1 . 1 2   The Inquiry Tool showing a partial list of available inquiry types

To try the Inquiry Tool, follow these steps:

1. On the Analyze tab of the ribbon, click Inquiry Tool.

2. Under Select An Inquiry Type, select Point ➢ Point Inverse.

3. When prompted to specify the first point, hold down the Shift key, right-click, and select Endpoint on the contextual menu that appears.

4. Click the southwestern endpoint of the line you drew earlier.

5. Use the Shift+right-click combination again to select Endpoint, and then click the opposite end of the line for the second point.

6. Scroll down to the Direction and Horizontal Distance values in the Inquiry Tool window. Note that they show the same bearing and distance you entered earlier.

THE ESSENTIALS AND BEYOND

Now that you have learned some of the basic controls, you are ready to take the car for its first spin around the block. As you are guided through more lessons, you will understand how to execute basic tasks such as "turn the wheel" and "step on the brake." You're not ready to navigate the streets of New York City yet, but you've certainly taken a major step.

Of course, driving is just an analogy, and what we're really talking about here is your ability to operate the basic controls of Civil 3D. With the skills and knowledge that you've gained in this chapter, you will be better equipped to execute the tasks in upcoming chapters that deal with specific Civil 3D functions. You'll become more efficient at using the software as you spend more time with it.

ADDITIONAL EXERCISES

1. For each command listed here, what is the name of at least one ribbon tab where it can be found?

   A. Match Properties

   B. Import Survey Data

   C. Add Labels

   D. Inquiry Tool

   E. Elevation Editor

   F. Toolspace

   G. Points From File

2. To practice becoming more fluent within the Civil 3D interface, open the drawing named User Interface 2.dwg, which is located in the Chapter 01 class data folder. Within this drawing, use at least one command or function from each of the following parts of the Civil 3D user interface:

   A. Application menu (this one's easy, because you have to use it to open the drawing)

   B. Command line

   C. Ribbon

   D. Prospector

   E. Transparent Commands

   F. Inquiry Tool

Visit www.sybex.com/go/civil2013essentials to download a video of the author completing this exercise. You can also download the Answers to Additional Exercises Appendix which contains even more information about completing this exercise.

CHAPTER 2

Leveraging a Dynamic Environment

Let's switch back to the 747 analogy again. So far, we've sat down in the cockpit and talked about the most important gauges and controls. In several cases, we've even pushed a few buttons and looked behind a few hidden panels. You now have a greater familiarity with the user interface.

In this chapter, we're going to take the plane for a ride and observe and discuss how it works. How does it turn? How fast can it go? And most important, how do the parts work together? You won't be able to fly solo after completing this chapter, but you will get the experience of applying specific instructions, producing specific results, and discussing those results.

How does this translate to the AutoCAD® Civil 3D® software? Civil 3D has a unique, dynamic environment that is all about leveraging interactions and relationships. When you capitalize on this while you're working with Civil 3D, you will be much more productive and efficient. After completing this chapter, you will already have an advantage over anyone who has learned Civil 3D from another source, because you will understand the dynamic capabilities of the Civil 3D environment and the importance of taking advantage of those capabilities.

- ▶ **Connecting objects and styles**

- ▶ **Connecting labels and label styles**

- ▶ **Connecting objects to objects**

- ▶ **Connecting objects to labels**

- ▶ **The richness of the 3D model**

- ▶ **Sharing data in a dynamic environment**

Connecting Objects and Styles

Certification Objective The word *object* is usually considered pretty generic, but in the world of Civil 3D, it means something very specific. A Civil 3D object is an intelligent piece of your design model that stores information about itself and has the ability to interact with other objects in the drawing. Another characteristic of a Civil 3D object is that it has the ability to be affected by a Civil 3D style. A Civil 3D *style* is a collection of settings that control the appearance and behavior of a Civil 3D object.

RECAP OF IMPORTANT DEFINITIONS

A Civil 3D *object* is an intelligent piece of your design model that stores information about itself and has the ability to interact with other objects in the drawing.

A Civil 3D *style* is a collection of settings that control the appearance and behavior of a Civil 3D object.

The relationship between objects and styles is one of several key relationships that you must understand and be able to take advantage of when using Civil 3D. Here are a few examples of Civil 3D objects that you'll encounter in this book as well as in a production environment:

Surface   A 3D model typically used to represent the shape of the ground, either existing or proposed

Alignment   A series of 2D lines, arcs, and spirals typically used to represent a linear feature such as a road centerline

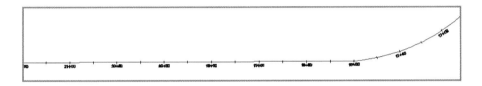

Profile   A series of lines and curves that represent changes in elevation along an alignment

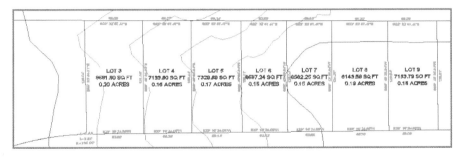

Parcel   A closed shape typically used to represent a legal property boundary

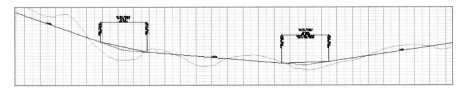

WHAT IS ELEVATION?

Depending on where you are in your civil engineering or surveying learning experience, the term *elevation* may be foreign to you. One way to visualize this concept is to think of it in terms of a piece of grid paper laid out over an area of land, with the horizontal lines running west to east and the vertical lines running south to north. Elevation would be coming straight up out of the paper. So, the top of a hill would have a greater elevation than the bottom of a ravine. Another way of thinking about this is in terms of an XYZ coordinate system. X and Y would be the lines on the grid paper and Z (elevation) would be coming out of it. Because Civil 3D combines general AutoCAD® software and civil engineering commands, elevation and the z-axis are the same.

One more thing—depending on where you live in the world, it may be appropriate to use the word *level* instead of *elevation*.

Each of the objects listed previously can be controlled by styles. For example, surface styles can be used to show a surface in many forms, including contour lines, a 3D grid, a series of arrows pointing downhill, shading representing different elevation ranges, and many more (Figure 2.1). In addition to changing the overall appearance of an object, styles can also control specific details that differ slightly between similar configurations. For example, in one case there may be surface contours that need to be shown on an existing layer, while in another case the same contours are shown on a proposed layer (Figure 2.2). The configuration is the same (contours), but the way that configuration is displayed (which layer) is different between two different styles.

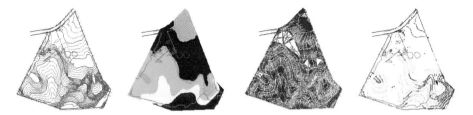

FIGURE 2.1 The same surface is shown in four different configurations using four different styles (from left to right): using contours, elevation banding, TIN lines and contours, and slope arrows.

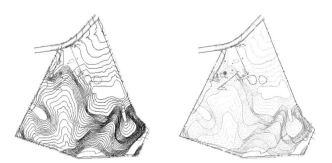

FIGURE 2.2 The contours on the left are displayed using proposed layers that are typically darker and more prominent. The contours on the right are displayed using existing layers that are typically lighter, so they appear more as background information.

To use styles to change the appearance and behavior of Civil 3D objects, follow these steps:

1. Open the drawing named Objects and Styles.dwg located in the Chapter 02 class data folder. The surface in the drawing should appear similar to the first image shown in Figure 2.1.

2. Click one of the contour lines in the drawing to select the surface object.

 3. Click Properties on the ribbon.

4. In the Properties window, change the Style property to Elevation Banding (2D). The surface will display as colored bands, representing different ranges of elevations, similar to the second image in Figure 2.1.

5. Change the Style property to Contours & Triangles. The surface should now appear similar to the third image in Figure 2.1. The triangles are the fundamental framework of the surface and give it the shape that it has.

Notice that when you click a contour, the entire surface object is selected, and all of the contours appear highlighted.

WHAT ARE CONTOURS?

Contours are lines that are used to represent topography or changes in elevation across the ground. Most people experience contours in things like trail maps that cover a large area (square miles or square kilometers) in comparison to what we typically see in Civil 3D. By definition, contours are lines that connect points of equal elevation. If you took a giant horizontal blade and passed it through the ground at equal elevation intervals, you would get contour lines. In flat areas, the lines would be far apart, and in steep areas, the lines would be close together. With practice, you can look at a contour map and visualize the 3D shape of the land that the map represents.

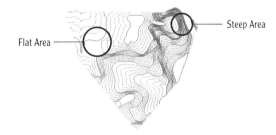

6. Change the Style property to Contours 1′ and 5′ (Design) (0.5m and 2.5m (Design)). The surface should now resemble the left image in Figure 2.2.

7. Change the Style property to Contours 1′ and 5′ (Background) (0.5m and 2.5m (Background)). This is the style that was assigned to the surface when you first opened the drawing. Note that both of the last two styles displayed contours but on different layers.

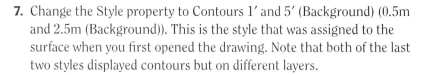

The Tin Surface: Existing Ground tab is an example of a special ribbon tab that is displayed because you selected a surface. These are often referred to as *contextual* ribbon tabs, as you may remember from the previous chapter.

8. With the surface still selected, click the Tin Surface: Existing Ground ribbon tab and then click Surface Properties ➤ Edit Surface Style.

9. Click the Display tab, and then click the color column next to Major Contour.

10. Choose a noticeable color and click OK. Click OK again to return to the drawing. Some of the contours will change to the new color as a result of this change.

As you worked through the previous exercise, did you notice that no extra steps were required to update or redraw the surface when a new style was assigned or the style was edited? The effect was immediate—as soon as you modified the assigned style or assigned a different style, the appearance of the surface changed. This is because of a dynamic relationship between the object and its style, a relationship that is honored throughout the software.

Editing a Style vs. Assigning a Different Style

In steps 5–7 of the previous exercise, you changed the appearance of the surface by assigning a different style to it. This is the way to do it 99 percent of the time. In steps 8–10, you edited the style that was already assigned to the surface. Editing styles is typically the responsibility of a CAD manager. In fact, in many companies end users are not permitted to modify or create styles. However, it is still important to understand that when a style is modified, any object using that style will change its appearance or behavior to honor the new version of the style.

Connecting Labels and Label Styles

Certification Objective

Labels are an important part of any design, because they provide specific information about the design that is often necessary for it to be properly constructed. Civil 3D enables you to create many different types of labels that associate themselves with the different types of Civil 3D objects. Labels are Civil 3D objects too, and just like the objects listed in the previous section, their appearance and behavior are controlled by styles. And just like the relationship between objects and their styles, labels also react when a different style is assigned or the assigned style is modified.

Here are some label types that correspond to the Civil 3D objects listed in the previous section.

Surface Spot Elevation Label   This type of label is typically used to display the elevation of a key point in the design, such as a low point where water will drain to or a high point that water will drain away from.

Alignment Station Offset Label   This type of label is used to express the location of a feature in reference to a linear object. For example, you could express the location of a manhole by saying that it is at a certain distance along the length of the road (station) and a certain distance to the left or right of it (offset).

Profile Grade Break Label   This type of label is used to show the location and elevation of a slope change along a profile. For example, if the profile slopes upward and then changes to a downward direction, the highest point where the change occurs is considered a grade break and is a common location to place a label.

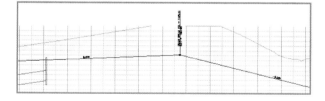

Parcel Segment Label   This type of label is typically used to express geometric information about a line or curve that forms part of a legal boundary. For example, it is common to label the bearing and distance of a straight line segment along a property boundary.

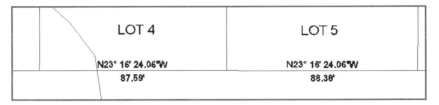

STATION AND OFFSET

Long linear designs such as roads and pipelines often use station and offset notation to express locations. Stations themselves are usually expressed in a special notation that has a plus sign in it.

For example, if you're working in imperial units, a station of 2+00 would refer to a location that is 200 feet "down the road" (assuming that the road begins at station 0+00). To get to station 2+00, offset 12′, you would travel down the road exactly 200 feet, turn right exactly 90 degrees, and travel exactly 12 feet.

If you're working in metric units, a common format is to use three digits after the plus sign. In this case, a station of 0+200 would refer to a location 200 meters "down the road." To get to station 0+200, offset 4m, you would travel 200 meters down the road, turn right exactly 90 degrees, and travel exactly 4 meters.

To use label styles to change the appearance and behavior of labels, follow these steps:

1. Open the drawing named Labels and Styles.dwg located in the Chapter 02 class data folder.

2. Zoom in to the station offset label located at the center point of the curve of the road centerline. Click the label, and then open the Properties window.

3. Change the value for Station Offset Label Style to Station And Offset, as shown in Figure 2.3. Notice how the content of the label changes.

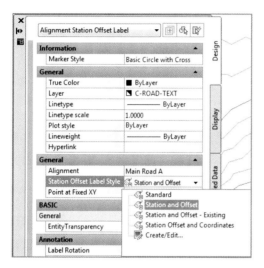

FIGURE 2.3 Assigning the Station And Offset label style to the label

4. Change the value for Station Offset Label Style to Station And Offset – Existing. This time, the content stays the same but the style of the text changes.

5. With the label still selected, click Label Properties ➢ Edit Label Style on the ribbon.

6. On the Station Offset Label Style dialog box, click Edit Current Selection, as shown in Figure 2.4.

FIGURE 2.4 Clicking the Edit Current Selection command for the selected label style

This is another example of a *contextual* ribbon tab.

7. In the Label Style Composer dialog box, click the Dragged State tab. Change the Visibility value for the leader to False, as shown in Figure 2.5.

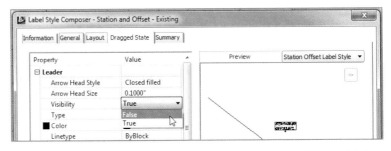

FIGURE 2.5 Changing the visibility of the leader by modifying a label style

8. Click OK twice to dismiss all dialog boxes and return to the drawing. The label is updated to reflect the change to the style and now no longer displays a leader.

STYLES AND COMPANY STANDARDS

Civil 3D styles can make it easier for end users to meet company standards and can make graphical output more consistent. With a good set of styles that integrate company standards, all an end user has to worry about is choosing the right style from a manageable list of choices. Conversely, if end users have to create their own styles, labels, and/or other graphical components, their drawings will most likely vary and may not comply with those standards.

Connecting Objects to Objects

Probably the most important type of relationship that you'll see in this chapter is the one between objects. A typical land development project is a collection of dozens of mini-designs that often tie in to one another. For example, a road is designed by first drawing the 2D path of its centerline, then the proposed changes in elevation along that centerline, and finally the lanes, curbs, and sidewalks extending outward from that centerline. To provide drainage during a rainstorm, ditches must be installed along the sides of the road. The location and depth of these ditches can be traced back through the design process the whole way to the layout of the road centerline. If the layout of the centerline needs to change for some reason, that change must propagate downstream through the design process, ultimately changing the location and depth of one or more ditches.

In Civil 3D, these connections between elements of the design are present regardless of the tool that is used. Before Civil 3D, these connections had to be managed manually by engineers and designers, and every aspect affected by a design change had to be manually fixed. With Civil 3D, these connections can be built into the design by establishing relationships between the road center-line and the roadside ditches and everything in between.

To demonstrate how object relationships are leveraged to make design changes in a drawing, follow these steps:

1. Open Object Relationships.dwg located in the Chapter 02 class data folder.

2. Press the F3 key, and observe the command line. If it reports <Osnap On>, then press F3 again. If it reports <Osnap Off>, this is the condition needed for this exercise, and you can move on to the next step.

3. Click the top-left viewport, which shows a profile of the road design. The black lines represent the elevations along the centerline of the new road. The blue lines represent storm drains and pipes connecting them.

4. Click the black line representing the road profile. Zoom in until you can clearly see the triangular grip located at the intersection of two lines.

5. Click the triangular grip and drag it upward to a location just below the top edge of the profile view grid, as shown in Figure 2.6. Watch the profile view and 3D view carefully. Notice how the 3D view of the road updates in the top-right view, including the height of the drain labeled Inlet 2. In the profile view (top left), the top of the drain is elevated to match the change in the road elevation.

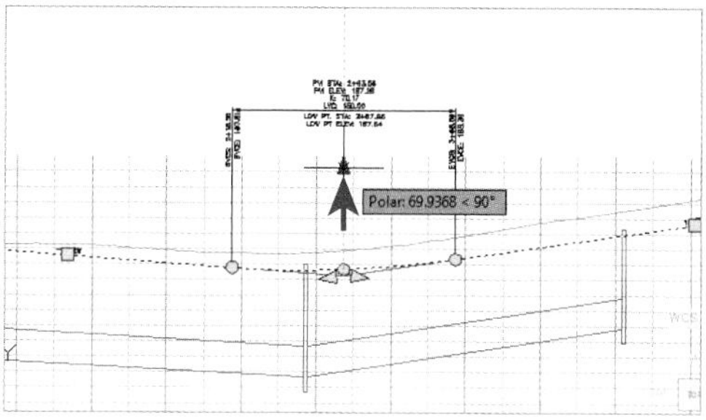

Be sure your command line is docked at the bottom of your screen and background color is set to white before proceeding with these steps.

<Osnap Off> will prevent your cursor from locking on to objects in the drawing that are near to it.

FIGURE 2.6 Grip editing the profile

This simple exercise illustrates the power of relationships between objects. The ease with which you just updated the design may cause you to take the underlying processes for granted; however, there is a lot happening behind the scenes. The following is a general account of the events that took place when you changed the location of the triangular grip:

▶ The slopes of the lines leading into that triangular grip were changed to match the new location of the grip.

▶ The parabolic curve geometry at the location of the grip was updated automatically.

▶ The corridor object, which represents a 3D model of the road, was automatically rebuilt and updated to match the new profile geometry.

▶ A surface representing the pavement and concrete elevations of the corridor was automatically rebuilt.

▶ The storm drain updated its top elevation to match the surface in the previous step.

▶ The 3D representation of the storm drain was automatically updated (top-right view).

▶ The profile view representation of the storm drain was automatically updated (top-left view).

A simple grip edit triggered a chain of events that might have taken an hour or more to update manually. In addition to all this, there were other changes that took place that did not affect the design of the storm drain. This is the power of the Civil 3D dynamic environment. You should know, however, that the existence of these relationships is not necessarily automatic. They have to be considered and at times consciously built into the design by the Civil 3D user.

Connecting Objects to Labels

There is also an important relationship between objects and labels. Labeling is one of the most time-consuming aspects of preparing a set of construction documents. Although it is a very important part of the process, it really has nothing to do with the design at all. Usually, labels are placed when the design is already complete as a means of communicating the necessary information for constructing the design in the field. The big advantage of the dynamic relationship between objects and labels is that it enables the user to create a single label that is valid for the life of the object. As the object changes, the label changes with it—so the label is always up to date and never has to be edited manually.

To demonstrate how dynamic labels respond when changes are made to the objects they annotate, follow these steps:

1. Open Objects and Labels.dwg located in the Chapter 02 class data folder. Notice the elevation label, which currently reads 190.02 (57.92).

2. Click one of the dark gray contour lines. On the ribbon, click Edit Surface ➢ Paste Surface.

3. Select Main Road A FG and click OK. Notice how the label updates and now reads 187.33 (57.07).

This step is like using a bulldozer to cut the road into the hillside, causing the elevation to drop about 3 feet (1 meter).

4. Take note of the station value of 10+95.68 (0+333.96) and the offset value of 68.49L (20.88m L) in the label to the south of the spot elevation. Click the road centerline to select it and display its grips. Then click the triangular grip and drag it west to a point near the west edge of the road, as shown in Figure 2.7. After a pause, while Civil 3D rebuilds several aspects of the design, the label updates once more. Since the road is no longer influencing the elevation of this spot, the label reverts to its original value of 190.02 (57.92). The station offset label now displays updated values for station and offset.

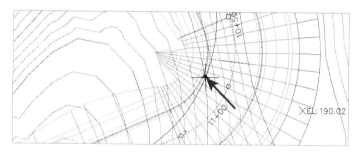

FIGURE 2.7 Grip editing the alignment

The Richness of the 3D Model

Even though this all probably seems very foreign at the moment, at some point, you will realize that all you're doing with Civil 3D is creating instructions for how to build something. If you've ever assembled a piece of furniture or a bicycle that you bought at the store, you can relate to this concept. The primary purpose of Civil 3D is to help you prepare the instructions for how to build a land development project.

Thirty years ago, the method used to prepare land development plans was relatively the same as it had been for millennia: plans were drawn on paper, providing only a two-dimensional depiction of what was to be built. The information that existed for the design was limited to what could be displayed on paper. Then, with the advent of computers, something magical started to happen. Virtual versions of design components could be modeled electronically. They could be represented in all three dimensions and even have additional information attached to them. Now, instead of using an ink line on paper to represent a pipe, you could do it with a 3D cylinder that also stored the pipe's material, structural characteristics, and flow characteristics. This "smart" object could be ported to hydraulic design software for further analysis in conjunction with local rainfall data to determine whether it was large enough to handle a storm with a specific likelihood of occurring within the lifespan of the pipe. And so on, and so on.

So, in 30 years, we have progressed from ink on paper to 3D intelligent objects. Early in that evolution was the step from drawing with a pen to drawing with a mouse—not 3D or intelligent, just lines on a screen that could be printed. Civil 3D contains all of the basic tools to represent your design in this manner, and unfortunately, many users are still working at this level even though they have access to the dynamic environment that you've seen in this chapter. My sincere hope is that you will not be this type of end user but will instead squeeze every dynamic relationship possible into the models that you build with Civil 3D. You may not realize the full potential of the dynamic relationships that you build until you have the opportunity to use them, but you can bet that they will pay dividends on every single project.

EXAMPLES OF PUTTING DYNAMIC MODELS TO USE

Here are a few examples of putting dynamic models to use.

Building Information Modeling

Building information modeling (BIM) has been a hot topic in the design, construction, and facilities management fields for quite some time now. Although some would argue that Civil 3D has little to do with the *B* (building), it definitely has the *I* (information) and the *M* (modeling) aspects. Many civil engineering projects are incidental to building construction and therefore present an opportunity for Civil 3D models to be integrated with BIM. No model, no BIM.

EXAMPLES OF PUTTING DYNAMIC MODELS TO USE *(Continued)*

GPS-Guided Machine Control

Imagine being able to download the instructions to assemble your bike and then upload them to your own personal robot, which would assemble it for you. That might sound like science fiction, but something similar to that is common practice in the land development industry. Models built with Civil 3D are being uploaded to GPS-guided earthmoving machines. These giant robots synchronize GPS-based locations of themselves and their digging implements with the dimensions of the Civil 3D model until the real dirt and rock are a match to the model. Without a model, there is no GPS-guided machine control.

Construction Simulation

If you think about it, one thing that Civil 3D enables you to do is simulate the project before having the contractor attempt to build it in the field. Why do this? It's a lot cheaper to undo a CAD command than to undo the placement of several truck loads of concrete. Contractors are taking this one step further by simulating the construction itself. The sequence of operations, staging of materials, arrangement of equipment, and many other aspects can all be simulated with several products available on the market. These 4D (3D + time) or even 5D (3D + time + cost) simulations are becoming commonplace in nearly all major construction projects. No model, no simulation.

Visualization

Visualization is itself a form of simulation. With design software now commonly producing 3D models, the leap to 3D visualization is much shorter and easier to accomplish than ever before. Clients, review agencies, and the public are now beginning to expect renderings and even animations of proposed designs to be available for them to assess. No model, no visualization.

Building your designs as dynamic models does take a bit more effort and time, but as you get more and more skilled, this extra time and effort are a small fraction of the overall process. The resulting models will be much more useful, much more information rich, and much more valuable to your clients and others involved in your projects. There's no telling how this information will be used, but one thing is for sure: it won't be used at all if it's not there.

In addition, building designs as dynamic models improves the quality and efficiency of the design process. Designers who make full use of the dynamic model produce better designs by creating more design iterations and what-if scenarios than those who don't. They can respond more quickly to design changes, reducing the overall cost involved in designing the project and increasing the bottom line. Leveraging the dynamic model isn't just cool, it's also practical and very smart from a business perspective.

Sharing Data in a Dynamic Environment

So far, you have studied many ways in which relationships and interaction are leveraged to make Civil 3D a powerful design solution; however, all of these relationships have been confined to a single drawing or a single user. What happens in a team environment? Are there ways in which whole drawings can interact with one another? Can multiple team members establish dynamic relationships between their designs? The answer is "yes" and the feature that makes it possible is the *data shortcut*.

Earlier, in the section titled "Connecting Objects to Objects," you observed how a profile, road design, and pipe system design could be related to one another. Now, imagine a design team where the profile is designed by Joe in one drawing, the road model by Susan in another drawing, and the pipe system design by Jill in yet another. Data shortcuts make it possible for these designs to be linked together just as you witnessed earlier—even across drawings.

A data shortcut is a link to a Civil 3D object that enables another drawing to get access to that object. For example, if you create a profile that represents the proposed centerline elevations of a road, you can publish a data shortcut for that profile that becomes "visible" to other drawings. You or someone else can then open another drawing and use that data shortcut to access the profile. Once you have accessed the profile, you can use it as part of another design, such as the case with the road model.

When a data shortcut is created, it is displayed in Prospector beneath the Data Shortcuts heading (Figure 2.8). Data shortcuts are stored within a *data shortcuts folder*. This enables related data shortcuts, such as those pertaining to a given project, to be grouped together in one location. The folder that contains data shortcuts folders is the *working folder*. It allows you to set up one location where all projects are stored.

Once a data shortcut is made available, you can then use it to create a *data reference* in another drawing. Objects that are data referenced, such as surfaces, alignments, and profiles, appear in Prospector along with other "native" objects. An icon next to them indicates that they are data references. In Figure 2.9, the Existing Ground surface and the Main Road A alignment have an icon next to them indicating that they are data references.

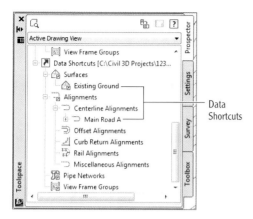

FIGURE 2.8 Data shortcuts shown within Prospector

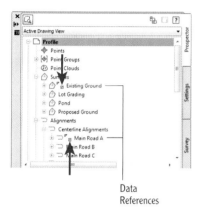

FIGURE 2.9 A surface data reference and an alignment data reference shown along with other surfaces and alignments in Prospector

To demonstrate how data shortcuts are utilized to share data between drawings, follow these steps:

1. Open the file named Surface.dwg located in the Chapter 02 class data folder.

2. If the Toolspace is not visible, click Toolspace on the Home tab of the ribbon.

3. On the Prospector tab of Toolspace, right-click Data Shortcuts and select Set Working Folder. The Browse For Folder dialog box opens.

4. Browse to the Chapter 02 class data folder and select Sample Working Folder. Click OK.

5. Right-click Data Shortcuts and select New Data Shortcuts Project Folder. The New Data Shortcut Folder dialog box opens.

6. Type **Sample Project** in the Name field and click OK.

7. Save the drawing. Click the Manage tab of the ribbon, and then click Create Data Shortcuts. The Create Data Shortcuts dialog box opens.

8. Check the box next to Existing Ground and click OK.

9. Open the file named `Alignment.dwg` located in the `Chapter 02` class data folder.

10. Repeat steps 7 and 8 for the alignment named Main Road A.

11. Open the file named `Profile.dwg` located in the `Chapter 02` class data folder.

12. On Prospector, expand Data Shortcuts ➢ Surfaces. Right-click Existing Ground and select Create Reference.

13. Click OK to accept the default settings on the Create Surface Reference dialog box. Contours in the drawing indicate a newly added surface.

14. Repeat steps 12 and 13 for the alignment data shortcut named Main Road A. A new alignment is created in the drawing.

15. On the Home tab of the ribbon, click Profile ➢ Create Surface Profile. The Create Profile From Surface dialog box opens.

16. Click Add, and then click Draw In Profile View. The Create Profile View – General dialog box opens.

17. Click Create Profile View. Pick a point in the open space to the right of the surface contours and other linework. A new profile is created that is the result of relating an alignment to a surface (Figure 2.10). This profile represents the interaction between three different drawings.

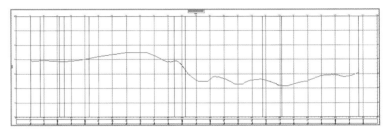

FIGURE 2.10 A profile created from an alignment data reference and a surface data reference

A NOTE ABOUT UNITS

Throughout this chapter, you'll notice that two values are provided for units of measurement. The first value is provided for the imperial system that is used in the United States, and the second value in parentheses is provided for the metric system that is used in many other countries. These values most often represent imperial feet and metric meters. It is important to note that generally only the numeric values are entered in the software, not terms like *feet* or *meters*. Also, you should know that the two numbers provided are not necessarily equal. In most cases, they are similar values that are rounded to work efficiently in their respective measurement systems.

THE ESSENTIALS AND BEYOND

Having completed this chapter, you should now have a better understanding and appreciation for the power of the relationships upon which Civil 3D is built. You have seen how styles relate to objects, objects relate to other objects, and labels relate to the things they annotate. These relationships take the repetition out of design work that used to plague it before Civil 3D was available. You are fortunate to be performing design with such powerful tools that enable you to focus more on applying your creativity and ingenuity than on performing repetitive tasks such as editing labels or fixing minor design discrepancies. From a designer's perspective, the relationships in Civil 3D simply make design more fun. From a business perspective, the relationships in Civil 3D make design more profitable.

ADDITIONAL EXERCISES

For these exercises, open the drawing named Parcels.dwg located in the Chapter 02 class data folder. Then use the objects, labels, and styles within it to study relationships that exist in a typical residential-subdivision design. Specifically, investigate the following:

1. Change the style applied to one or more parcels to display them as open space rather than single-family.

2. Change the style assigned to one or more parcel area labels to display more than just the parcel number.

(Continues)

THE ESSENTIALS AND BEYOND *(Continued)*

3. Use grip editing to change the geometry of the road centerline, and observe what happens to the geometry of the parcels. Consider the relationships that make this behavior possible.

4. Use grip editing to move several parcel lines that are perpendicular to the road. Observe how the adjacent parcels and their labels respond. Consider the relationships that make this behavior possible.

5. Create a data reference to the Existing Ground surface using the data shortcut created in the previous exercise; then create a profile of this surface along the Main Road A alignment.

Visit www.sybex.com/go/civil2013essentials to download a video of the author completing this exercise. You can also download the Answers to Additional Exercises Appendix which contains even more information about completing this exercise.

CHAPTER 3

Establishing Existing Conditions Using Survey Data

With our tour of the AutoCAD® Civil 3D® user interface and our study of its capabilities behind us, it's time now to do what we came here to do: use Civil 3D to complete a land development project. To begin to understand the task ahead, let's imagine land development as creating a sculpture but on a very large scale. If a sculptor were creating a work of art from wood, he or she would probably begin by studying the original piece of wood, assessing its dimensions, shape, and surface features. These elements would all factor into how the sculptor would approach his or her work. A sculptor with some computer savvy might even model the original piece of wood on a computer and plan out each cut of material.

In this chapter, we are going to explore the first activities that are performed during a land development project: the measurement, mapping, and modeling of the land in its existing form. To plan out how the land will be reshaped, you must first understand how it is shaped right now. This is analogous to the sculptor's measurement and assessment of his medium. The work that is required to map an existing piece of land is done by a surveyor.

- ▶ **What is survey data?**

- ▶ **Creating a survey database**

- ▶ **Importing survey data**

- ▶ **Automating field-to-finish**

- ▶ **Editing survey points**

- ▶ **Editing survey figures**

- ▶ **Creating additional points**

What Is Survey Data?

Think back to the last time you played connect-the-dots to draw a picture. Ever wonder who made the dots and how they were made? I'm no expert, but I'm guessing someone took the original picture, laid a piece of tracing paper over it, and made dots along the edges of key features in the picture. Someone skilled at this would make just enough dots to define the features but not so many as to make them confusing or wasteful. The dots are a way of capturing an image and transferring it to another location.

In land development, the land is the picture, and the surveyor is the one who makes the dots—referred to as *points*. Obviously, tracing paper cannot be used, so the surveyor lays an imaginary grid over the land (a coordinate system) and creates the points as information by recording their coordinates on this grid paper. The tools that the surveyor uses are extremely accurate and are able to capture the location of each point within a tolerance of about ⅛ of an inch (3 mm). Something different about the surveyor's "dots" is that their location is recorded in all three dimensions. This enables a technician to play connect-the-dots in 3D to create a 3D model in addition to a 2D map of the features of the land. Another difference is that a surveyor's dots have description codes next to them instead of just numbers. A description code identifies the type of feature that a dot is intended to represent (see Figure 3.1).

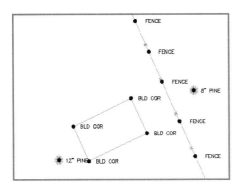

FIGURE 3.1 Survey points shown as dots, giving a sense of how they are used to create mapping

If you're thinking that it takes a lot of points to capture several acres of land, you're absolutely right. How can you keep track of all those points? How can they be easily turned into a 3D model of the land? Is there some way of automating the connect-the-dots process? Civil 3D has the answers to these questions, and in this chapter you'll learn how you can use Civil 3D to transform raw field points into maps and 3D models of the land.

Creating a Survey Database

In Chapter 2, you learned about the importance of relationships in Civil 3D and saw firsthand how Civil 3D makes use of interactions between different object types. When dealing with survey data, these relationships are managed in a *survey database*. In the survey database, the raw data is linked with the screen representation of the points, which is linked with the linework generated by connecting those points, and so on. The survey database is unique within Civil 3D in that it is stored outside of the drawing file.

Creating and configuring a survey database is relatively simple. Follow these steps to see for yourself:

1. Open Civil 3D and click New on the Application menu. When prompted for a template, browse to the Chapter 03 class data folder and open Essentials.dwt.

2. Click the Survey tab of the Toolspace.

3. Right-click Survey Databases and select Set Working Folder.

4. Browse to and select the Chapter 03 class data folder and click OK.

THE SURVEY WORKING FOLDER

The working folder is simply the location where survey databases will be stored. In the next step, you will create a survey database named Essentials. This will create a folder within Chapter 03 named Essentials.

---

5. Right-click Survey Databases and click New Local Survey Database.

6. Type Essentials as the new database name and click OK.

7. The Essentials database is now shown on the Survey tab. Note the components of the survey database, such as Import Events, Networks, Figures, and Survey Points (Figure 3.2). The survey database establishes and manages relationships between these different components.

If the Toolspace is not visible, you can click Toolspace on the Home tab of the ribbon. If the Survey tab is not visible, click the Survey icon to the right of the Toolspace icon.

On Prospector, you will see a series of Essentials survey databases that you will use in upcoming exercises.

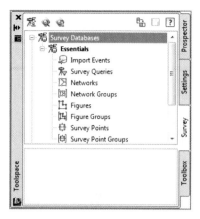

FIGURE 3.2 The Essentials survey database shown in Prospector after the completion of step 7

Importing Survey Data

After creating a survey database to receive the data, the next step is to transfer the raw data into Civil 3D so that the analysis and mapping can begin. There are several ways to accomplish this, but in this chapter, you're going to do it the way a surveyor would do it. The process of importing data requires some important questions to be answered, but for your first try, you're going to accept all the defaults and see what happens. To import survey data into a drawing, follow these steps (note: the previous exercise must be completed for this exercise to work properly):

The *Essentials 1* database is the result of correctly completing the previous exercise. This database is provided to ensure that you start the current exercise with the correct version.

If no survey database existed, you could have created one by clicking **Create New Survey Database**.

1. Open the drawing named Import Survey Data.dwg located in the Chapter 03 class data folder.

2. On the Home tab of the ribbon, click Import Survey Data.

3. Select the Essentials 1 survey database and click Next.

4. Under Data Source Type, select Point File.

5. Click the plus icon under Selected Files and browse to the Chapter 03 class data folder.

6. Select Topo Survey.txt and click Open.

7. Under Specify Point File Format, select PNEZD (Comma Delimited).

8. Click Next. In the Specify Network dialog box, note that <none> is selected for the current network. Click Next.

9. In the Import Options dialog box, check the boxes next to Process Linework During Import and Insert Survey Points.

10. Verify that Current Figure Prefix Database and Current Linework Code Set are both set to Sample.

PNEZD represents the order of the data columns in the text file: Point number, Northing, Easting, Z coordinate (elevation), Description.

SURVEY DATA SOURCES

Survey data can come in several forms, depending on the hardware and/ or software utilized to create it. Here are a few of the most common forms:

Field Book File   This is considered a legacy format unique to Autodesk® products such as Land Desktop and older versions of Civil 3D. Many surveyors have moved on from field book files but have done so fairly recently. For that reason, you might still find them to be quite common. One difference with field book files is that they can store the measurements exactly as they were taken in the field. The other formats listed here contain points that have been reduced to coordinates.

LandXML File   Many civil engineering and surveying programs can export data in the form of LandXML, including Civil 3D. This nonproprietary format enables data to be exchanged between programs created by different software companies.

Point File   The point file is probably the most generic and universally accepted way of delivering point data. This type of file is plain text and can be opened in a program like Microsoft Notepad. Regardless of age, cost, or origin, nearly all surveying and civil engineering programs are able to produce this type of file.

Points from Drawing   With this option, you can open a drawing that already contains points and add them to your survey database. Remember that the survey database is stored outside the drawing, so the points you see in the drawing are a representation of what is stored there.

WHAT IS A NETWORK?

Surveying is a complicated business. For some surveying projects, key measurements are related to one another so that accuracy can be adjusted across the entire project simultaneously. The network is the way of setting up these relationships and performing accuracy adjustments. The survey data used in this exercise is a simple form that does not contain any of these relationships; therefore no network is needed.

11. Click Finish.

12. Zoom in to the drawing and examine what you see (Figure 3.3).

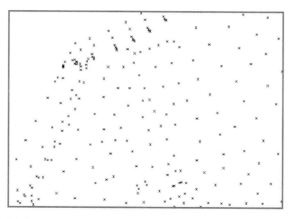

FIGURE 3.3 So far, importing data shows only a bunch of relatively meaningless x markers in the drawing.

IMPORTING POINTS WITHOUT A SURVEY DATABASE

Sometimes you may want to import points straight into your Civil 3D drawing without the extended data management capabilities of the survey database. You can do this using the Points From File command on the Insert tab of the ribbon, as shown in the following illustration.

IMPORTING POINTS WITHOUT A SURVEY DATABASE   *(Continued)*

The resulting dialog box (shown below) provides only one choice for file format, a text file, and no association with a survey database or linework code is set.

For that reason, some of the features you will learn about later in this chapter will not be utilized. These include the automatic generation of linework, accuracy adjustment, and others.

The differences continue as you work with the points you've imported. Points created without the management of the survey database are easily edited. You will find that points created using the Points From File command can be moved as easily as moving a circle or a polyline. They can also be freely edited using the Properties window.

Using the Points From File function is definitely quicker and simpler than using the Import Survey Data command; however, there are considerable differences in functionality. When you choose which method to use, be sure to consider the level of protection, ease of editing, ability to generate linework, and interrelationship between points and survey measurements. Each method serves a different purpose and should be chosen appropriately.

Automating Field-to-Finish

The term *field-to-finish* refers to the process of transforming raw survey field data into a finished drawing. Before computers, the point data collected in the field was plotted on paper by hand, and draftspeople skillfully connected the

A *topographic map* can be thought of as a 3D map: the 2D outlines of surface features combined with contour lines representing the third dimension.

dots and employed other methods to create the desired topographic map. The process was manual in the truest sense of the word. Next came the first CAD programs in which points could be plotted on a computer screen and the dots connected using primitive entities such as lines, arcs, polylines, and blocks. This is what many would now refer to as a "manual" process.

As you might guess, the process of making a drawing out of point data is quite tedious and presents an opportunity for automation. Imagine using the result from the steps in the previous section (Figure 3.3) to create a map of the land. With no information accompanying the points, it would be nearly impossible. In this section, you'll see how to use several Civil 3D features to automate this process, resulting in a drawing that is 80 to 90 percent complete immediately after importing the raw field data. However, as is usually the case, the more automation you want, the more setup you are required to do. Automation is another way of saying that you're going to make a bunch of decisions ahead of time and ask the computer to carry out those decisions when needed.

The following Civil 3D features enable you to convert raw field data into drawing information.

Linework Code Set

To create linear features using connected points, someone has to tell those features when to start, when to end, when to draw curves, when to draw straight lines, and so on. In other words, it can be a bit more complicated than "Draw a line from point 1 to point 2." Field crews use codes to carry out these geometric instructions. For example, they might include the string BEG when locating the first point on a fence line, which means to begin a new feature at that point. The linework code set correlates these field codes with instructions that control the generation of linework in the drawing. This is the way of telling Civil 3D that BEG means "begin drawing here," BCV means "begin curve here," and so on. Another way to think of a linework code set is as a translator between field language and Civil 3D language.

The *Essentials 2* database is the result of correctly completing the previous exercise. This database is provided to ensure that you start the current exercise with the correct version.

To assign a linework code set to your drawing and apply it to points that have been imported, follow these steps:

1. Open the drawing named Linework Code Set.dwg located in the Chapter 03 class data folder.

2. Click the Survey tab of the Toolspace.

3. If the contents beneath the Essentials 2 survey database are not visible, right-click Essentials 2 and select Open For Edit.

4. Expand Import Events. Right-click Topo Survey.txt and select Properties.

 5. Click the browse icon next to File to open the text file. Notice the codes BEG, BCV, ECV, and END. These are the codes used in the field to represent Begin Feature, Begin Curve, End Curve, and End Feature. If you scroll down within the text file, you will also see the CLS code, which represents Close Feature.

6. Close the text file and click Cancel to dismiss the Import Event Properties dialog box.

7. Click the icon in the top-left corner of the Survey tab to edit the survey user settings.

8. Click the folder icon next to Linework Code Sets Path, browse to the Chapter 03 class data folder, and click OK. Click OK to dismiss the Survey User Settings dialog box.

9. On the Survey tab, right-click Linework Code Sets and select Refresh. Click the plus sign next to Linework Code Sets. You should now see Essentials listed as a Linework Code Set.

10. Under Linework Code Sets, right-click Essentials and select Make Current.

11. Under Linework Code Sets, right-click Essentials and select Edit. Notice that the codes used for Begin, End, Begin Curve, End Curve, and Close now match what you saw in the text file. The codes in the linework code set named Sample were different, and therefore no linework was drawn when you imported the survey data.

12. Click Cancel to dismiss the Edit Linework Code Set dialog box.

13. Under Import Events, right-click Topo Survey.txt and select Re-Import.

14. For Current Linework Code Set, select Essentials and click OK.

15. On the Duplicate Point Number dialog box, verify that Resolution is set to Overwrite. Then check the box next to Apply To All Duplicate Point Numbers and click OK. This time, linework is drawn as the data is imported.

If you receive an error message here, you may not have installed the datasets correctly. Refer to the Introduction for instructions on installing the datasets.

Point Styles

Not all points are meant to be connected with other points. Some represent stand-alone features such as power poles, manholes, or trees. These types of features are typically represented with a symbol that either resembles their true form or uniquely identifies them. With the Point Styles feature, a symbol can be used to mark a point, meaning that the likeness of a power pole, manhole, or tree can be used instead of an *x* or a dot.

Point Label Styles

For some points, you might want labeling to be included automatically. For example, you may want trees to be labeled with their common names or manholes to be labeled with their top elevations. When the annotation is very uniform, Point Label Styles can be employed to automatically provide the desired labels.

Description Keys

Certification Objective

As discussed, it takes a lot of points to effectively capture several acres of land. To make things even more challenging, field crews often use abbreviated versions of descriptions to represent points, such as EP for edge of pavement, CLRD for centerline of road, and so on. The result is hundreds or even thousands of points all clumped together and labeled with cryptic abbreviated descriptions.

Description keys solve this problem by automatically sorting the points onto the appropriate layers, rewriting the abbreviated descriptions to full-length descriptions, and automatically applying point styles to control the appearance of the points. For example, a description key will take a point coded as PP, place it on the utility layer, display it as a power pole, and rewrite the description to say POWER POLE. Imagine the time saved when this is done automatically for 10,000 points.

To use a description key to apply this type of automation to the tree points in your drawing, follow these steps:

1. Open the drawing named Description Keys.dwg located in the Chapter 03 class data folder.

2. Click the Settings tab of the Toolspace and expand Point ➢ Description Key Sets.

3. Right-click Essentials and select Edit Keys.

4. Click the style cell for code TR* to open the Point Style dialog box.

5. Select Tree as the point style and click OK.

 6. Click the green check mark to dismiss Panorama.

7. Click the Prospector tab, and then click Points.

8. In the listing of points at the bottom of Prospector, scroll to the right and click the Raw Description column heading to sort the points by that property.

9. Scroll to the bottom of the list where all of the TR points are now located.

10. Right-click one of the points and select Apply Description Keys. One of the points in the drawing should become a tree symbol.

11. Select all of the TR points and use the Apply Description Keys command to change them. All of the trees in the drawing are now clearly visible and appropriately represented.

12. Return to the Settings tab and edit the Essentials description key set once again. This time, assign a point label style of Description Only to the TR* code. Apply description keys to the TR points from within Prospector as you did before. The trees in the drawing are now labeled, although the label is the actual field code. A better result would be a more "polished" description.

13. Edit the TR* description key code once again, this time changing the Format value to $1" $2 ($1mm $2). Apply the description keys to the TR points once again. This time, the labels make more sense and read 12" (300mm) PINE, 15" (375mm) MAPLE, and so on.

Raw description is usually the code that is entered in the field and is often abbreviated to save time and make it easier on field crews under potentially harsh conditions.

WHAT'S UP WITH THE DOLLAR SIGNS?

In the previous step, you used a code of $1" $2 to create the full description for the trees. The $ is a special code that tells Civil 3D that you want to use part of the raw description in the full description. The parts of the raw description are separated by spaces and numbered from left to right, starting at zero. So, in the raw description TR 12 OAK, the TR is $0, 12 is $1, and OAK is $2. So $1" $2 becomes 12" OAK. With metric values in the raw description TR 300 OAK, the TR is $0, 300 is $1, and OAK is $2. So $1mm $2 becomes 300mm OAK. This is a great way for the person in the field to control the outcome in the drawing with as few keystrokes as possible.

Figure Prefix Database

Certification Objective

As discussed, the linework code set handles how the field codes are translated into linework commands, but what happens to those features once they are drawn? What layer are they drawn on? Do they have any special purpose such as a property line or breakline? The Figure Prefix Database is the means by which these decisions can be made up front for specific codes. For example, any feature drawn through points coded EP will be drawn on the pavement layer and tagged as a key component for establishing a "hard edge" in the 3D model of the terrain, also known as a breakline.

To assign a Figure Prefix Database to your drawing and apply it to survey data that has been imported, follow these steps:

1. Open the drawing named `Figure Prefix Database.dwg` located in the `Chapter 03` class data folder.

2. On the Survey tab of the Toolspace, click the Edit Survey User Settings icon in the top-left corner.

3. Click the browse icon next to Figure Prefix Database Path. Browse to and select the `Chapter 03` class data folder.

4. Click OK to dismiss the Survey User Settings dialog box. Right-click Figure Prefix Databases and select Refresh. Click the plus sign next to Figure Prefix Databases to expand its contents. You should now see Essentials listed under Figure Prefix Databases.

5. Right-click Essentials and select Make Current. Right-click Essentials again, and this time, select Manage Figure Prefix Database.

6. Scroll down and examine the codes in the Name column. These match the codes that you saw in the text file containing the survey data. Notice that some of the codes are designated as breaklines, such as EP (edge of pavement), TOPD (top of ditch), and TOB (top of bank). The breakline designation means that these lines can be used to define hard edges in a surface model. Also note the layers that are assigned by code.

7. Click Cancel to dismiss the Figure Prefix Database Manager dialog box.

8. If the contents of the `Essentials 3` survey database are not visible, right-click `Essentials 3` and select Open for Edit.

9. Expand Import Events. Right-click `Topo Survey.txt` and select Process Linework.

The *Essentials 3* database is the result of correctly completing the previous exercise. This database is provided to ensure that you start the current exercise with the correct version.

▶

10. In the Process Linework dialog box, select Essentials for Current Figure Prefix Database and click OK. Civil 3D will redraw the linework, this time doing so on the appropriate layers. This is evident in the linetypes that are applied to the treelines and fence lines, which are now appropriately represented on the drawing (Figure 3.4).

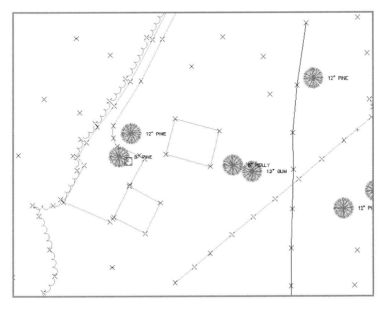

F I G U R E 3 . 4 The appearance of the drawing makes more sense now that features such as fence lines and treelines have been drawn on the appropriate layers.

SURVEY FIGURES

At this point you may be wondering what the word *figure* means or, specifically, what a survey figure object is. A Civil 3D survey figure object is the program's way of representing a linear feature that has been defined using survey data. A survey figure is commonly used to represent visible features such as fence lines, edges of pavement, and treelines, as well as topographic features such as tops and bottoms of embankments. The topographic feature line layers are usually turned off when the drawing is plotted. Survey figures can be referenced by other Civil 3D objects such as surfaces, feature lines, and corridors, enabling design work to tie into existing features and topography where applicable.

Point Groups

Certification
Objective

Point groups are another way of managing large amounts of point data. This feature enables you to sort points based on a number of factors, such as description, elevation, point number, or manual selection. You can set up point groups ahead of time so that points can be automatically sorted into groups as they are imported into the drawing. You can also create new point groups on the fly to sort points as you go.

Once points have been grouped, you can use them to study and manipulate multiple points at once. The groups are listed in Prospector, and you can view the points contained in each group by simply clicking the group name and viewing the contents of the point group in the item view at the bottom (Figure 3.5). In addition, many point editing commands allow you to select points by group, enabling you to modify large numbers of points at once.

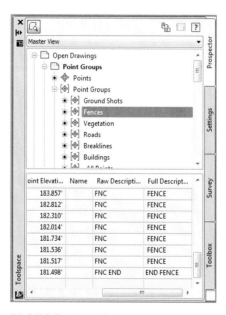

FIGURE 3.5 The contents of a specific
point group shown in the item view of Prospector

Point groups also enable you to assign default point styles and label styles to points within the group. With this capability, you can make points in a certain group take on specific graphical characteristics by controlling the point style and point label style.

To use point groups to organize points in your drawing and control their appearance, follow these steps:

1. Open the drawing named `Point Groups.dwg` located in the `Chapter 03` class data folder.

2. On Prospector, right-click Point Groups and select New.

3. On the Information tab of the Point Group Properties dialog box, type **Buildings** in the Name field. Select Basic as the Point Style and <None> as the Point Label Style.

4. Click the Raw Description Matching tab. Check the box next to BLD* and click OK.

5. Expand Point Groups and click the Buildings point group in Prospector. Examine the list of points shown in the Prospector item view at the bottom. Note that they all are points with a BLD description.

6. Create the following point groups with the associated raw descriptions listed. Use a default Point Style of Basic and a default Point Label Style of <None> for each point group.

   ▶ Breaklines: **BOB, BOTD, SWL, TOB, TOPD**

   ▶ Roads: **CLRD, DW, EP, ES**

   ▶ Vegetation: **ESHB, TL, TR**

   ▶ Fences: **FNC**

   ▶ Ground Shots: **GS**

7. Click the Settings tab and expand Point ➢ Description Key Sets.

8. Right-click Essentials and select Edit Keys.

9. Hold down the Shift key to select all rows except the last one (TR*). Then right-click the Style column heading and select Edit.

10. Select <default> and click OK. Click the green check mark to close Panorama.

11. On Prospector, right-click the _All Points point group and select Apply Description Keys. This applies the new style choice of <default> to all points except trees. Now, the point style assigned by the point groups is able to have an effect, and most of the points change from *x* markers to circle markers.

_All Points is a special point group that must exist in all drawings. As the name implies, it always contains all of the points in the drawing.

12. On Prospector, right-click the Ground Shots point group and select Properties.

13. On the Information tab, select Ground Shot as the default Point Style and Elevation Only as the default Point Label Style. Click OK and notice what happens to all of the ground shot points in the drawing.

14. Click the Output tab of the ribbon, and then click Export Points.

15. Check the box next to Limit Points To Point Group and choose the Roads point group.

16. Click OK and browse to your Chapter 03 class data folder. Enter **Road Points** as the name of the file and click Open. Then click OK to dismiss the Export Points dialog box.

This is an example of using a group to make a selection of points. Imagine selecting all these road points one by one.

POINT GROUPS VS. DESCRIPTION KEYS

At this point, you may be scratching your head a bit, thinking that a few minutes ago, you learned that description keys control the point style and point label style assigned to a point. Well, you're right—they do. However, you may have also noticed that when you assign these styles using description keys, the choice at the top of the list in each case is <default>. This choice could (and maybe should) be changed to say ByPointGroup, because that's what it essentially means. When you configure your description keys to use <default> as the style, you're deferring the decision about what style to use to the point groups. If you choose anything else, you're making that decision right then and there.

Feel better about it? Well, unfortunately, there's another feature to consider that makes this a little more complicated but also gives you even more flexibility when stylizing points. One of the properties of a point group is the ability to set up an override. When you set up a point style or point label style as an override, that means you're going to apply that style regardless of whether it's <default> or something else. There is an Overrides tab on the Point Group Properties dialog box that enables you to do this.

If you're wondering whether point groups or description keys are best to use, the answer is *both*. By thoroughly understanding how each method can be applied to your point data, you can leverage both point groups and description keys to stylize and organize your points in the best way possible. When starting out, however, you might want to pick one method or the other and completely develop that method; then sprinkle in the other method little by little, observing and understanding how the two work together.

In the previous exercises, you made some corrections and assigned a specific linework code set and figure prefix database to the data you imported. In an actual production environment, the changes you make to the description key set should be incorporated into the company template so that the tree points are handled correctly for all future jobs. The point groups you create could also be included in the company template so that they're available on all future jobs. In addition, the linework code set and figure prefix database that you use could be assigned as defaults so that they are automatically applied to future data imports. This type of configuration management is typically handled by a CAD manager, but the needs for the changes are usually identified by end users like you. When you are working with Civil 3D in a production environment, be sure to work with your CAD manager to make sure you and your coworkers are leveraging the configuration of Civil 3D as much as possible.

Editing Survey Points

As we've discussed, it takes many points to survey a piece of land—that's hundreds or even thousands of individual measurements and hand-typed field codes. On nearly every project, there will be items that require editing. Once the data has been imported into Civil 3D, the field crew is off on its next job and the task of fixing things up will belong to you.

A Note About Units

Throughout this chapter, you'll notice that two values are provided for units of measurement. The first value is provided for the imperial system that is used in the United States, and the second value in parentheses is provided for the metric system that is used in many other countries. These values most often represent imperial feet and metric meters. It is important to note that generally only the numeric values are entered in the software, not terms like *feet* or *meters*. Also, you should know that the two numbers provided are not necessarily equal. In most cases, they are similar values that are rounded to work efficiently in their respective measurement systems.

For several reasons, editing survey points is a bit different from editing "regular" points, properly referred to as COGO points. One reason is that surveyed points are considered "sacred" and are not typically moved or modified in any way without considerable thought and/or the supervision of a surveyor. The second reason, related to the first, is that Civil 3D uses a separate survey database system to store points. The points in the drawing are essentially locked and cannot be changed unless the information in the survey database changes. With this system, a surveyor can send out the drawing file without sharing the survey database that goes with it. When the points in the drawing are separated from the survey database, they become locked and cannot be easily modified. In this way, the survey database gives control of the points to the person who created them.

To edit a survey point to correct an error in field coding, follow these steps:

1. Open the drawing named `Edit Survey Points.dwg` located in the `Chapter 03` class data folder. If a survey database is open, right-click it and select Close Survey Database.

2. Locate and zoom in to the red point along the west treeline, as shown in Figure 3.6.

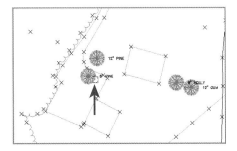

FIGURE 3.6 An error has caused this point to display incorrectly.

SURVEY POINTS VS. COGO POINTS

As previously mentioned, there are two types of points: COGO points and survey points. How can you tell the difference? Here are a few characteristics of each to help you distinguish between the two.

Survey Point Characteristics

▶ Only survey points display on the Survey tab (COGO points do not).

▶ Survey points display on both the Prospector and the Survey tabs.

▶ Survey points have an icon next to them that looks like a survey target (an hourglass inside of a box overlaid on crosshairs).

▶ Survey points cannot be moved.

▶ Survey points cannot be edited in the Properties window.

SURVEY POINTS VS. COGO POINTS   *(Continued)*

COGO Point Characteristics

▶ COGO points do not display on the Survey tab.

▶ COGO points have an icon next to them that looks like a circle overlaid on crosshairs.

▶ COGO points can be moved, even with the AutoCAD® software move command.

▶ COGO points can be edited in the Properties window.

> The survey database is needed to edit the points. This is how the points are kept safe when the drawing is shared outside the survey office.

3. Open the Properties window and then select the red point. Note that there is a typo in the raw description. It should say TR 12 PINE (TR 300 PINE) instead of TTR 12 PINE (TTR 300 PINE). You cannot edit the raw description here, because the data is actually stored in the survey database.

4. With the point still selected, click Survey Point Properties on the ribbon. A dialog box will open, informing you that you must open a survey database.

5. Click OK to dismiss the dialog box. Then right-click the Essentials 4 survey database on the Survey tab and select Open For Edit.

> The *Essentials 4* database is the result of correctly completing the previous exercise. This database is provided to ensure that you start the current exercise with the correct version.

6. With the red point still selected, click Survey Point Properties on the ribbon.

7. Edit the description to say **TR 12 PINE (TR 300 PINE)** and click OK.

8. Press Enter to end the command. You will then be prompted to update linework in the drawing. Answer No since the change you made does not affect linework.

9. Click the red point, right-click, and select Apply Description Keys. The effect of the description key will put the point on the correct layer, change its marker to a tree symbol, and provide a label indicating that it is a 12" (300mm) PINE.

Editing Survey Figures

Mistakes in the field can also lead to errors in the way linework is drawn. Once again, the changes need to be made a certain way because you are dealing with special survey objects, this time survey figures. Survey figures are linked to the survey database. Unlike survey points, they can be edited without accessing the survey database, but at that point in time, they are no longer in sync with the survey database. It is important to use the correct commands and keep your edits in sync with the survey database to ensure that the correct data is utilized in the future.

The *Essentials 5* database is the result of correctly completing the previous exercise. This database is provided to ensure that you start the current exercise with the correct version.

1. Open the drawing named Edit Survey Figures.dwg located in the Chapter 03 class data folder.

2. If the contents beneath the Essentials 5 survey database are not visible, right-click Essentials 5 and select Open For Edit.

3. Zoom in to the building that is missing its north side. You'll find it between the driveway and the fence line near the northwest corner of the site.

4. Click the building figure line, and then click Survey Figure Properties on the ribbon. Notice that point 285 is missing a CLS (close) code that would provide the north side of the building by closing the rectangle.

5. Click point 285 in the point list; then set the Closed value to Yes and click OK. The shape of the building is now closed. Because you used the Survey Figure Properties command to edit this figure, the drawing and the survey database are in sync.

At this point, you could back out and fix the point description, but for the purposes of this exercise, you'll edit the figure instead.

6. Press Esc to clear the previous selection. Pan to the southeast until you can see the building to the west of the 6" (150mm) pine. This building should appear as two separate buildings. Click the building figure, and then click Survey Figure Properties on the ribbon.

7. In the Figure Properties dialog box, click point 288 and then click the red X icon. Remove points 289, 290, and 291 in the same manner.

8. Click OK to close the Figure Properties dialog box. Now, only the north building is shown in the drawing.

9. Right-click Figures on the Survey tab and select Create Figure Interactively.

10. When prompted, enter **BLD2** as the figure name and click OK.

11. Click the four points that make up the smaller building, and then press Enter.

12. In the Figure Properties dialog box, set the Closed value to Yes. Adjust the order of the points using the arrow buttons, if necessary. Click OK when the blue figure outline appears as a rectangle in the drawing.

The figure seems to disappear in this step. It actually was never drawn and has to be inserted from the survey database.

13. On the Survey tab, click Figures. Scroll down until you can see BLD2 in the list of figures. Right-click BLD2 and select Insert Into Drawing.

14. Click somewhere on the Survey tab other than Figures to remove the blue highlighting. If the building rectangle is not closed, use the Survey Figure Properties command to close it as you did in steps 4 and 5. The building figure now appears as it should and the two separate buildings are represented properly, as shown in Figure 3.7.

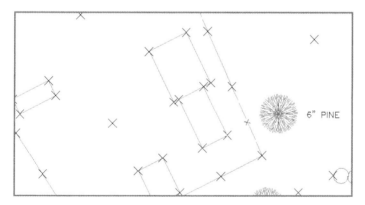

FIGURE 3.7 The result of editing the building figures

Creating Additional Points

You may occasionally need to create your own points to establish key locations in the drawing. For example, early in the design, you may want to show specific locations for proposed test borings or property corners that need to be found. Another example is that you may have a point file that you would like to import

Certification Objective

into the drawing without including it in a survey database. Civil 3D has a multitude of tools designed to create points easily and efficiently. They are found on a special toolbar that opens when you click the Point Creation Tools command on the Home tab of the ribbon.

In many ways, the points you create using these tools are treated just the same as those created by importing survey data. They can be placed in point groups and can respond to description keys. They can also be affected by point styles and point label styles. There are differences, however, between these points and those created by importing survey data. For example, Civil 3D cannot automatically generate linework by importing points in this manner. Also, these points do not have the protection of the survey database, allowing them to be edited by anyone who opens the drawing. Regardless of how they are created, all points can be exported to a file that can be uploaded to a portable device and taken to the field to be staked out.

To create additional points in the drawing by importing point data and creating points within the drawing, follow these steps:

Stake out **is a term used by surveyors to refer to placing markers in the field at predetermined locations, often calculated in the office.**

1. Open the drawing named `Stake Out.dwg` located in the `Chapter 03` class data folder. This drawing contains a calculated property boundary reconstructed from a deed or other source of information. It also contains a preliminary layout of the road centerlines that will be used to determine soil test boring locations. You'll begin by inserting points into the drawing that represent property corners located in the field.

2. On the Insert tab of the ribbon, click Points From File.

3. In the Import Points dialog box, select PNEZD (Comma Delimited) as the format. Then click the plus sign icon and browse to the `Chapter 03` class data folder.

4. For Files Of Type, select the Text/Template/Extract File (*.txt) option. Then select `Found Corners.txt` and click Open.

5. Click OK to dismiss the Import Points dialog box.

There are points in the drawing that have the same numbers. This is resolved by increasing the incoming point numbers by 1000.

6. On the Duplicate Point Number dialog box, under Resolution, select Add An Offset. Type **1000** in the box below Add An Offset From and click OK.

7. On Prospector, expand Point Groups. Right-click Found Corners and select Update. This will apply the default styles from the point group

to the newly imported points. Found corners will appear with red markers and text.

8. Notice that two points are missing along the south property boundary as well as one point on the east property boundary and one at the northwest corner (four points in all). Finding and locating these corners in the field will greatly improve the accuracy and validity of the property survey.

9. On the Home tab of the ribbon, click Points ➢ Point Creation Tools.

10. On the Create Points toolbar, click the button on the far left to launch the Miscellaneous Manual tool. Snap to the locations of the missing points.

11. On Prospector, right-click the Corners To Be Found point group and select Update. These points display in blue.

12. On the Create Points toolbar, click the chevron on the far right to expand the toolbar.

13. Expand Points Creation and enter BORE as the Default Description.

14. Click the down arrow on the button farthest to the left, and then click Measure Object.

15. Click one of the magenta road centerlines. Press Enter three times to accept the default starting station, ending station, and offset.

16. Type an interval of 250 (80) and press Enter. The points will be created at a 250-foot (80m) interval along the polyline you've selected.

17. On Prospector, update the Test Borings point group.

18. Repeat steps 14 to 17 for the remaining road centerlines.

19. On the Output tab of the ribbon, click Export Points.

20. For format, select PNEZD (Comma Delimited). Check the box next to Limit To Points In Point Group and select Corners To Be Found.

21. Click OK and browse to the Chapter 03 class data folder. Specify a filename of Corners to be Found.txt.

22. Repeat steps 19 to 21 for the Test Boring point group to create a Test Borings.txt point file.

THE ESSENTIALS AND BEYOND

In this chapter, you learned the necessary steps to convert raw survey data into meaningful drawing information. As you saw, this is done by importing raw data into a survey database while having the proper configuration in place to display the points and draw linework according to the appropriate graphical standards. You also learned how to edit the resulting drawing information and add more data to it that can be exported back out to the field personnel for stakeout or additional location.

ADDITIONAL EXERCISE

In this exercise, you will continue configuring Civil 3D so that it can properly display property information gathered in the field. Use the Property Survey.dwg file and Essentials 6 survey database located in the Chapter 03 class data folder to do the following:

1. Set up the following description keys within the Essentials description key set:

NEW DESCRIPTION KEYS

Code	Style	Point Label Style	Format	Layer
ROW*	Bound	<default>	$*	V-NODE-BNDY
PROP*	Iron Pin	<default>	$*	V-NODE-BNDY

2. Set up the following figure prefixes within the Essentials figure prefix database:

NEW FIGURE PREFIXES

Name	Breakline	Lot Line	Layer	Style	Site
ROW	No	Yes	V-RWAY	Basic	Survey Site
PROP	No	Yes	V-PROP-BNDY	Basic	Survey Site

3. Set up a new point group named Property Corners that includes points with a raw description matching ROW* and PROP*. Assign a default point label style of Point# and Description. The default point style won't matter, because it is being assigned by the description key.

THE ESSENTIALS AND BEYOND *(Continued)*

4. Import the Property Survey.txt point file located in the Chapter 03 class data folder. It should be a second import event within the Essentials 6 survey database.

5. If everything is done properly, right-of-way lines should be drawn along the road with square symbols marking the corners. Property lines should be drawn around the project with circular symbols marking the corners. A new parcel should be created with a label near the center of the property. Click this label, and then click Parcel Properties on the ribbon. Change the style of the parcel to Property.

Visit www.sybex.com/go/civil2013essentials to download a video of the author completing this exercise. You can also download the Answers to Additional Exercises Appendix which contains even more information about completing this exercise.

CHAPTER 4

Modeling the Existing Terrain Using Surfaces

In Chapter 3, you learned how to establish the existing conditions of a project by playing a very elaborate game of connect-the-dots. Thus far, you've been solving the connect-the-dots puzzle in only two dimensions— creating the tree lines, fence lines, buildings, trees, and so on. Now, you'll use the same data to establish the third dimension of your existing conditions model, and you'll do that using AutoCAD® Civil 3D® surfaces.

Many would say that the goal in this process is to generate existing contours for the project. Twenty years ago, that would have been true, but in this era of 3D modeling, the result of your efforts will serve a much greater purpose. Although it's true that you'll be able to create contours from your surface model, you'll also create an accurate 3D representation of the ground that can be used in many ways throughout the project.

- ▶ **Understanding surfaces**

- ▶ **Creating a surface from survey data**

- ▶ **Using breaklines to improve surface accuracy**

- ▶ **Editing surfaces**

- ▶ **Displaying and analyzing surfaces**

- ▶ **Annotating surfaces**

Understanding Surfaces

As you might guess, the game of 3D connect-the-dots is a bit more sophisticated than the 2D version. In addition, you need the result to be a 3D model rather than just lines. To accomplish this, you need to apply a computer algorithm that connects the dots in the most efficient and accurate way possible. This algorithm is known as a *Triangular Irregular Network* or *TIN*.

The TIN algorithm works by connecting one point to at least two of its neighbors using 3D lines. Because each point connects to two or more of its neighbors, the resulting model looks something like a spider web made up of triangles (the *T* in TIN). Because the spacing between points is typically nonuniform, the triangles come in many shapes and sizes—which is why it's called irregular (the *I* in TIN). The network (the *N* in TIN) part comes from all of the points being connected by lines, and the points and lines being related to one another. Figure 4.1 shows a surface with its TIN lines visible.

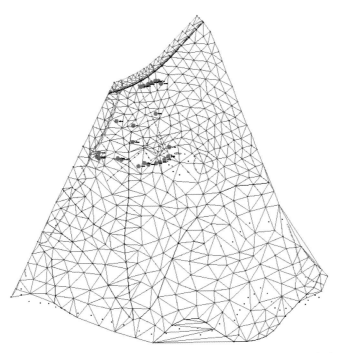

FIGURE 4.1 A surface model displayed as TIN lines. Note the irregular triangular shapes that make up the surface model.

There's even more to it than the triangles, though. In fact, the triangles are just a handy visual representation of the algorithm at work, and by themselves, they really aren't all that useful. What *is* useful is that the algorithm can calculate the elevation of any point within the area covered by the TIN model. So, even if you pick a point in the open space inside a triangle, the elevation will be calculated. This is what makes the TIN model a true model. It can be sliced, turned on its side, have water poured on it, excavated, and filled in—all virtually, of course. The capability to use surface models for these types of calculations and simulations is what makes them so useful and puts them at the core of Civil 3D functionality.

Creating a Surface from Survey Data

You create a surface in Prospector by simply right-clicking the Surfaces node of the tree and selecting Create Surface, as shown in Figure 4.2. The newly created surface appears in Prospector immediately but cannot be seen in the drawing until some data is added to it. The fundamental components of a surface are points and lines. It is your job to supply the source of the points, and Civil 3D will take care of drawing the lines. At this phase of the project, you will be using survey points as the initial source of surface point data.

Certification
Objective

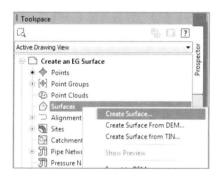

FIGURE 4.2 Creating a surface from within Prospector

Follow these steps to create the surface from survey data:

1. Open the drawing named Create an EG Surface.dwg located in the Chapter 04 class data folder.

2. On Prospector, right-click Surfaces and select Create Surface.

3. In the Create Surface dialog box, enter **EG** in the Name field.

4. For Style, select C-Existing Contours (1′) (C-Existing Contours (0.5m)). Click OK to dismiss the Create Surface dialog box.

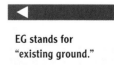

**EG stands for
"existing ground."**

5. In Prospector, expand Surfaces ➤ EG ➤ Definition. Study the items listed beneath EG in the tree (Figure 4.3).

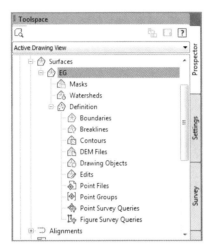

FIGURE 4.3 The contents of a surface shown in Prospector

6. Right-click Point Groups and select Add.

7. Select Ground Shots and click OK. The surface is now visible in the drawing in the form of contours.

8. Click one of the contours in the drawing to select the surface. Right-click and select Object Viewer.

9. In the Object Viewer window, select the 3dWireframe visual style, as shown in Figure 4.4.

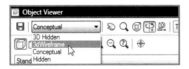

FIGURE 4.4 Changing the visual style to 3dWireframe within the Object Viewer window

This change in appearance is a function of the surface style.

10. Click near the bottom of the Object Viewer window and drag upward to change the view. The appearance of the surface will change to show the TIN lines.

11. Change the visual style of the Object Viewer window to Conceptual and look at the model from several different viewpoints. This way of studying the surface gives a real sense of the surface as a solid model in which the area inside the triangles has "substance." It is also a great visual representation of the TIN algorithm and the surface model (Figure 4.5).

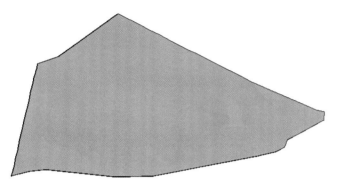

FIGURE 4.5 A surface shown using the Conceptual visual style

COMPONENTS OF A SURFACE

As shown in Figure 4.3, you can use many potential types of information to create a surface and control its shape. The following list describes each one briefly.

Boundaries   Boundaries are used to control where the surface *is*. A boundary around the edge of a surface can keep it contained within a certain area. Another type of boundary can keep a surface out of an interior area like a pond or building.

Breaklines   Breaklines force TIN lines to align with them. In this way, they help to define "hard edges" such as edges of embankments, curb lines, ditch lines, and so on.

Contours   Usually, we think of contours as the end product of building a surface, but they can also be used as a source of data for a surface.

DEM Files   DEM stands for digital elevation model and is typically associated with large-scale mapping that has relatively low accuracy. DEMs can often be found alongside large-scale mapping data and are typically only accurate enough for rough analysis or calculations.

(Continues)

COMPONENTS OF A SURFACE *(Continued)*

Drawing Objects   Drawing objects are AutoCAD® entities such as lines, blocks, and even text. These items can be used to help define a surface as effectively as survey points, as long as they've been created at the appropriate elevations.

Edits   Edits aren't actual data, but they do contribute to the makeup of a surface. There are many ways in which a surface can be edited to improve its accuracy or usability. Some of these editing methods will be covered in this chapter.

Point Files   You've already learned that a point file is a text file containing *x*, *y*, and *z* data. So far, you've used these files to create Civil 3D points in the drawing, but the same data can also be imported directly into a surface.

Point Groups   In Chapter 3, you learned that one of the benefits of point groups is that they enable multiple points to be selected simultaneously. Using one or more point groups to define a surface is one of the most important and most common uses of point groups in Civil 3D.

Using Breaklines to Improve Surface Accuracy

Certification
Objective

The TIN algorithm creates surfaces by drawing 3D lines between points that are closest to each other. In certain instances, this is not the most accurate way to model the surface, and the TIN lines must be forced into a specific arrangement. This arrangement typically coincides with a linear feature such as a curb, top of an embankment, or wall. This forced alignment of TIN lines along a linear feature is best handled with a breakline. In Figure 4.6, the blue lines represent the edges of a channel and the TIN lines are shown in red. In the image on the top, the blue lines have not been added to the channel surface as breaklines, resulting in a rough and inaccurate representation of the channel. In the image on the bottom, the breaklines have been applied and force the TIN lines to align with the edges of the channel, producing a much smoother and more accurate model.

From Prospector, you can add breaklines by right-clicking the Breaklines node for a given surface and selecting Add (Figure 4.7). When it comes to survey data, there is an even easier way. From the Survey Toolspace, you can right-click Figures and select Create Breaklines. This will open a list of all your survey figures with some checked as breaklines and some not (Figure 4.8). How does it know which is which? It was specified in the figure prefix database that you learned about in Chapter 3. As the figures were created, they were automatically tagged as breaklines or non-breaklines according to the code assigned to the points that define them.

FIGURE 4.6 The effect of breaklines on a surface

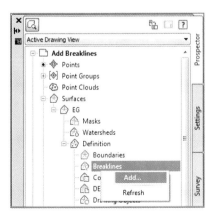

FIGURE 4.7 Adding breaklines from within Prospector

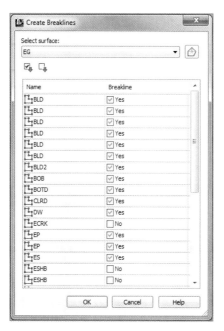

FIGURE 4.8 Creating breaklines from survey figures. Note how some figures are checked as breaklines and some are not.

To add breaklines to a surface and observe their effect on the accuracy of the surface, follow these steps:

1. Open the drawing named Add Breaklines.dwg located in the Chapter 04 class data folder.

2. On the Survey tab of the Toolspace, right-click Survey Databases and select Set Working Folder.

3. Browse to and select the Chapter 04 class data folder. Click OK. You should see a different survey database named Essentials.

4. Right-click the Essentials survey database and select Open For Edit.

5. Expand the Essentials database. Right-click Figures and select Create Breaklines.

6. Scan the list of figures and note which ones are tagged as breaklines. Click OK.

BREAKLINES IN THE FIELD

As you study the list of figures in this exercise, are you wondering why some are designated as breaklines and others are not? Breaklines are linear features that mark a change in the slope of the ground. Some of these are quite obvious, such as a set of bottom of bank (BOB) points and top of ditch (TOPD) points. Others serve double-duty, such as an edge of pavement (EP). This survey figure marks the line where pavement ends and dirt begins, but typically, there is also a change in slope at this line between the slope of the ground and the man-made slope of the road. For this reason, EPs are often tagged as breaklines. Other features obviously have nothing to do with the slope of the ground, such as a right of way (ROW), treeline (TL), and fence line (FENC); therefore, they are not checked as breaklines.

7. In the Add Breaklines dialog box, change the Mid-ordinate Distance value to **0.1** and click OK (see the "Breakline Settings and Options" sidebar for more information). You should notice a change in the contours along the red breaklines. These breaklines define the swales, edges, and ridges that were recognized in the field and explicitly located as terrain features. In addition, notice that contours now cover the road area to the north. The surface in this area is made strictly of breaklines.

8. Click one of the surface contours, and then click Surface Properties on the ribbon.

9. On the Information tab of the Surface Properties dialog box, change the Surface style to Triangles. Click OK. Notice how TIN lines do not cross the breaklines.

10. Open Surface Properties once again. On the Definition tab, uncheck the box next to Add Breakline, as shown in Figure 4.9. Click OK, and then click Rebuild The Surface. You have removed the effect of the breaklines temporarily. Notice how the TIN lines cross back and forth over the swale and ridge lines, creating a rough edge where there should be a sharp, well-defined edge.

FIGURE 4.9 Unchecking the Add Breakline operation for the surface

This exercise shows you the importance of breaklines. Connecting a bunch of points together with 3D triangular shapes does not necessarily generate an accurate surface. In certain areas, the shapes themselves have to be manipulated so they align with terrain features in order to accurately model their form. Figure 4.10 compares the surface with and without breaklines in both 2D and 3D views.

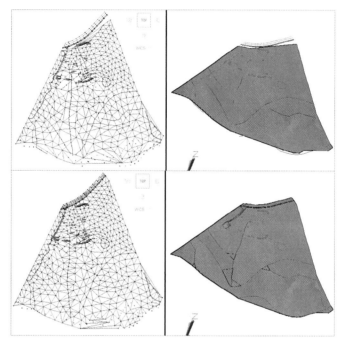

FIGURE 4.10 The two top views show the surface in 2D and 3D without the breaklines; the two bottom views show the surface with the breaklines included.

BREAKLINE SETTINGS AND OPTIONS

The Add Breaklines dialog box has several options and values to choose from. Here is a brief explanation of each:

Type Of the five types listed here, only two are important to discuss at this time: proximity and standard. Standard breaklines have two jobs. First, they control the alignment of TIN lines, as discussed previously. Second, their vertices are a source of additional point information in the drawing. As you might recall, the only point group you added to the surface is Ground Shots, so you'll need the points to come along with these breaklines as well. For this to work, the vertices of the breaklines must be 3D and must be at the correct elevations.

BREAKLINE SETTINGS AND OPTIONS *(Continued)*

Proximity breaklines have only one job, which is to control the alignment of TIN lines. Therefore, proximity breaklines only need to be 2D, but they must have points in their *proximity* so that they can "steal" their elevations. If you had added all of the survey points to your surface, then the survey figures could have been added as proximity breaklines.

Weeding Factors   Sometimes, the items you use for breaklines can have too many vertices on them, and you'll want to eliminate some of them so that your surface isn't overloaded with data. The selective removal of points based on distance and angle is known as weeding.

Supplementing by Distance   Sometimes your breaklines will have long stretches without any vertices in them. Since new TIN lines are only created where there are points, and points are only created where there are vertices, some supplemental vertices may be needed to improve the accuracy of the surface. When you check the box next to Distance, Civil 3D will create more points along the breakline that are spaced out according to the value you provide.

Supplementing by Mid-ordinate   Curves are a bit of a challenge because TIN lines are straight and curves are…curved. For that reason, any curves in a breakline are approximated with a series of short TIN lines. Just how short and numerous these lines are depends on the mid-ordinate setting. Mid-ordinate is a geometric term that refers to the perpendicular distance between an arc and its chord. When this distance is short, the chord is also short and multiple instances of it can fit within the length of the arc. This might seem like a strange way to define this behavior, but what's handy about it is that a single mid-ordinate value works pretty well for a fairly wide range of curve radii. The following image shows the effect of the mid-ordinate setting on a surface. The image on the left uses a value of 0.1, and the image on the right uses a value of 1.0.

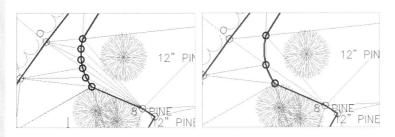

Editing Surfaces

Certification
Objective With the inclusion of points and breaklines in the surface, you have essentially provided all the data that will be needed to create the surface model. However, you should continue manipulating this data until you achieve the most accurate representation of the existing ground surface possible. You can edit surfaces in many ways. In this section, you will learn about three surface editing methods: adding boundaries, deleting lines, and editing points.

Adding Boundaries

As discussed earlier, boundaries are a way of defining where the surface is and where it is not. In the example project, you do not want the surface to exist outside of the area that has been surveyed. Why would the surface extend beyond the survey data? If the edge of an area represented by the points happens to bend inward, the lines will extend across the "bay" (Figure 4.11) and will create misrepresented surface data in that area. One way to avoid or correct this situation is to provide an outer boundary that prevents the surface from existing in these areas.

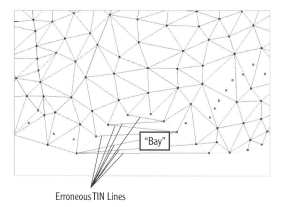

Erroneous TIN Lines

FIGURE 4.11 Erroneous TIN lines created across a "bay" in the surface data

Another common example of surfaces being where they shouldn't is within the shape of a building. It is considered poor drafting practice to show contours passing through a building. After all, the ground surface is not accessible in that location. Another type of boundary, called a *hide boundary,* can be used to remove surface data from within a surface, thus creating a void or "hole" in the surface.

TYPES OF BOUNDARIES

The four types of boundaries that you can create with Civil 3D are as follows:

Outer   An outer boundary establishes a perimeter for the surface. No surface data can exist outside an outer boundary. This type of boundary is commonly used in most surfaces.

Hide   A hide boundary creates a void or hole in the surface. Hide boundaries are commonly used to remove surface data within buildings.

Show   A show boundary creates an island of data within a hide boundary. An example of a show boundary is a courtyard within the footprint of a building.

Data Clip   The first three types of boundaries hide the surface data after it has been created. A data clip boundary is a special type of boundary that prevents data outside it from ever becoming part of the surface at all. Data clip boundaries are used in cases where a small surface is made from source data that covers a large area.

Follow these steps to add boundaries around the buildings that will remove surface data from within their footprints:

1. Open the drawing named Surface Boundaries.dwg located in the Chapter 04 class data folder.

2. In Prospector, expand Surfaces ➢ EG ➢ Definition.

3. Right-click Boundaries and select Add.

4. Enter **Bld1** as the boundary name and select Hide as the type. Make sure the box next to Non-destructive Breakline is checked and click OK.

5. Select one of the buildings in the drawing and press Enter. You should immediately see the contour lines removed from within the building. It appears that they have been trimmed, but actually, the surface data has been removed from within the shape of the building.

6. Repeat steps 3 to 5 for the other buildings, even if contours do not pass through them.

7. Click one of the contours to select the surface, right-click, and select Object Viewer. Set the visual style to Conceptual so that the surface is shaded in the Object Viewer window. As you view the surface from

The Non-destructive Breakline option creates a clean edge along the boundary by trimming some TIN lines and adding others.

Remember that contours aren't the only things for which you use surfaces. No matter how you look at this surface, you don't want data to appear where the buildings are.

a 3D perspective, notice that there are now voids where the buildings are located, as shown in Figure 4.12.

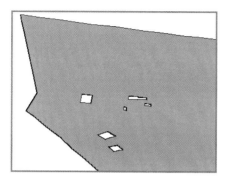

FIGURE 4.12 The effects of hide boundaries added at building locations

Deleting Lines

Another, less eloquent way of removing unwanted TIN lines is to delete them from the surface rather than using a boundary to do it for you. This method is best when you need to remove only a few TIN lines in isolated areas. There are two important things to remember when deleting TIN lines. The first is that in order for the lines to be deleted, they must be visible, which means you must apply a style that displays them. The second thing to remember is that you cannot use the AutoCAD ERASE command to remove them; instead, you must use the Delete Line command created especially for surfaces.

To delete unwanted TIN lines from a surface, follow these steps:

1. Open the drawing named Delete TIN Lines.dwg located in your Chapter 04 class data folder.

2. In Prospector, expand Surfaces. Right-click EG and select Surface Properties.

3. On the Information tab, change the Surface style to Triangles and click OK.

4. Zoom in to the southern edge of the surface and note the TIN lines that extend across the bend in the stream (shown previously in Figure 4.11).

5. On Prospector, expand Surfaces ➤ EG ➤ Definition. Right-click Edits and select Delete Line. Select the erroneous lines as indicated previously in Figure 4.11. Press Enter after you've made your selection.

6. Pan around the edge of the surface and delete any other TIN lines that look like they don't belong. The resulting surface should look similar to Figure 4.13.

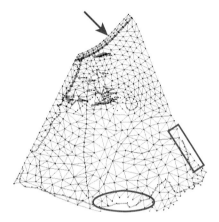

FIGURE 4.13 The extents of the surface after erroneous TIN lines have been removed, with the areas of removal highlighted

Editing Points

As you have learned, the fundamental building blocks of surfaces are points and lines. The points are derived from some other source of data such as standard breaklines, contours, survey points, and so on. If there is an error in one of those source objects, there will be an error in the surface as well. When this occurs, you can either edit the source data and rebuild the surface or edit the surface itself. You have already learned about editing survey source data (survey points and survey figures), so now follow these steps to edit the surface:

1. Open the drawing named Editing Points.dwg located in your Chapter 04 class data folder. This drawing has been split into two views, both zoomed in to the location where the driveway meets the road on the north side of the property. In this area, one of the surface points is incorrect. In the plan view on the left, the effects of the incorrect point can be seen in the densely packed contours. In the 3D view on the right, the erroneous point is quite obvious.

 2. Click one of the contours to select the surface, and then click Surface Properties on the ribbon.

3. In the Surface Properties dialog box, click the Information tab and change the Surface style to Triangles And Points. Click OK. The display of the surface will change to lines and points, with the points appearing as plus-sign markers.

 4. Click any TIN line to select the surface, and then click Edit Surface ➢ Modify Point on the ribbon.

5. When prompted to select a point, click the point in the 3D view that is located well below the other points (Figure 4.14). Press Enter.

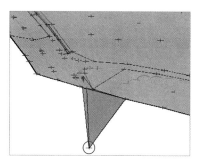

FIGURE 4.14 3D view of incorrect surface point

6. At the command line, type **190.76 (58.144)** and press Enter. Notice how the surface is modified but the survey figure is left behind. Depending on the situation, it may be prudent to go back to the source data for the survey figure and correct that as well.

7. Press Enter to exit the Modify Point command. Change the style of the surface back to C-Existing Contours (1′) (C-Existing Contours (0.5m)). Notice that the closely spaced contours are no longer there.

Displaying and Analyzing Surfaces

Certification
Objective

Because you're working with a surface object in Civil 3D, you can do much more than simply show contours. Civil 3D surfaces can help you tell many different stories about the shape of the land and how water will flow across it. They are able to do this through multiple types of analyses as well as the ability for styles to display analysis results in nearly any way you wish. With these tools at your disposal, you will be able to study the terrain thoroughly and make smart choices about the direction of your design early in the process.

Analyzing Elevation

Elevation analysis allows you to delineate any number of elevation ranges and then graphically distinguish the different ranges by color. This is a useful tool in many instances, especially when you are working with someone who doesn't know how to read contours.

To perform an elevation analysis on a surface in your drawing, complete these steps:

1. Open the drawing named Elevation Analysis.dwg located in the Chapter 04 class data folder.

2. Click one of the contours to select the surface, and then click Surface Properties on the ribbon.

3. Change the surface style to Elevation Banding (2D).

4. Click the Analysis tab. Verify that the Analysis Type is Elevations and the number of ranges is 8.

5. Click the downward-pointing arrow to populate the Range Details section of the dialog box with new data.

6. Click OK to return to the drawing. The surface undergoes an obvious change and is now displayed as a series of colored bands, with red signifying the lowest elevations and purple signifying the highest.

7. Change the style of the surface to Elevation Banding (3D). Now, the 3D view displays the colored bands as a 3D representation with exaggerated elevations. This tells a clear story about the existing shape of the land for this site (Figure 4.15).

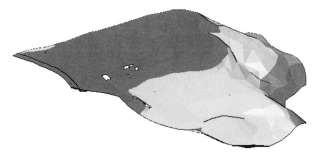

FIGURE 4.15 A 3D view of a surface using the Elevation Banding (3D) style

Analyzing Slope

Another important aspect of the terrain is the slope. Areas with very steep slopes are difficult to navigate either by construction vehicles or the eventual occupants of the property. Flat slopes are much more accessible, but if they are too flat, then drainage problems often occur. One of your tasks as a designer is to ensure that your project has the right slopes in the right areas. By studying the slopes of the existing topography, you can locate features where slopes are good or determine that terrain modifications will be necessary to create good slopes.

Civil 3D can display slopes in two ways. The first is to show the slopes as colored ranges like the ones you saw in the previous section. The second is to use slope arrows that can be color-coded to indicate what range they're in, with the added benefit of always pointing downhill to show you the direction of water flow.

To perform a slope analysis on a surface in your drawing, complete these steps:

1. Open the drawing named Slope Analysis.dwg located in the Chapter 04 class data folder.

2. Click one of the contours to select the surface, and then click Surface Properties on the ribbon.

3. On the Information tab of the Surface Properties dialog box, change the Surface Style to Slope Banding (3D).

4. Click the Analysis tab. Change the Analysis Type to Slopes and click the downward-pointing arrow.

5. Click OK. In the 3D image on the right, the darkest reds signify the steepest slopes. This enables you to see that the area north of the farm is fairly flat pasture land while the area to the south of the farm slopes dramatically toward the stream farther to the south (Figure 4.16).

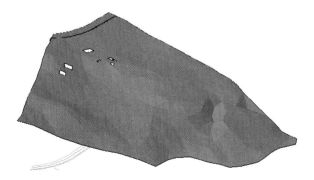

F I G U R E   4 . 1 6 Slope analysis of surface shown in 3D

6. Access Surface Properties again and change the style to Slope Arrows.

7. On the Analysis tab, choose Slope Arrows as the Analysis Type and click the arrow once again.

8. Click OK to return to the drawing. In this view, the darker blues are the steepest slopes and the arrows themselves always point downhill. As you study the arrows, you should notice a drainage divide that runs west-to-east behind the farm buildings. Rain falling to the north of this area drains to the road and rain falling south of it drains to the stream.

Performing Other Types of Analysis

In addition to analyses of elevations, slopes, and slope arrows, you can also perform the following types of analyses:

Contours   Contours can be used to analyze a surface. They can be color coded, and a legend table can be created that shows the area and/or volume that the contours represent.

Directions   With this type of analysis, you can see a visual representation of your surface slopes. For example, you can use it to see which parts of your surface flow to the south and which flow to the north.

User-Defined Contours   Contours are usually placed at even intervals, such as the 1′ (0.5 meter) contours you have been working with so far. What if you want to show a contour that represents elevation 92.75? That's done as a user-defined contour. A user-defined contour is an individual instance of a contour, usually at an irregular interval that exists between the regular intervals.

Watersheds   A watershed analysis will outline areas within the surface where rainfall runoff flows to a certain point or in a certain direction. This type of analysis is yet another way of studying the drainage characteristics of the terrain.

Exploring Even More Analysis Tools

There are even more ways of analyzing your surface that are not found in Surface Properties. For example, the following tools are especially useful on many projects:

Water Drop Tool   With the Water Drop tool, you can click any point on your surface and Civil 3D will trace the path from that point downhill until it reaches a low point or encounters the edge of the surface. This is a very detailed way to study how water will flow across the ground.

Catchment Area Tool   With this tool, you can click a point on the surface and Civil 3D will draw a closed shape that represents the area that flows to that point. This is very useful when you're analyzing the effects of rainfall on your project.

Quick Profile   With the Quick Profile tool, you can display a slice of your surface to get an "edge-on" view of it. This can help you understand the slope of the land and the location of high and low points.

Annotating Surfaces

Certification
Objective

As you have read, surfaces are used to tell a story about the shape of a piece of land. I have presented nearly a dozen different ways to tell that story but have yet to discuss the most obvious and most common way to tell that story: with text. In this section, you will use the following three types of labels to annotate a surface:

▶ Spot elevation labels

▶ Slope labels

▶ Contour labels

Adding Spot Elevation Labels

To annotate a surface using spot elevation labels, follow these steps:

1. Open the drawing named `Labeling Surfaces.dwg` located in the Chapter 04 class data folder.

2. Zoom in to the north end of the project near the location where the magenta centerline meets the centerline of the existing road. Your task is to label the elevation of the existing road where these two centerlines meet.

 3. Click one of the contours to select the surface, and then click Add Labels ➢ Add Surface Labels on the ribbon.

4. In the Add Labels dialog box, select Spot Elevation as the Label Type.

5. Verify that the spot elevation Label Style is set to Elevation Only – Existing and the Marker Style is set to Spot Elevation.

6. Click Add. Snap to the northern endpoint of the magenta centerline. A label is placed at the location you selected (Figure 4.17).

7. Keep this drawing open for the upcoming exercise.

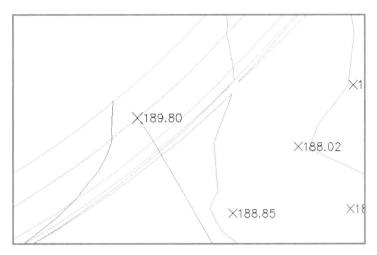

FIGURE 4.17 Spot elevation label showing 189.80′ (57.851m) added where the new road meets the existing road

A NOTE ABOUT UNITS

Throughout this chapter, you'll notice that two values are provided for units of measurement. The first value is provided for the imperial system that is used in the United States, and the second value in parentheses is provided for the metric system that is used in many other countries. These values most often represent imperial feet and metric meters. It is important to note that generally only the numeric values are entered in the software, not terms like *feet* or *meters*. Also, you should know that the two numbers provided are not necessarily equal. In most cases, they are similar values that are rounded to work efficiently in their respective measurement systems.

Adding Slope Labels

To annotate a surface using slope labels, follow these steps:

1. With the Labeling Surfaces.dwg drawing from the previous exercise still open, pan to the south where the road centerline bends at a 90-degree angle. Note the steep slope to the south of the road in this area. You want to measure and label the slope in this area to determine whether homes can be built here and/or if guardrails will be required for the road.

2. If the Add Labels dialog box is already open, skip to the next step. If not, click one of the contours to select the surface, and then click Add Labels ➢ Add Surface Labels on the ribbon.

3. For Label Type, select Slope.

This will create a label that points directly downhill at the one point you select. With two-point labels, you control the direction.

4. Verify that Slope Label Style is set to Percent-Existing and click Add.

5. When prompted at the command line, press Enter to accept the default of <One-point>.

6. Click a point to the south of the road to label the slope. Press the Esc key to end the command.

7. Click the label, and then click the square grip at the midpoint of the arrow. Move your cursor across the drawing and note how the label changes.

This dynamic label behavior is consistent throughout Civil 3D.

8. Keep this drawing open for the upcoming exercise.

Adding Contour Labels

To annotate a surface using contour labels, follow these steps:

1. If the Add Labels dialog box is already open (in the Labeling Surfaces.dwg drawing from the previous exercise), skip to the next step. If not, click one of the contours to select the surface, and then click Add Labels ➢ Add Surface Labels on the ribbon.

2. For Label Type, select Contour – Multiple. Verify that the names of all three label styles begin with Existing and click Add.

3. Click two points in the drawing that stretch across several contours. Contour labels will appear where contours fall between the two points you've selected (Figure 4.18). In fact, you've actually drawn an invisible line that intersects with the contours.

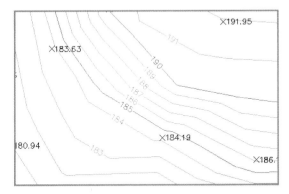

FIGURE 4.18 Contour labels

4. Press Esc to clear the previous command, and then click one of the newly created labels. Notice the line that appears. Click one of the grips and move it to a new location to change the location of the line. The contour labels go where the line goes, even if you stretch it out and cause it to cross through more contours, in which case it will create more labels.

5. Continue placing contour labels until you've evenly distributed labels throughout the drawing.

THE ESSENTIALS AND BEYOND

Although survey data is the ideal choice for creating existing ground surfaces, there will be many times when you are asked to create surfaces from alternate sources of data. For example, to do a preliminary hydrologic analysis, terrain data is needed for a large area that drains to the stream on the south side of the project. It is not feasible to survey an area this large with conventional surveying—in fact, that level of accuracy is not needed for this type of analysis. For this reason, GIS contours will be used to create an existing ground surface.

(Continues)

THE ESSENTIALS AND BEYOND *(Continued)*

ADDITIONAL EXERCISE

Open the drawing named Surface From Contours.dwg located in the Chapter 04 class data folder. Do the following:

1. Create a surface from the contour data in the drawing.

2. Use the green polyline in the drawing to create an outer boundary for the surface.

3. Perform an elevation analysis to illustrate the distribution of high and low elevations across the surface.

4. Assign the C-Existing Contours (5′) (C-Existing Contours (2m)) style to the surface.

5. Create several spot elevation and slope labels on the surface.

6. Create contour labels for the surface.

Visit www.sybex.com/go/civil2013essentials to download a video of the author completing this exercise. You can also download the Answers to Additional Exercises Appendix which contains even more information about completing this exercise.

CHAPTER 5

Designing in 2D Using Alignments

Now that the existing conditions of the project have been thoroughly established, you are ready to move on to designing the new work to be constructed on the site. A common way of beginning this design is to lay out a 2D version of some of the key features of the project. If this were a commercial site project, you might start by drawing the outlines of buildings, sidewalks, and parking lots. For an environmental project such as wetland relocation, you might begin by drawing a 2D outline of the new wetland boundary. Since our example project is a single-family residential development, the key features are the roads. So, you would begin your design by drawing a basic version of them in 2D. As you are about to learn, AutoCAD® Civil 3D® alignments are the best tool for establishing this basic geometry and then using it as the basis for additional design.

▶ **Understanding alignments**

▶ **Creating alignments from objects**

▶ **Creating alignments using the Alignment Creation Tools**

▶ **Editing alignments**

▶ **Applying design criteria files and check sets**

Understanding Alignments

You can think of the basic road geometry discussed in the chapter introduction as a single-line form of the roads, as shown in Figure 5.1. The lines that you draw will typically represent the centerlines of the roads, and eventually, you will build the rest of each road around those centerlines.

Civil 3D alignments are designed specifically for the task of representing the initial single-line version of a linear design feature. They are also used to establish the backbone of a linear design such as a road, railroad, channel, pipe line, and many other examples. The lines, arcs, and spirals that make up an alignment have the ability to interact with one another. This enables you to edit part of the alignment and have the other parts fix themselves automatically. Also, more design objects can be built around alignments, such as profiles, cross-sections, and corridors, which will be discussed later in this book.

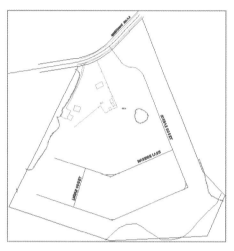

FIGURE 5.1 A single-line drawing of the subdivision roads (in red)

Creating Alignments from Objects

Certification
Objective

A common way of creating an alignment is to use the basic AutoCAD® geometry that's already in the drawing. You may be using someone's "sketch," or maybe you've chosen to draw the initial version of the layout this way because of the simplicity of the AutoCAD tools. Whatever the case, Civil 3D makes it fairly easy to convert simple AutoCAD entities into alignments.

To create alignments from objects in your drawing, complete the following steps:

Notice on the command line that the Create Alignment From Objects command accepts lines, arcs, and polylines.

▶

1. Open the drawing named Alignment from Objects.dwg located in the Chapter 05 class data folder.

2. On the Home tab of the ribbon, click Alignment ➤ Create Alignment From Objects.

3. When the command line prompts you to select an object, click the longest magenta polyline that is labeled Jordan Court.

4. Press Enter. A black arrow should appear on the polyline, indicating the program's guess at the direction of the alignment.

5. If the arrow is pointing toward the south, press Enter. If it is pointing north, press R and then press Enter.

6. In the Create Alignment From Objects dialog box, do the following:

   ▶ For Name, verify that it says Jordan Court.

   ▶ For Site, verify that <None> is selected.

   ▶ For Alignment Style, verify that Proposed is selected.

   ▶ For Alignment Label Set, verify that _No Labels is selected.

   ▶ Uncheck the box next to Add Curves Between Tangents.

   ▶ Check the box next to Erase Existing Entities.

   ▶ Click OK.

7. Click the newly created alignment, and then click one of the magenta polylines. Notice how the polyline grips are different than the alignment grips (Figure 5.2). Experiment with moving the grips and compare the behavior of a Civil 3D alignment with the behavior of a polyline.

Believe it or not, the choice here is very important. The direction of the alignment will affect the configuration and labeling of many more components of this design as it progresses.

ALIGNMENTS ARE SMARTER

As you investigate the grip editing behavior of the alignment versus the polyline, what do you find? You should notice that the alignment wants to follow a very basic geometric rule that the polyline isn't too worried about: maintaining tangency. Whether you move or stretch a straight line portion (aka tangent) or modify a curve, the adjacent lines and curves morph themselves to remain tangent (shown here). This is a good thing because driving your car down a road where the curves and lines are not tangent could be hazardous to your health.

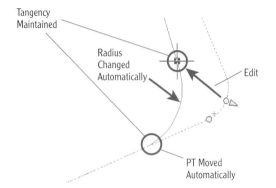

Tangency Maintained

Radius Changed Automatically

Edit

PT Moved Automatically

8. Repeat steps 2 through 6 to create the Madison Lane and Logan Court alignments.

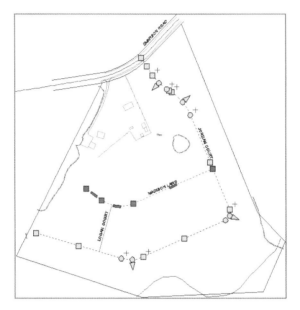

FIGURE 5.2 The object with the dark blue grips is a polyline, and the object with the light blue grips is an alignment. Alignments have more types of grips that enable more geometric editing functionality.

Creating Alignments Using the Alignment Creation Tools

 Certification Objective

In many cases, you will want to create alignments "from scratch," meaning that the exact geometry of the alignment is not already in place as it was in the previous section. In this case, you may use a different approach: the Civil 3D Alignment Creation Tools.

The Alignment Creation Tools are housed within Civil 3D's version of a toolbar and consist of a comprehensive set of commands to create and edit the lines, curves, and spirals that make up an alignment.

To create an alignment using the Alignment Creation Tools, follow these steps:

1. Open the drawing named Alignment Creation Tools.dwg located in the Chapter 05 class data folder.

2. Examine the blue geometry and accompanying dimensions and notes. This geometry is described in detail in the "Using Temporary Geometry" sidebar.

ALIGNMENT TERMINOLOGY

Before jumping into the next exercise, you may want to review the following list of terms that you will find throughout the Alignment Creation Tools commands as well as other places within Civil 3D.

Tangents (alignment segments): The straight-line portions of an alignment

Tangent (geometric condition):

▶ Touching or passing through at a single point

▶ In the case of a line and arc: perpendicular to a line drawn from the intersection point to the center point of the arc

▶ In the case of two arcs: intersecting in such a way that a line drawn from the center point of one arc to the center point of the other arc passes through the intersection point

Curves: The curved portions of an alignment that have a constant radius

Spiral: The curved portions of an alignment that change in radius from one end to the other

PI (point of intersection): The place where two tangents intersect or would intersect if they were extended

PC (point of curvature): The place where the curve begins

PT (point of tangency): The place where the curve ends

Free: A line, curve, or spiral that is dependent on another alignment segment at both ends

Floating: A line, curve, or spiral that is dependent on another alignment segment at one end

Fixed: A line, curve, or spiral that is not dependent on another alignment component at either end

3. On the Home tab, click Alignment ➤ Alignment Creation Tools.

4. In the Create Alignment – Layout dialog box, click OK to accept the defaults.

5. On the Alignment Creation Tools toolbar, click the black triangle on the first button on the left to expand it downward (see Figure 5.3). Then click Tangent-Tangent (With Curves).

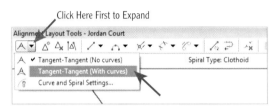

FIGURE 5.3 Selecting the Tangent-Tangent (With Curves) command

6. Snap to the center of the circle marked A.

7. Snap to circles B through E and press Enter. The Jordan Court alignment is created.

8. Repeat steps 3 through 5 and create the Madison Lane alignment using the circles marked F through H.

9. Repeat steps 3 through 5 once again, this time drawing the Logan Court alignment from circle I perpendicular to the Madison Lane alignment.

Using Temporary Geometry

The layout of any land development design is almost always influenced by existing physical and legal boundary features. In a residential project such as the example in this book, the goal is to create as many optimum-sized lots as possible within the available area. Every lot must also be accessible from roads built through the site. With these things in mind, along with the geometry of the existing property boundaries, terrain, and other constraints, it is often helpful to create some temporary geometry to guide you in the creation of the alignments.

In the drawing for this exercise, the blue linework is provided for you and represents reference geometry to existing features of the site. Dimensions and notes have also been provided to help explain the reasoning behind this geometry. The following list represents key considerations when creating this temporary geometry:

- ▶ 150′ (45m) offset from road centerline to back of lots to accommodate 50′ (15m) right-of-way, adequate front yard, single-family residence, and adequate rear yard

- ▶ Perpendicular intersection with existing road that is ideal for safety and accessibility

USING TEMPORARY GEOMETRY *(Continued)*

- ▶ Avoidance of steep area to the south

- ▶ Uniform geometric properties where possible, such as 90 degree angles, parallel lines, and so on. This is recommended for simpler, more efficient stake-out and construction

- ▶ Avoidance of the farmhouse and buildings, because that part of the property will be deeded back to the original owner

In the real world, you will need to come up with this temporary geometry on your own. In fact, this is what design is really all about: using your knowledge and creativity to come up with a technical solution to a need or problem. Creating the alignment is the easy part. Coming up with the temporary geometry as described here is the real challenge.

Editing Alignments

Of course, nobody gets it right the first time. In fact, as a general rule, you'll find yourself laying things out about 10 percent of the time and spending the remaining 90 percent making edits. That's totally OK, because that's really the way Civil 3D was designed to be used. In fact, it's highly recommended that you do a rough layout of the basic design elements at the beginning of a project and then spend the rest of the time adjusting, refining, and improving that initial layout until it's the way it needs to be. This is also a great approach because it matches with the general nature of land development designs, which typically change frequently throughout the life of the project.

Editing Alignments with Grips

As you learned in the first section of this chapter, alignments are different. They're smarter and more sophisticated than basic AutoCAD entities. They have more types of grips, and the way they respond to geometric changes is more intelligent. You can leverage this to make quick visual edits to your alignment without ever typing a number or entering a command. To experiment with using grips to edit alignments, follow these steps:

1. Open the drawing named Graphical Editing.dwg located in the Chapter 05 class data folder.

This exercise goes more smoothly if Osnaps are turned off. If they are turned on, you can press F3 to turn them off.

2. Click the Jordan Court alignment to display its grips. Click the upright triangular grip on the second curve and drag it to a new location. This grip is located at the PI. As you move it, the curve always remains tangent and the radius of the curve remains constant (Figure 5.4).

3. Click the circular grip at either end of the curve and move it to a different location. These grips are located at the PC and PT. As you move them, the radius changes and tangency is maintained at both ends of the curve (Figure 5.5). They can be used to graphically set the exact beginning point or ending point of a curve.

FIGURE 5.4 Moving a PI grip   FIGURE 5.5 Moving a PC or PT grip

A NOTE ABOUT UNITS

Throughout this chapter, you'll notice that two values are provided for units of measurement. The first value is provided for the imperial system that is used in the United States, and the second value in parentheses is provided for the metric system that is used in many other countries. These values most often represent imperial feet and metric meters. It is important to note that generally only the numeric values are entered in the software, not terms like *feet* or *meters*. Also, you should know that the two numbers provided are not necessarily equal. In most cases, they are similar values that are rounded to work efficiently in their respective measurement systems.

4. Click the circular grip at the midpoint of the curve and move it to a different location. This grip is located at a pass-through point and forces the curve to pass through that point while maintaining tangency at both ends. This is accomplished by changing the radius of the curve (Figure 5.6). This grip can be used to make the curve pass through a specific point.

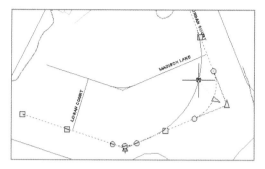

FIGURE 5.6 Moving the pass-through-point grip

5. Click the triangle grip located near the midpoint of the curve and place it in a new location. This grip controls the radius of the curve, while maintaining tangency at both ends of the curve (Figure 5.7).

FIGURE 5.7 Moving the radius grip

6. Click the square grip at the end of the Jordan Court alignment and place it in a different location. This type of grip is located at either the beginning or the end of the alignment. As it is moved, the geometry adjacent to it will respond. In the case of this alignment, the curve just before the endpoint changes the locations of its beginning and ending points to remain tangent at both ends (Figure 5.8).

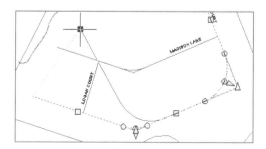

FIGURE 5.8 Moving the start point or endpoint grip

7. Click the square grip located at the midpoint of the last tangent in the alignment and move it to a different location. This grip moves the tangent while maintaining its orientation in the drawing. Adjacent geometry responds as needed to meet its geometric rules. In the case of this alignment, the PI to the left of this grip changes location and the curve to the right changes its beginning and ending points to remain tangent (Figure 5.9).

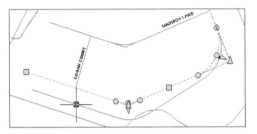

FIGURE 5.9 Moving the tangent midpoint grip

Editing Alignments Using the Alignment Layout Tools

Grips are wonderful tools to edit geometry that is already there, but what if you need to add a PI or draw a curve? For that, you need the Alignment Layout Tools toolbar (Figure 5.10). This toolbar is the same one that you used to initially lay out the alignment.

FIGURE 5.10 Alignment Layout Tools toolbar

To edit an alignment using the Alignment Layout Tools, follow these steps:

1. Open the drawing named Editing Tools.dwg located in your Chapter 05 class data folder.

2. Click the Jordan Court alignment, and then click Geometry Editor on the ribbon. This opens the Alignment Layout Tools toolbar.

3. On the Alignment Layout Tools toolbar, click Insert PI. Then snap to the center of the circle marked A.

4. Click Delete Sub-entity, and then click the curve at the PI marked B.

5. Click the tangent between A and B to remove it as well. The alignment should now look like Figure 5.11.

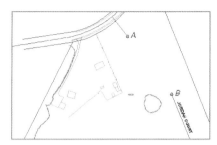

FIGURE 5.11 Alignment after removing tangent and curve

6. Expand the curve button and click More Floating Curves ➢ Floating Curve (From Entity End, Radius, Length).

7. Click the tangent near point A.

8. Type O and press Enter to indicate a counterclockwise direction.

9. Enter a radius of 100′ (30m).

10. Enter a curve length of 100′ (30m). A short curve is placed at the end of the tangent.

11. On the Alignment Layout Tools toolbar, expand the curves button and select Free Curve Fillet (Between Two Entities, Radius).

12. Click the curve you just created in the previous steps.

13. Click the red tangent that begins at point B.

14. Press Enter to indicate that the solution is less than 180 degrees.

15. Press R and then Enter to indicate that it is a reverse curve.

16. Enter 100′ (30m) for the radius, and then press Enter to end the command. The new curve is created in the drawing, as shown in Figure 5.12.

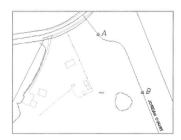

FIGURE 5.12 Alignment after addition of reverse curve

Editing Alignments Numerically

At times, you may want to adjust your design by telling Civil 3D the exact dimension of a portion of the alignment. This can be done in one of two different ways. The first is Alignment Grid View, which opens a tab in Panorama. This tab shows the geometry of the alignment in table form and enables you to edit some of the values to adjust the design.

To edit alignments numerically using Alignment Grid View, follow these steps:

1. Open the drawing named Numerical Editing.dwg located in the Chapter 05 class data folder.

2. Click the Jordan Court alignment, and then click Geometry Editor on the ribbon.

3. Click Alignment Grid View to open the Alignment Entities tab and display the tabular version of the alignment geometry, as shown in Figure 5.13.

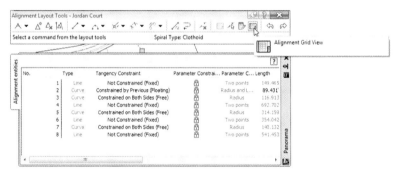

F I G U R E 5 . 1 3 The Alignment Entities tab of Panorama showing the tabular data of the alignment

The item number is found in the No. column.

4. Change the Radius value for items 2 and 3 to **150′ (45m)**. Notice that the alignment updates automatically in the drawing. Keep this drawing open for the next exercise.

Another method for editing the alignment design numerically is referred to as Component-Level Editing. With this approach, you open the numerical data for a piece of the alignment (such as a line, curve, or spiral) in a separate window. This is done by clicking the Sub-entity Editor button on the Alignment Layout Tools toolbar and then using the Pick Sub-entity tool to choose the part of the alignment you want to edit.

To edit alignments numerically using Component-Level Editing, follow these steps (you should still have Numerical Editing.dwg open from the previous exercise):

1. Close Panorama. Click Sub-entity Editor on the Alignment Layout Tools toolbar to display the Alignment Layout Parameters dialog box. (This dialog box is blank when it first appears.)

2. Click Pick Sub-entity (Figure 5.14), and then click the curve at the 90-degree bend on Jordan Court. This will populate the Alignment Layout Parameters dialog box with data, as shown in Figure 5.14.

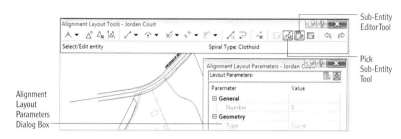

F I G U R E 5 . 1 4 The Sub-entity Editor Tool, Pick Sub-entity Tool, and Alignment Layout Parameters dialog box

3. Change the Radius value to 50′ (15m).

4. Close the Alignment Layout Parameters dialog box and the Alignment Layout Tools toolbar.

Applying Design Criteria Files and Check Sets

When you're laying out a design, how do you know whether you're doing it right? What should the curve radii be? Should there be a minimum tangent length between curves, or is it OK to have back-to-back curves? How does the expected speed of traffic affect the answers to these questions?

The answers to these types of questions can differ, depending on the project. For road design, the government entity that accepts responsibility for the road is most likely calling the shots when it comes to design standards. That may be the state Department of Transportation (DOT), county planning commission, or even the community homeowners association. In other cases, you may be designing roads or other linear features on private property that is not governed by any official design standards. In this case, you will have to utilize your knowledge and experience to create the best design. Whether the design standards come from you or someone else, it's helpful to have tools that ensure your design meets the requirements that have been assigned to it.

Design criteria and *check sets* are two ways of telling Civil 3D what your design standards are and asking Civil 3D to tell you when you've violated those standards by displaying a warning symbol (Figure 5.15). These two features are customizable, so you can use them to represent any standard or combination of standards that is necessary.

FIGURE 5.15 Tooltip relaying details about a design check set violation

PRELOADING YOUR DESIGN STANDARDS

If you work for a company that does projects in different jurisdictions that have different design requirements, it would be a good idea to talk with your CAD manager about separate templates, one for each jurisdiction. These templates not only can establish graphical standards as discussed previously, but they also can be set up with preloaded design criteria files and design check sets that represent applicable design standards. With this type of setup, you can simply choose the right template before starting your design and proceed with confidence that a warning symbol will pop up if you have not met a requirement of the county, state, or client you're designing for.

Applying Design Check Sets

A *design check set* is a collection of one or more design checks. There are four types of design checks: line, curve, spiral, and tangent intersection. When a design check set is applied to an alignment, Civil 3D will flag any violations with a triangular yellow shield marked with an exclamation point. You can hover over the shield to get more information about the violation, as shown in Figure 5.15.

To apply a design check set to an alignment and edit the alignment based on what it reports, follow these steps:

1. Open the drawing named Design Check Set.dwg located in the Chapter 05 class data folder.

2. Click the Jordan Court alignment, and then click Alignment Properties on the ribbon.

3. In the Alignment Properties dialog box, click the Design Criteria tab.

4. Change the Design Speed value to **25 mi/h (40 km/hr)**.

5. Check the box next to Use Criteria-based Design.

6. Uncheck the box next to Use Design Criteria File.

7. Verify that Use Design Check Set is checked and select Subdivision.

8. Click OK to close the Alignment Properties dialog box. Press Esc to clear the grips on the alignment. You should see three yellow shields in the drawing, as shown in Figure 5.16.

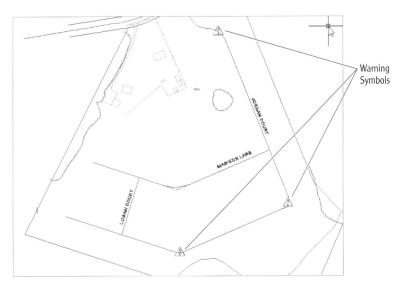

FIGURE 5.16 Warning symbols indicating design check set violations within the alignment

9. Zoom in to the curve farthest to the south. Hover your cursor over the yellow shield. A tooltip should appear, indicating that the Subdivision Curve design check has been violated.

10. Use grips to increase the radius of the curve until the shield disappears.

If no tooltip appears, type **rollovertips** at the command line; then type **1** and press Enter.

11. Click the Jordan Court alignment, and then click Geometry Editor on the ribbon.

12. On the Alignment Layout Tools toolbar, click Alignment Grid View. Notice the yellow shields in the No. column as well as the bold values in the Radius column and several other columns (Figure 5.17). This tells you which items have violations as well as which specific values are causing them.

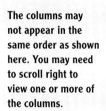

The columns may not appear in the same order as shown here. You may need to scroll right to view one or more of the columns.

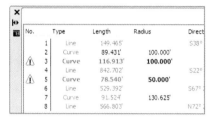

FIGURE 5.17 Warning symbols in Panorama indicate design check set violations.

13. Change the radius of item 3 to **150′ (45m)**. The shield disappears and the bold values for item 3 now show in normal print. The curve at item 5 will remain set to a 50′ (15m) radius.

Applying Design Criteria Files

AASHTO stands for the American Association of State Highway and Transportation Officials. It is the basis for many of the state DOT standards in the United States.

Design criteria files are another way of having Civil 3D check your design as you go. From an end-user standpoint, there is not much difference between a design check set and design criteria file: they're both something you assign to your alignment so that certain design parameters can be checked. From a setup standpoint, they're quite different. Design check sets are a group of design checks that are relatively simple and are managed through the Settings tab of the Toolspace. A design criteria file is a single file and is potentially much more sophisticated. There is a special tool for editing design criteria files called the Design Criteria Editor. Civil 3D comes with AASHTO design criteria files that can be used as is or copied and modified to meet local requirements. Autodesk also provides numerous country kits that include even more design criteria files that meet the requirements of various design authorities around the world.

To apply a design criteria file to an alignment and then adjust the design of the alignment based on what is reported, follow these steps:

1. Open the drawing named `Design Criteria Files.dwg` located in the `Chapter 05` class data folder. Note that currently there is only one warning symbol shown for the Jordan Court alignment.

   2. Click the Jordan Court alignment and select Alignment Properties on the ribbon.

   3. Click the Design Criteria tab. Check the box next to Use Design Criteria File.

   4. Click the button to the right of the file path and select the file named Autodesk Civil 3D Imperial (2004) Roadway Design Standards.xml (Autodesk Civil 3D Metric (2004) Roadway Design Standards.xml). Click Open.

   5. Uncheck the box next to Use Design Check Set.

   6. Click OK and press Esc to clear the grips. New warning symbols appear on the first, second, and fourth curves. As you can see, the design criteria file is a bit more stringent than the design check set of the previous exercise.

   7. Hover your cursor over the warning symbol farthest to the north. The tooltip informs you that the required radius is 154′ (47m).

   8. Select the alignment and click Geometry Editor on the ribbon.

   9. Click Alignment Grid View on the Alignment Layout Tools toolbar.

   10. Note that the Minimum Radius is listed in Panorama. Change the radius of items 2, 3, and 7 to **155′ (48m)**. Do not edit item 5; it should remain set to 50′ (15m).

   11. Close Panorama and observe the change to the alignment. With the exception of one curve, the alignment meets the requirements of both the design criteria file and the design check set.

You Have the Power

Design check sets and design criteria files do not change your design. They simply tell you when one of the rules has been broken. Depending on many factors, there will be times when you fix the issue to satisfy the rule and times when you don't. In the previous case of the 50′ (15m) radius, you know that Phase II of the project will create a T intersection at this location, which makes the sharp turn OK.

THE ESSENTIALS AND BEYOND

In this chapter, you were given specific instructions about laying out and editing the example alignments for the project. For a learning environment, specific instructions are necessary so that your results are predictable and understood. Real design is rarely like this, however. Instead, you are typically given some broad parameters, and you need to rely on your own skills and creativity to come up with a solution. The better you understand the tools that you have (Civil 3D in this case), the more quickly you can create solutions. The more quickly you can create solutions, the more scenarios you can test and the more likely you are to achieve the best design possible.

ADDITIONAL EXERCISE

Open the drawing named Road Layout Alternate.dwg located in the Chapter 05 class data folder. Save the file as **Road Layout Alternate 1.dwg** and use alignments to create a new road layout based on the parameters listed after this paragraph. Repeat this for second and third alternates. For at least one of the three alternate layouts, try just roughing something in and relying on the editing tools to get it just right. You can grip edit, add and remove components, and edit numerically at will. With practice, this approach becomes much more efficient than spending a lot of time laying out temporary construction geometry, as you saw in the second exercise in this chapter.

Here are the alignment design parameters:

▶ 150′ (45m) minimum offset from road centerline to back of lots to accommodate 50′ (15m) right-of-way, adequate front yard, single-family residence, and adequate rear yard.

▶ Perpendicular intersection with existing road that is ideal for safety and accessibility.

▶ Avoidance of steep area to the south.

▶ Uniform geometric properties where possible, such as 90-degree angles, parallel lines, and so on. This is recommended for simpler, more efficient stake-out and construction.

▶ Avoidance of the farmhouse and buildings, because that part of the property will be deeded back to the original owner.

Visit www.sybex.com/go/civil2013essentials to download a video of the author completing this exercise. You can also download the Answers to Additional Exercises Appendix which contains even more information about completing this exercise.

CHAPTER 6

Displaying and Annotating Alignments

As you will find with nearly every design component that you create for a land development project, creating the design is only half the job. Alignments serve as the basis for further design of a linear feature, but they also serve as a means of expressing the geometry of the feature to reviewers and contractors. The alignment by itself does not tell this story in enough detail and must therefore be stylized and annotated appropriately. In addition, alignments often serve as baselines used to express the location of other features within the project.

In this chapter, you'll learn how to use various styles and annotations to convey important information about alignments.

▶ **Using alignment styles**

▶ **Applying alignment labels and label sets**

▶ **Creating station/offset labels**

▶ **Creating segment labels**

▶ **Using tag labels and tables**

Using Alignment Styles

Certification
Objective

As with other styles you have learned about, alignment styles are used to control the appearance and behavior of alignments. By applying different styles, you can graphically distinguish between existing centerlines, proposed centerlines, and so on. You can even use styles to display alignments as something completely different, such as a property line or even utility line. Figure 6.1 illustrates how styles enable alignments to represent many different things.

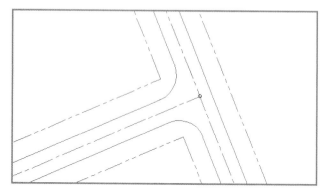

FIGURE 6.1 Different alignment styles are used to represent the right-of-way, edges of pavement, and centerlines in this drawing.

Alignment styles have two major ways of affecting the appearance of alignments. First, they control which components of the alignment are visible, and second, they control the graphical properties such as layer, color, and linetype of the components that are displayed.

To use alignment styles to control the appearance of alignments in a drawing, complete the following steps:

1. Open the drawing named Alignment Styles.dwg located in the Chapter 06 class data folder. The drawing contains a dozen different alignments that are intended to serve different purposes. Currently all alignments look the same because they have all been assigned a style of Standard.

2. Select the alignment representing the centerline of Emerson Road, right-click, and select Properties.

3. Change the style to C-ROAD-CNTR-E, as shown in Figure 6.2. This will display the alignment as a simple series of lines and curves on the existing road centerline layer.

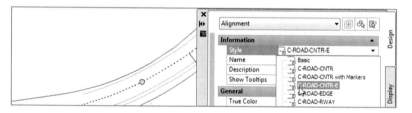

FIGURE 6.2 Assigning an alignment style within the Properties window

4. Press Esc to clear the selection of the alignment. Select the Jordan court centerline alignment and change its style to C-ROAD-CNTR. This will display this alignment as a simple series of lines and curves on the proposed road centerline layer.

5. Now change the style of the Jordan Court centerline alignment to C-ROAD-CNTR With Markers. With this style, markers are placed at the beginning, end, points of curvature (PCs), points of tangency (PTs), points of reverse curvature (PRCs), and points of intersection (PIs). In addition, line extensions are displayed with the tangents extending to the PI markers. You would use this style for the polished look of a final plan but probably not for design.

6. Change the style of the Madison Lane centerline alignment to Layout. You would use this style for analysis purposes during design, not for the polished look of a final plan.

7. For the alignments that run parallel to the Jordan Court centerline and extend the full length of the centerline, assign the C-ROAD-RWAY style. This displays the alignments on the right-of-way layer, enabling them to take on the appearance of property lines.

You can select both right-of-way alignments and assign the C-ROAD-RWAY style to both of them at once using the Properties window.

8. For the remaining alignments that represent the edges of pavement, change the style to C-ROAD-EDGE. This displays the alignments on the edge-of-pavement layer.

Applying Alignment Labels and Label Sets

Alignments (and, as you'll learn later, profiles) have a special kind of annotation that is applied either to the entire alignment at once or to a range of stations within the alignment. This annotation repeats at specified increments or when specific types of geometry are encountered. This type of annotation is very useful because it changes as the alignment changes, even if new geometry is added or the length of the alignment changes. In all, you can add seven types of alignment labels in this way. This chapter does not cover all seven types, but you will learn about the following three alignment label types:

Certification Objective

Major station labels: Placed at the major station increment, which is larger than the minor station increment. They typically include a tick mark along with a numerical label calling out the station.

Minor station labels: Placed at the minor station increment, which is smaller than the major station increment. These typically consist of tick marks.

Geometry point labels: Placed at key geometric points along the alignment, such as the beginning of the alignment, ending of the alignment, places where there are curves, and so on.

Applying Labels to Alignments

To apply alignment labels to an alignment, complete the following steps:

1. Open the drawing named Alignment Labels.dwg located in the Chapter 06 class data folder.

2. Click the Jordan Court alignment. Then click Add Labels ➢ Add/Edit Station Labels on the contextual ribbon tab.

3. In the Alignment Labels dialog box, do the following:

    a. For Type, verify that Major Stations is selected.

    b. For Major Station Label Style, verify that Parallel With Tick is selected.

    c. Click Add.

    d. For Increment, enter **50 (20)** to indicate the number of feet (meters) to increment.

    e. Click OK.

4. Zoom in and examine the labels that have been created. Notice that a tick mark and label have been placed at 50-foot (20-meter) increments along the alignment.

5. Click the Jordan Court alignment and launch the Add/Edit Station Labels command as you did in step 2.

6. In the Alignment Labels dialog box, do the following:

    a. For Type, select Minor Stations.

    b. For Minor Station Label Style, verify that Tick is selected.

    c. Click Add.

    d. Change the Minor Station Increment to **10 (5)** to indicate the number of feet (meters) to increment.

    e. Click OK.

Remember that values listed in parentheses are not conversions but values that would make sense in a metric environment. Fifty feet and 20 meters are not even close to equal, but each is a reasonable increment for stationing.

7. Examine the alignment once more. Now, you should see tick marks at 10-foot (5-meter) increments, which means that there are four (three) minor tick marks between the major tick marks and labels.

 8. Launch the Add/Edit Station Labels command once again, as you did in step 2. In the Alignment Labels dialog box, do the following:

   a. For Type, select Geometry Points.

   b. For Geometry Point Label Style, verify that Perpendicular With Tick And Line is selected.

   c. Click Add.

   d. In the Geometry Points dialog box, uncheck all boxes except Tangent-Curve Intersect, Curve-Tangent Intersect, and Reverse Curve-Curve Intersect.

   e. Click OK to dismiss the Geometry Points dialog box.

   f. Click OK to dismiss the Alignment Labels dialog box.

9. Examine the alignment labels and note the labels at the PCs, PTs, and PRC, as shown in Figure 6.3.

> ◀
>
> **You can use the button at the top-right corner of the dialog box to quickly clear all check boxes. The boxes you check will take care of PCs, PTs, and PRCs, respectively.**

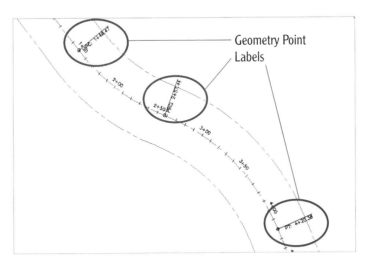

FIGURE 6.3 Geometry point labels displayed on the Jordan Court alignment

Using Alignment Label Sets

As you might guess, the collection of labels used in the previous exercise is quite common: station and tick at the major station, just a tick at the minor station, and labels calling out key geometric features. What if you could gather those three label types together in a nice, neat package and apply them all at once? That's exactly what a *label set* is used for.

Complete the following steps to create a label set and then apply it to another alignment:

1. Open the drawing named `Alignment Label Sets.dwg` located in the Chapter 06 class data folder.

2. Click the Jordan Court alignment. Then click Add Labels ➤ Add/Edit Station Labels on the contextual tab of the ribbon.

3. In the Alignment Labels dialog box, click Save Label Set.

4. In the Alignment Label Set dialog box, enter **M50 Stations & m10 Ticks & Geometry Points** (M20 Stations & m5 Ticks & Geometry Points) in the Name field.

5. Click OK to close the Alignment Label Set dialog box.

6. Click OK to close the Alignment Labels dialog box.

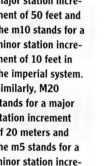

7. Press Esc to clear the selection of the Jordan Court alignment. Click the Madison Lane alignment, and then click Add Labels ➤ Add/Edit Station Labels on the contextual tab of the ribbon.

8. In the Alignment Labels dialog box, click Import Label Set.

9. Select M50 Stations & m10 Ticks & Geometry Points (M20 Stations & m5 Ticks & Geometry Points), and then click OK.

10. Click OK to dismiss the Alignment Labels dialog box.

11. Examine the Madison Court alignment (Figure 6.4), and note that the label set applied here is the same as the label set that was applied to Jordan Court.

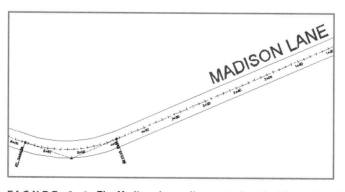

FIGURE 6.4 The Madison Lane alignment after the label set has been applied

Editing Alignment Labels

Working with alignment labels is a bit different from working with other labels, because alignment labels exist in groups. If you click a major station label, for example, all the major station labels for the entire alignment will be selected. So, what if you want to change something about just one label? The answer is to use your Ctrl key when selecting individual labels within a group.

This Ctrl-key trick works for many types of labels that exist in groups.

Another type of label edit you'll be introduced to in this chapter is *flipping*. Flipping a label simply means switching it over to the other side of the line.

To practice making edits to alignment labels, complete the following steps:

1. Open the drawing named Editing Alignment Labels.dwg located in the Chapter 06 class data folder.

2. Click one of the geometry point labels on the Jordan Court alignment. Then click Edit Label Group on the contextual ribbon tab that appears.

3. For Geometry Points, change the Style to Perpendicular With Tick And Line - Offset.

4. Click OK to dismiss the Alignment Labels dialog box. The labels are now shown outside the right-of-way line (Figure 6.5).

Notice that the right-of-way line is passing through the geometry point labels. These labels should be moved beyond the right-of-way line, which you will do in the next few steps.

5. While holding your Ctrl key down, click the first PC label. Right-click and select Flip Label. The label is flipped to the opposite side of the road.

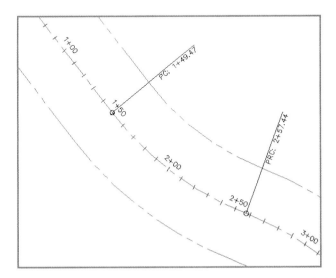

FIGURE 6.5 Changing the style of the geometry point labels improves their appearance and readability by moving them outside the right-of-way line.

6. Zoom to the intersection of Madison Lane and Jordan Court. Note how the 0+00 (0+000) station label for Madison Lane is conflicting with the centerline of Jordan Court.

7. Click the 0+00 (0+000) station label of Madison Lane, and then click the square grip that appears above the label. Drag the grip to a clear area in the drawing. The station label is more readable in its new location, and a leader appears that indicates the actual location of the station.

DRAGGED STATE

In step 7, when you used a special grip on a label to drag it to a new location, a leader magically appeared. This happened because the leader was turned on within the *dragged state* configuration of the label style. The dragged state of a label can dramatically change the look of that label when it's dragged to a new location. In addition to the appearance of a leader, you might see a change in text height or orientation, the appearance of a border around the text, and several other changes.

A NOTE ABOUT UNITS

Throughout this chapter, you'll notice that two values are provided for units of measurement. The first value is provided for the imperial system that is used in the United States, and the second value in parentheses is provided for the metric system that is used in many other countries. These values most often represent imperial feet and metric meters. It is important to note that generally only the numeric values are entered in the software, not terms like *feet* or *meters*. Also, you should know that the two numbers provided are not necessarily equal. In most cases, they are similar values that are rounded to work efficiently in their respective measurement systems.

Creating Station/Offset Labels

As mentioned earlier, an alignment is often used as a baseline, enabling other features to express their locations in relation to that baseline. This is typically done with station offset notations, and of course, the AutoCAD® Civil 3D® program provides you with labels to do just that. This type of label is referred to as a *station/offset* label.

Unlike the label groups you learned about earlier, station/offset labels stand alone and must be created one by one. They are capable of reporting the station and offset of a point you select as well as the alignment name, coordinates of the point, and other types of information.

You can create station/offset labels as either fixed or floating labels. If they are fixed, then they hold their positions and update the station and offset values when the alignment is edited. If they are not fixed, then they maintain their station and offset values and move with the alignment when it is edited. Like spot elevation labels, station/offset labels are paired with a marker.

To create station/offset labels in a drawing, complete the following steps:

1. Open the drawing named Station Offset Labels.dwg located in the Chapter 06 class data folder. This drawing is zoomed in to the intersection between Jordan Court and Madison Lane. Your task will be to label the station and offset of either end of each curve that forms the intersection between the two roads.

2. Click the Jordan Court alignment, and then click Add Labels ➤ Station/Offset - Fixed Point on the contextual ribbon tab.

3. While holding down the Shift key, right-click, and select Endpoint.

4. Click the northern end of the northern arc. A new label is created at this location that references the Jordan Court alignment.

5. While holding down the Shift key, right-click, and select Endpoint. Then click the southern end of the southern arc. Another label is created.

6. Press Esc twice to end the command and clear the selection of the alignment. Click the Madison Lane alignment, and then click Add Labels ➤ Station/Offset - Fixed Point on the contextual ribbon tab.

7. While holding down the Shift key, right-click, and select Endpoint. Click the western end of the northern arc.

8. While holding down the Shift key, right-click, and select Endpoint. Then click the western end of the southern arc. This label and the one created in step 7 provide the station and offset in reference to the Madison Lane alignment.

9. Press Esc twice to end the labeling command and clear the selection of the alignment. Click one of the labels, and then click the square grip and drag it to a new location that is clear of other lines and text. Repeat this for the other labels to improve their appearance and readability. The result should look similar to Figure 6.6.

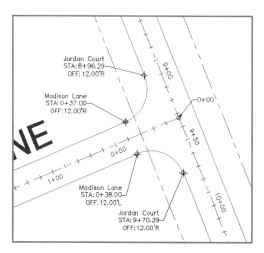

FIGURE 6.6 Station/offset labels applied to the edge-of-pavement arcs at the intersection of Madison Lane and Jordan Court

Creating Segment Labels

So far, you have seen label groups that label the entire alignment at once and station/offset labels that are typically used to label something other than the alignment. What about the individual parts of the alignment? How do you tell reviewers and contractors how to re-create those alignments in the field? The answer is *segment labels*. Segment labels allow you to label things such as bearings and distances for tangents and curve data for curves. By providing this information as text in the drawing, you give viewers of the drawing the information they need to stake out the alignment in the field. You are also sharing information about the geometric "performance" of the alignment that might answer questions such as these: "Are the curves too sharp for the expected speed?" "Is the alignment parallel to other important features?" "Are intersecting roads perpendicular to one another?"

Segment labels stand alone like station/offset labels; however, you can create them in bulk if you so desire. For example, all of the tangents of an entire alignment can be labeled at once if you choose that option when creating the labels.

To create some segment labels in your drawing, complete the following steps:

1. Open the drawing named Segment Labels.dwg located in the Chapter 06 class data folder.

2. Click the Madison Lane alignment, and then click Add Labels ➢ Add Alignment Labels.

3. In the Add Labels dialog box, do the following:

    a. For Label Type, select Single Segment.

    b. For Line Label Style, verify that Bearing Over Distance is selected.

    c. For Curve Label Style, verify that Curve Data is selected.

    d. Click Add.

4. Zoom in and click one of the tangents of Madison Lane. Notice the bearing and distance label that is created.

5. Press Esc to end the labeling command. Click the newly created label, right-click, and select Flip Label. This swaps the position of the bearing and distance.

6. Select the label once again, right-click, and this time select Reverse Label. Notice what happens to the bearing: it switches from SW to NE, but the numbers don't change.

7. Click Add in the Add Labels dialog box. Then click the curve and the other tangent of Madison Lane. This will create two new labels in the drawing.

8. Press Esc to end the labeling command. Click the curve label, and then click the label's square grip and drag it to a clear location in the drawing. This will improve the appearance and readability of the label and automatically create a leader pointing back to the curve.

◀

Be careful to click the line, not one of the station labels or tick marks. You may need to zoom in a bit to do this.

WHY BE A BEAR ABOUT BEARINGS?

If this is the first time you've seen bearings, you may not know what is going on here. A *bearing* is a way of expressing the direction of a line. In this exercise, the bearing of the eastern tangent of Madison Lane is S67°27′02.54″W. That means if you face south and then turn yourself toward the west about 67°, you'll be facing roughly in the direction that this line is pointing. Since there are 90° between south and west, you'll actually be facing more west than south.

When the bearing is reversed, it's like you've done an about-face and you're now facing 67° east of north. This doesn't change the appearance of the line at all, and it might seem picky to distinguish between SW and NE in this case. But when you think about it, the stationing of this road is increasing in a certain direction (west in the case of Madison Lane), which establishes the direction of the alignment. For consistency, it's a good idea for the direction of your bearing labels to agree with the direction of your alignment.

9. In the Add Labels dialog box, change the Label Type to Multiple Segment. Change the Curve Label Style back to Curve Data.

10. Click Add, and then click anywhere on the Jordan Court alignment. All tangents and curves are labeled at once.

11. Move the curve labels for Jordan Court to open areas in the drawing so that they are easier to read (Figure 6.7).

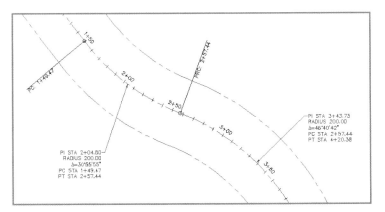

FIGURE 6.7 Curve labels added to the Jordan Court alignment. To improve readability, the labels have been dragged away from the alignment and into clear areas.

Using Tag Labels and Tables

Sometimes, it is better to put all the geometric data for an alignment in a table rather than labeling it right on the alignment itself. This can clear up a cluttered drawing and provide space for other types of annotation. You can accomplish this in Civil 3D by using tag labels and tables.

Creating Tag Labels

A tag label is a special kind of label that assigns a number to a curve, tangent, or spiral. Common examples are C1, S1, or L1 for a curve, spiral, or tangent, respectively. Tag labels can be created ahead of time if you know you're going to use a table, or you can convert "regular" labels to tag labels on the fly. In fact, you can convert just a few of the labels to tag labels and use a combination of a table and in-place labels to convey alignment information. This is common in cases where certain segments of an alignment are too short to have a label fit on them nicely.

Complete the following steps to create tag labels in a drawing:

1. Open the drawing named Tag Labels.dwg located in the Chapter 06 class data folder.

2. Click the Jordan Court alignment, and then click Add Labels ➣ Add Alignment Labels on the contextual ribbon tab.

3. In the Add Labels dialog box, select Multiple Segment as the Label Type.

4. Verify that Circle Tag is selected for both the Line Label Style and Curve Label Style.

5. Click Add, and then click anywhere on the Jordan Court alignment. As you can see in Figure 6.8, curve and line tag labels have been created, but the numbering is not what it should be. You will address this in the next exercise.

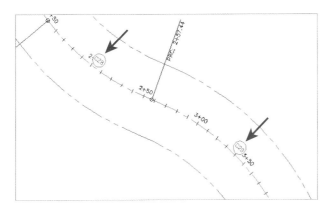

FIGURE 6.8 Curve tag labels on the Jordan Court alignment

Renumbering Tag Labels

As Murphy's law would have it, the numbers you get when creating tag labels are almost never what you want them to be. This is no fault of the software; in fact, the reason for this happening so frequently is that the software is doing its job. Each time you create a tag label, Civil 3D bumps the next tag number up by one. Since most designs are laid out and labeled more than once (lots more in most cases), your next tag number is likely to be set to something other than 1.

Fortunately, Civil 3D is quite good at enabling you to correct your tag labels. In fact, there is a Renumber Tags command designed for that specific purpose.

To renumber tag labels in your drawing, complete the following steps:

1. Open the drawing named Renumber Tags.dwg located in the Chapter 06 class data folder.

2. Click the Jordan Court alignment, and then select Renumber Tags on the contextual ribbon tab.

3. On the command line, type **S** for settings and press Enter.

4. Change all values to 1 in the Table Tag Numbering dialog box and click OK.

5. Starting at the beginning of the Jordan Court alignment, click each tag label in order from start to end.

There are eight tags in all: L1–L4 and C1–C4.

Creating Tables

Once you have created all of the tag labels and numbered them correctly, you're ready to create a table. Civil 3D provides four types of alignment tables that you can insert into your drawing: Line, Curve, Spiral, and Segment. A segment table is a combination of the other three tables.

When you create a table in your drawing, you have full control over which data is included in your table. You can choose to provide table data for the entire alignment, you can tell Civil 3D to seek out certain label styles and include them in your table, or you can hand pick the labels from the drawing by selecting them directly.

As you will find with all Civil 3D tables, they are dynamically linked to the objects for which they display data. In the case of alignments, as the alignment is modified, the table updates automatically. There is even an option to create additional table entries as new tangents, curves, or spirals are created in the process of editing. Imagine how much time is saved by not having to go back and check all of the numbers in a table each time an alignment is tweaked.

Complete the following steps to create an alignment table in a drawing:

1. Open the drawing named Create Table.dwg located in the Chapter 06 class data folder.

2. Click the Jordan Court alignment, and then click Add Tables ➢ Add Segments on the contextual ribbon tab.

3. In the Alignment Table Creation dialog box, click the Select By Label Or Style option.

4. If you are unable to read the label style names, click and drag the lower-right corner of the dialog box to increase its size. Then click and drag the line between the Label Style Name and Selection Rule column headings to widen the Label Style Name column. Repeat these actions as needed until you can see the full names of the label styles listed.

5. Check the box in the Apply column for Alignment Curve: Circle Tag and Alignment Line: Circle Tag.

6. Click OK. Click a point in an open area of the drawing to insert the table. The table reflects the geometric data for the alignment (Figure 6.9).

Jordan Court				
Number	Radius	Length	Line/Chord Direction	Start Station
L1		149.47	S38° 17' 44.49"E	0+00.00
C1	200.00	107.97	S53° 45' 42.11"E	1+49.47
C2	200.00	162.94	S45° 53' 18.59"E	2+57.44
L2		762.92	S22° 32' 57.46"E	4+20.38
C3	50.00	78.54	S22° 27' 02.54"W	11+83.29
L3		504.04	S67° 27' 02.54"W	12+61.83
C4	200.00	140.13	S87° 31' 23.49"W	17+65.88
L4		541.45	N72° 24' 15.56"W	19+06.01

FIGURE 6.9 An alignment segment table for Jordan Court

THE ESSENTIALS AND BEYOND

Having completed this chapter, you should now be able to provide basic labeling for alignments. This includes station label groups (incremental station labels, ticks, and geometry points), station/offset labels, segment labels, tag labels, and tables. The ability to effectively communicate your design through annotation is almost as important as the design itself. Although it is changing very quickly, the current state of the industry is such that most land development projects are constructed from paper plans. When this is the case, your annotations become even more important than your design, because they provide the labeled stations, bearings, distances, and curve data that are used to stake out the road.

(Continues)

THE ESSENTIALS AND BEYOND *(Continued)*

ADDITIONAL EXERCISE

For this exercise, open the drawing named Alignment Labels Beyond.dwg located in the Chapter 06 class data folder. The road layout in this drawing is more complete than the other drawings you have opened in this chapter, but there are no labels. Add annotations to this drawing as follows:

1. For all centerline alignments, apply a label set that labels stations, ticks, and geometry points.

2. Create station/offset labels for the endpoints of all right-of-way geometry, such as beginning/endings of curves, beginning/endings of straight segments, and corners.

3. Create tag labels that start at the beginning of Jordan Court with the number 1. Madison Lane should be next in the series, and Logan Court should be last.

4. Create a table in the drawing for each of the three proposed alignments.

5. In all cases, reposition labels that clash with other labels or geometry.

Visit www.sybex.com/go/civil2013essentials to download a video of the author completing this exercise. You can also download the Answers to Additional Exercises Appendix which contains even more information about completing this exercise.

Designing Vertically Using Profiles

Now that the paths of the roads have been established as alignments representing their centerlines, the next question to ask is, what will it be like to travel along those paths? Will the terrain be steep or flat? Will it change much from one end of the road to the other? Will it require earth to be moved to smooth out the bumps in the road?

In Chapter 4, you learned how existing ground surfaces can be used to analyze the shape of the ground. Although surfaces can be quite effective for this purpose, you're looking for something that tells you specifically what the terrain is like in relation to the road alignment. Once you have learned that, you'll be looking for an effective way to redesign the terrain to create a nice, smooth road.

Whether analyzing the terrain along an alignment or redesigning it, the tool that is most effective is the *profile*. Profiles allow you to show a slice through the ground along a specific alignment. This provides you with a clear and direct visualization of changes in terrain so that you can assess existing conditions and improve your design if necessary.

▷ **Creating surface profiles**

▷ **Displaying profiles in profile views**

▷ **Creating design profiles**

▷ **Editing profiles**

▷ **Using design check sets and criteria files**

Creating Surface Profiles

Certification
Objective

One of the first steps in designing the vertical aspect of a linear feature is to analyze the shape of the *existing* terrain along that feature. You've learned how surfaces are used to create a 3D model of the shape of the ground. You've also learned that there are many potential uses for surfaces other than displaying contours or labeling spot elevations. One of these uses is the creation of profiles from surface data, which helps with the design of linear features such as roads, channels, pipelines, and so on.

When a profile is created based on the data within a surface, it is aptly named a *surface profile*. A surface profile maintains a dynamic link to the surface that it references. In fact, a surface profile is tied to both the alignment and surface that were used to create it. If either one changes, the surface profile is updated.

To create a surface profile, complete the following steps:

1. Open the drawing named Surface Profile.dwg located in the Chapter 07 class data folder.

2. Click the Jordan Court alignment in the drawing, and then click Surface Profile on the contextual ribbon tab.

3. In the Create Profile From Surface dialog box, verify that Jordan Court is selected as the Alignment.

4. Under Select Surfaces, select EG.

5. Click Add, and then click OK. Although nothing changes in the drawing, you may notice that the Events tab opens in Panorama, informing you that a profile has been created.

6. On Prospector, expand Alignments ➤ Centerline Alignments ➤ Jordan Court ➤ Profiles. You should see EG - Surface (1) listed under Profiles.

7. Right-click EG - Surface (1) and select Properties.

8. On the Information tab of the Profile Properties dialog box, change the Name to **Jordan Court EGCL**. Click OK.

EGCL stands for *existing ground* *centerline.*

A NOTE ABOUT UNITS

Throughout this chapter, you'll notice that two values are provided for units of measurement. The first value is provided for the imperial system that is used in the United States, and the second value in parentheses is provided for the metric system that is used in many other countries. These values most often represent imperial feet and metric meters. It is important to note that generally only the numeric values are entered in the software, not terms like *feet* or *meters*. Also, you should know that the two numbers provided are not necessarily equal. In most cases, they are similar values that are rounded to work efficiently in their respective measurement systems.

Although Prospector shows you that a profile has been created, you have nothing graphical to look at. To display a graphical representation of the profile in your drawing, you need a profile view, which takes us to the next section.

Displaying Profiles in Profile Views

In the AutoCAD® Civil 3D® software, you must use a *profile view* to display a profile. A profile view is basically a grid that represents stations in the *x* direction and elevations in the *y* direction. The stations along the alignment and their corresponding elevations are plotted on this grid, and the resulting line represents changes in the terrain along the alignment. The profile view also includes various types of labels such as axis labels and axis titles to provide context to the display of the profile. Profile views can be further augmented with bands, which is something that will be covered in the following chapter.

To display a profile in a profile view, complete the following steps:

1. Open the drawing named Profile View.dwg located in the Chapter 06 class data folder.

2. Click the Jordan Court alignment, and then click Profile View on the contextual ribbon tab.

3. In the Create Profile View - General dialog box, click Create Profile View.

4. When prompted for the profile view origin, click a point in the open area to the east of the project. A new profile view will be inserted into the drawing, as shown in Figure 7.1.

Certification Objective

There are tons of settings here, but for now you'll just accept the defaults and skip right to creating the profile view.

The profile view origin is the lower-left corner of the profile view.

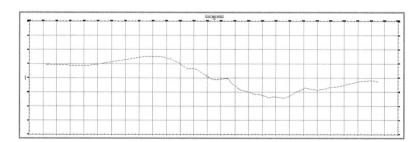

FIGURE 7.1 The newly created profile view

Now, you have your first picture of the nature of the terrain along the Jordan Court alignment. As you study the profile, you see a relatively flat area at the beginning, a fairly steep drop into a low area, and then a gradual rise for the remaining third of the alignment. The appearance of the line is somewhat jagged, which indicates moderately rough terrain. In just a short time, you have created a graphical depiction of what it would be like to travel down the path of the road as it exists right now. From this image, you can begin to visualize the adjustments that will be needed to create a smooth and safe driving experience.

Creating Design Profiles

Certification Objective

Earlier, you used a surface profile to determine the nature of the existing terrain along the path of Jordan Court. As the surface profile shows, the current state of this path is not suitable for driving, so it must be transformed into something with much more subtle geometry. In other words, a new profile must be *designed* for the road. In Civil 3D, this type of profile is often referred to as a design profile or *layout profile*.

PROFILE TERMINOLOGY

Familiarizing yourself with the following terms will be helpful as you work with design profiles:

Tangent: The straight-line portions of a profile.

PVI (point of vertical intersection): The location where two tangents intersect.

PVC (point of vertical curvature): The beginning of a vertical curve.

PVT (point of vertical tangency): The end of a vertical curve.

Parabolic curve: A vertical curve that does not have a constant radius and follows the shape of a parabola.

Circular curve: A vertical curve that has a constant radius.

Asymmetric curve: A vertical curve that is created from two back-to-back parabolic curves.

Crest curve: A vertical curve at the top of a hill where the grade leading into the curve is greater than the grade leading out. The PVI is located above the curve.

Sag curve: A vertical curve at the bottom of a valley where the grade leading into the curve is less than the grade leading out. The PVI is located below the curve.

Like alignments, design profiles consist of straight line segments (called *tangents*) and the curves that connect them. The curve geometry is a bit different, but essentially you can think of a design profile as an alignment turned on its side. The process of laying out a profile is very similar to laying out an alignment, right down to the Profile Layout Tools toolbar, which bears a striking resemblance to the Alignment Layout Tools toolbar.

To create a design profile, complete the following steps:

1. Open the drawing named `Design Profile.dwg` located in the `Chapter 06` class data folder.

2. Click one of the grid lines for the Jordan Court profile view, and then click Profile Creation Tools on the contextual ribbon.

3. In the Create Profile - Draw New dialog box, enter **Jordan Court FGCL** for the Profile Name.

FGCL stands for finished ground centerline.

4. Verify that the Profile Style is set to Design Profile and the Profile Label set is set to _No Labels. Click OK.

5. On the Profile Layout Tools toolbar, click the small black triangle on the far left button to expand it, and then click Draw Tangents With Curves (Figure 7.2).

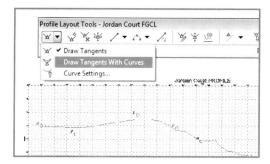

FIGURE 7.2 Invoking the Draw Tangents With Curves command

6. Right-click the OSNAP icon at the bottom of your screen. Turn on Center and Enabled.

This will configure Civil 3D so that your cursor will recognize center points and lock on (snap) to them automatically.

7. Click the center of the circle marked A. Then click the remaining circles in order from left to right. The newly created profile consists of a PVI at each point you clicked. Because you used the Draw Tangents With Curves command, all PVIs (except for the beginning and ending points) also include a vertical curve.

Editing Profiles

As you learned in Chapter 5, it is common (and often recommended) to lay out a rough version of a design and then apply a series of refinements to achieve the final design. This is especially true with profiles, because the first pass is usually an attempt to match existing ground as closely as possible, without creating too many of your own bumps in the road. Why try to match existing ground? Quite simply, it's cheaper. The closer your new road matches the existing terrain, the less earth will need to be moved to construct it. The cost of earth-moving is measured by the volume of earth that is excavated, so less digging equals less cost.

After you create the initial profile that roughly matches existing ground, you must then refine the design based on various factors such as performance requirements for the road, avoiding overhead and underground obstacles, and ensuring that rainwater will drain properly. Many times, the adjustments that you make are based not only on your own ideas but also on the input of others involved in the project. Whatever the case, a good set of tools for editing profiles is going to come in quite handy. Civil 3D provides a robust set of tools for editing profiles graphically and numerically.

Editing Profiles with Grips

In yet another respect, profiles are similar to alignments in that they come equipped with specialized grips that enable editing to be done efficiently. To use grips to edit a profile in your drawing, follow these steps:

1. Open the drawing named `Graphical Editing.dwg` located in the Chapter 06 class data folder.

2. Click the blue Jordan Court FGCL profile to display its grips. Click the upright triangular grip located within the circle marked A1 and drag it to the center of the circle marked A2, as shown in Figure 7.3. This is an example of moving the PVI grip, which changes the slope of both tangents, maintains the length of the curve, and keeps the curve tangent at both ends.

3. At the circle marked B1, click the triangle grip on the right and drag it to the center of the circle marked B2, as shown in Figure 7.4. This type of grip moves the PVI along the slope of one of the tangents.

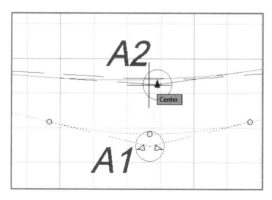

FIGURE 7.3   Moving a PVI grip

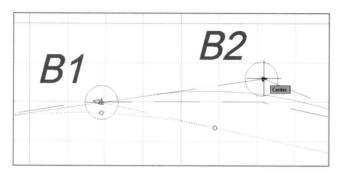

FIGURE 7.4   Moving a tangent slope grip

4. Click the square grip at the center of circle C1 and move it to the center of circle C2, as shown in Figure 7.5. This grip moves a tangent while keeping its slope constant. The result is that the PVIs at either end of the tangent are raised or lowered and the curve geometry associated with them must update.

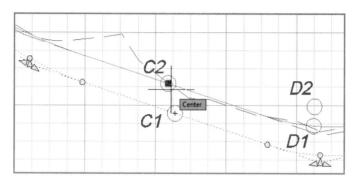

FIGURE 7.5   Moving a tangent midpoint grip

5. Click the circular grip located at the center of circle D1 and move it to the center of circle D2, as shown in Figure 7.6. This is an example of moving the pass-through grip, forcing the curve to pass through a given point while adjusting the length of the curve.

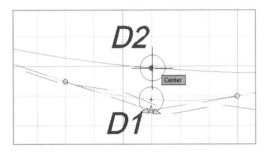

FIGURE 7.6   Moving the pass-through point grip

For vertical curves, the curve length refers to the horizontal distance from the beginning of the curve to the end.

6. Click the circular grip at the center of circle E1 and move it to the center of circle E2, as shown in Figure 7.7. This is an example of moving the endpoint grip of the curve, which also moves the start point to adjust the length of the curve.

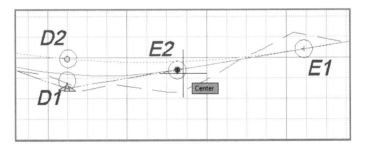

FIGURE 7.7   Moving the start point or endpoint grip

Editing Profiles Using the Profile Layout Tools

Grips are wonderful tools for editing geometry that is already there, but what if you need to add a PVI or draw a curve? For that, you need the Profile Layout Tools toolbar (Figure 7.8). This toolbar is the same one that you would use to create a profile initially.

FIGURE 7.8   Profile Layout Tools toolbar

To use the Profile Layout Tools to edit a profile in your drawing, complete these steps:

1. Open the drawing named Editing Tools.dwg located in your Chapter 07 class data folder.

2. Click the Jordan Court FGCL profile, and then click Geometry Editor on the ribbon. This opens the Profile Layout Tools toolbar.

3. On the Profile Layout Tools toolbar, click Insert PVI. While holding down the Shift key, right-click, and select Endpoint.

4. Zoom in to the left end of the profile and click the sharp break in the existing ground profile that is located at the center of the circle marked A. This sharp break is the edge of the existing road that the new road will tie into.

5. On the Profile Layout Tools toolbar, click Delete PVI. Then click within the circle marked B. This will delete the PVI at this location and remove the slight bend in the profile.

6. On the Profile Layout Tools toolbar, click Insert PVIs - Tabular.

7. In the Insert PVIs dialog box, enter **19+10 (0+582)** for the Station and **174.00 (53.000)** for the Elevation.

8. Press the Enter key to create a new line. Then enter **21+55 (0+655)** for the Station and **173.5 (52.750)** for the Elevation. Click OK. This creates two new PVIs located near the centers of the circles marked C and D.

9. On the Profile Layout Tools toolbar, click the black triangle to the right of the curves button to view the curves menu. Select More Free Vertical Curves ➢ Free Vertical Parabola (PVI Based), as shown in Figure 7.9.

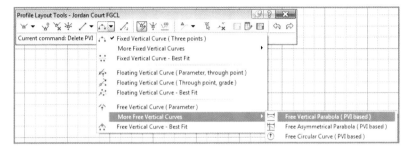

F I G U R E   7 . 9   Clicking the Free Vertical Parabola (PVI Based) command

10. Click within the circle marked C. Type **150 (45)** and press Enter to provide the curve length.

11. Click within the circle marked D. At the command line, type **200 (60)** for the curve length and press Enter.

12. Press Enter to end the command. You have successfully edited the design profile using the Profile Layout Tools toolbar.

Editing Profiles Numerically

At times, you may want to adjust your design by telling Civil 3D the exact dimension of a portion of the profile. You can do this in one of two different ways. The first is Profile Grid View, which opens a tab in Panorama. This tab shows the geometry of the profile in table form and enables you to edit some of the values to adjust the design.

To edit a profile numerically using Profile Grid View, follow these steps:

1. Open the drawing named Numerical Editing.dwg located in the Chapter 07 class data folder.

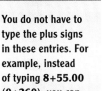

2. Click the Jordan Court FGCL profile, and then click Geometry Editor on the ribbon.

3. Click Profile Grid View to open the Profile Entities tab and display the numerical version of the profile geometry.

4. Change the Station value for Item 3 to **2+70.00 (0+080.00)** and the PVI Elevation value to **188.00 (57.00)**.

5. Change the remaining items as follows:

Item	Station	PVI Elevation
4	8+55.00 (0+260)	196.50 (60.0)
5	10+50.00 (0+320)	188.50 (57.5)
6	16+90.00 (0+515)	164.00 (50.0)

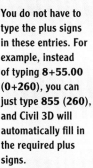

You do not have to type the plus signs in these entries. For example, instead of typing 8+55.00 (0+260), you can just type 855 (260), and Civil 3D will automatically fill in the required plus signs.

6. Close Panorama. The drawing may not look much different than it did before, because the changes you made were very subtle. Keep the drawing open and the Profile Layout Tools toolbar open for the next exercise.

KEEP IT SIMPLE

As you might have guessed, the main objective of this exercise is simplification of the profile design. In most cases, the stations or elevations do not need to be located with a precision of 0.01, so why not round them off to nice even numbers? The contractor and surveyor who are staking out the design in the field will appreciate this rounding, because there will be fewer digits to keep track of and a bit less potential for error.

The PVIs of items 1, 2, and 9 were not rounded because these are specific locations and elevations that need to be met. Items 7 and 8 were already entered as round numbers when you used the Insert PVIs - Tabular command in the previous exercise.

The second method for editing the profile design numerically is referred to as Component-Level Editing. With this approach, you open the numerical data for a piece of the profile (such as a line or vertical curve) in a separate window. You do this by clicking the Sub-entity Editor button on the Profile Layout Tools toolbar and then using the Pick Sub-entity tool to choose the part of the profile you want to edit.

To make numerical edits to a design profile using Component-Level Editing, complete the following steps (you should have Numerical Editing.dwg open from the previous exercise):

1. Click Profile Layout Parameters on the Profile Layout Tools toolbar to display the Profile Layout Parameters dialog box. (This dialog box is blank when it first appears.)

2. Click Select PVI, and then click near the curve at the lowest point on the Jordan Court FGCL profile. This will populate the Profile Layout Parameters dialog box with data.

3. Change the Profile Curve Length to **275 (80)**.

4. Close the Profile Layout Parameters dialog box and the Profile Layout Tools toolbar. Again, the drawing doesn't appear to change much because the edit you made was so subtle.

Using Design Check Sets and Criteria Files

You first learned about design criteria files and check sets in Chapter 5. These two features enable you to check your design on the fly to catch any errors or design flaws as you work. Of course, what's considered right can differ from place to place and from design type to design type, so these checking tools are customizable. The task of setting them up is usually left to a CAD manager or one of the top CAD users in your company or organization. This is true of most Civil 3D customizations.

As discussed in Chapter 5, the actual details of how design criteria files and check sets are configured can be driven by government entities, such as a department of transportation or planning commission, or according to your own personal design standards or those adopted by your company. Whatever the case, you should be careful not to rely on them 100 percent. Even while using design criteria files and check sets, a solid understanding of design principles is a must. These tools are just a way of making sure that you're applying what you already know, not a substitute for knowing it in the first place.

Using Design Check Sets

As you learned earlier, a design check set is a collection of one or more design checks. For profiles, there are two types of design checks: line and curve. When a design check set is applied to a profile, Civil 3D will flag any violations with a triangular yellow shield marked with an exclamation point. You can hover over the shield to get more information about the violation.

To apply a design check set to a profile, complete the following steps:

1. Open the drawing named Design Check Set.dwg located in the Chapter 07 class data folder.

2. Click the Jordan Court FGCL profile, and then click Profile Properties on the ribbon.

3. In the Profile Properties dialog box, click the Design Criteria tab.

4. Select the Use Criteria-Based Design box.

5. Select the Use Design Check Set box, and select Subdivision.

6. Click OK to close the Profile Properties dialog box. Press Esc to clear the grips on the profile. You should see two yellow shields near the right end of the profile, as shown in Figure 7.10.

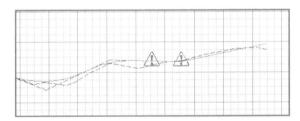

FIGURE 7.10 Warning symbols indicating design
check set violations

7. Zoom in to the area where the warning symbols are displayed. Hover
   the cursor over the symbol on the left. The tooltip reports that the
   slope check is being violated for this tangent.

8. Click the profile to display its grips. Then click the PVI grip to the left
   of the warning symbol and move it upward. This warning symbol disappears, but a new warning symbol may appear on the tangent to the
   left because the slope of this tangent now exceeds 5 percent.

9. Move the PVI down little by little until both tangent warning symbols
   disappear. Now you have satisfied the design check for both tangents.

10. Hover your cursor over the remaining warning symbol. This tooltip
    indicates that the minimum curve length of 3× (1×) the design
    speed is not being met.

11. Click the profile to display the grips, and then click one of the circular grips
    at either end of the curve and move it outward to lengthen the curve. If
    you lengthen the curve enough, the warning symbol will disappear.

Using Design Criteria Files

As you did with alignments, you can assign design criteria files to a profile. The general behavior of design criteria files is the same as it is for design checks: they display
warning symbols when certain design parameters are not met. However, behind the
scenes, design criteria files are much more sophisticated than design check sets, and
you can use them to check more types of geometric criteria.

   To apply a design criteria file to a profile in your drawing, complete these steps:

1. Open the drawing named Design Criteria File.dwg located in the
   Chapter 07 class data folder.

2. Click the Jordan Court FGCL profile and select Profile Properties on
   the ribbon.

3. Click the Design Criteria tab. Check the boxes next to Use Criteria-Based Design and Use Design Criteria File.

4. Click the button to the right of the file path and select the file named Autodesk Civil 3D Imperial (2004) Roadway Design Standards.xml (Autodesk Civil 3D Metric (2004) Roadway Design Standards.xml). Click Open.

5. Verify that the box next to Use Design Check Set is unchecked.

6. Click OK. New warning symbols appear on several of the vertical curves.

7. Hover your cursor over the warning symbol farthest to the left. The tooltip reports that minimum passing sight distance is not being met (Figure 7.11). Since passing will not be allowed anywhere within the subdivision, this warning can be ignored.

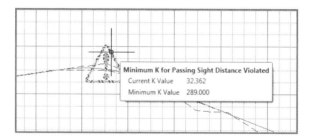

FIGURE 7.11   Warning symbol with tooltip reporting that the passing sight distance criterion is not being met

8. Hover your cursor over the warning symbol at the lowest point of the profile. Notice that this curve is not meeting the requirement for minimum headlight sight distance. This is a requirement that should be honored.

9. Click the Jordan Court FGCL profile, and then click Geometry Editor on the contextual ribbon tab.

10. On the Profile Layout Tools toolbar, click Profile Grid View.

11. In Panorama, scroll to the right until you can view the Minimum K For Headlight Sight Distance column. Note that a warning symbol appears in the row for Item 6 and that the required K value is 26.000 (9.000), as shown in Figure 7.12.

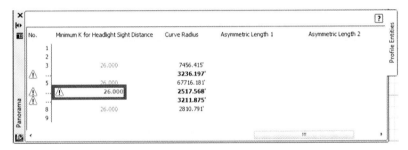

FIGURE 7.12   A warning symbol in Panorama indicating a violation of the headlight sight distance criteria

12. Scroll to the left until you can see the K Value column. Change the K value for Item 6 to **26 (9)**. This removes the warning symbol and changes the curve length to 215.128 (74.914). To practice good design, you'll round that value in the next step.

13. Change the Profile Curve Length for Item 6 to **225 (75)**. This generates a K value of 27.193 (9.010), so the warning symbol is still suppressed.

WHAT'S SO SPECIAL ABOUT K?

The K value is a way of expressing the abruptness of a vertical curve. If you've ever been driving on a country road and caught air at the top of a hill or smacked your head on the dashboard at the bottom of a hill, then you've experienced a K value that is too low for your speed. The K value is calculated as a ratio between the curve length and the change in grade. Longer, more subtle curves have a higher K value, which equates to greater safety because the change in grade is spread out over a longer distance.

Headlight sight distance is an important design parameter for all road designs. If the peaks and valleys of the road do not allow headlights to illuminate obstacles within an acceptable distance, then the road is considered unsafe. The acceptable distance varies based on design speed. Obstacles need to be detected much farther away at higher design speeds to allow the driver enough time to react.

THE ESSENTIALS AND BEYOND

In this chapter, you were given very specific instructions for laying out and editing the example profiles for the project. This is necessary for a learning environment so that your results are predictable and understood.

Now that you have been exposed to methods for creating profiles, creating profile views, editing profiles, and ensuring proper design, you can use what you've learned to create the remaining design profiles for the project. In the exercise that follows, you will not be given specific instructions but more generalized tasks to complete your design. This is a much better representation of how design takes place in a real production environment.

ADDITIONAL EXERCISE

Open the drawing named All Profiles.dwg located in the Chapter 07 class data folder. Complete the following steps to create profiles for Madison Lane and Logan Court.

1. Create a surface profile using the EG surface.

2. Create a profile view using the default profile view style and band settings.

3. Create a layout profile that roughly matches the existing ground profile.

4. Round off the station and elevation values of each PVI to the nearest 5′ (1m) for Station and 0.5′(0.25m) for Elevation.

5. Ensure that the profile meets the criteria of the Subdivisions design check set.

Visit www.sybex.com/go/civil2013essentials to download a video of the author completing this exercise. You can also download the Answers to Additional Exercises Appendix which contains even more information about completing this exercise.

CHAPTER 8

Displaying and Annotating Profiles

Now that you have captured the nature of the existing ground along the road centerlines using surface profiles, and reshaped it using layout profiles, it's time to specify how you intend your design to be built. A wavy line in the drawing simply isn't enough information for a contractor to build with. You need to provide specific geometric information about the profile so that it can be re-created in the field. This is done with various types of annotations.

In addition, it is also important that the framework within which the profiles are displayed is properly configured. As you learned in the previous chapter, the grid lines and grid annotation behind your profiles is a *profile view*. In this chapter, you'll look at applying different profile view styles to control what information about your profiles is displayed and in what manner.

Finally, it is often necessary to show other things in a profile view that might impact the construction of whatever the profile represents. Pipe crossings, underground structures, rock layers, and many other features may need to be displayed so that you can avoid them or integrate your design with them. One way of showing these items in your profile view is through an AutoCAD® Civil 3D® software function called *object projection*.

▶ **Applying profile styles**

▶ **Applying profile view styles**

▶ **Applying profile view bands**

▶ **Applying profile labels**

▶ **Creating and applying profile label sets**

▶ **Creating profile view labels**

▶ **Projecting objects to profile views**

Applying Profile Styles

Certification
Objective

Like any object style, you can use profile styles to show profiles in different ways for different purposes. Specifically, you can use profile styles to affect the appearance of profiles in three basic ways. The first is to control which components of the profile are visible. You might be surprised to know that there are potentially 8 different components of a profile. The second is to control the graphical properties of those components such as layer, color, linetype, and so on. Finally, a profile style enables you to control the display of markers at key geometric points along the profile. Once again, you might be surprised at the number of types of points that can be marked along a profile: there are 11 of them.

To see how different profile styles can be used to affect the display of profiles in your drawing, follow these steps:

Be sure your background color is set to white before proceeding with these steps.

1. Open the drawing named Profile Styles.dwg located in the Chapter 08 class data folder.

2. On the Jordan Court profile view, click the red existing ground profile, and then click Profile Properties on the ribbon.

3. On the Information tab of the Profile Properties dialog box, change the style to _No Display. Then click OK. The profile disappears from view.

USING A STYLE TO HIDE AN OBJECT

In step 3, you used the style _No Display to hide the profile, something you might have normally done by turning off or freezing a layer. This method of making things disappear via style is used quite a bit in Civil 3D. In fact, if you look inside the stock template that ships with Civil 3D, you'll see a _No Display style for nearly every object type.

Using this approach has a couple of advantages over turning layers on and off. First, many Civil 3D objects have multiple components that can be displayed on different layers. Changing one style is more efficient than changing several layers, so it becomes easier and quicker to control the visibility of components by style. Second, you may not know which layer or layers need to be turned off to make the object disappear from view. By simply applying the _No Display style, you make the items disappear without considering layers at all.

4. Press Esc to clear the selection of the existing ground profile. Then click the black design profile for Jordan Court. Right-click and select Properties.

5. In the Properties window, change the Style property to Layout and press Esc to clear the grips. The profile now shows curves and lines as different colors and includes markers that clearly indicate where there are key geometry points (Figure 8.1). This might be helpful while you're in the process of laying out the profile, but it may not work well when you're using the profile to create a final drawing.

You can also use the specific Profile Properties command to access the style assignment, but to show it a different way, in this step you're using the generic Properties command instead.

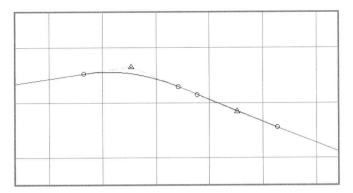

FIGURE 8.1 The Layout profile style displays lines and curves with different colors as well as markers at key geometric locations.

6. Select the Jordan Court profile once again. In the Properties window, change the style to Basic. This is a very simple style that just shows the basic geometry, with no markers or color differences.

7. Change the style to Design Profile With Markers. This style displays the lines and curves on the standard road profile layer, includes markers that are typically used for annotation, and shows the line extensions as gray dashed lines. This style is an example of how you might represent a profile in a final drawing.

8. In Prospector, expand Alignments ➤ Centerline ➤ Jordan Court ➤ Profiles. Right-click Jordan Court EGCL and select Properties, as shown in Figure 8.2.

Remember that this profile was set to _No Display, so the only way to get to it is through the Prospector tab.

9. Change the style to Existing Ground Profile so it looks like it did when you started this exercise.

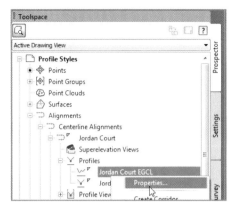

FIGURE 8.2 Using Prospector to access the Properties command for the Jordan Court EGCL profile

A NOTE ABOUT UNITS

Throughout this chapter, you'll notice that two values are provided for units of measurement. The first value is provided for the imperial system that is used in the United States, and the second value in parentheses is provided for the metric system that is used in many other countries. These values most often represent imperial feet and metric meters. It is important to note that generally only the numeric values are entered in the software, not terms like *feet* or *meters*. Also, you should know that the two numbers provided are not necessarily equal. In most cases, they are similar values that are rounded to work efficiently in their respective measurement systems.

Applying Profile View Styles

Certification
Objective

Styles are especially important when you're working with profile views because of their potential to dramatically affect the appearance of the data that is being presented. Among other things, profile view styles can affect the vertical exaggeration, spacing of the grid lines, and labeling.

IT'S OK TO EXAGGERATE SOMETIMES

Vertical exaggeration is a common practice used to display information in profile view. In most places, the earth is relatively flat and the changes in elevation are quite subtle. To make the peaks and valleys stand out a bit more, the elevations are exaggerated while the horizontal distances are kept the same. The result is a profile that appears to have higher high points, lower low points, and steeper slopes in between. This makes the terrain easier to visualize and analyze. When this technique is used, you will likely see a pair of scales assigned to the drawing: one that represents the horizontal scale and one that represents the vertical scale. For example, a drawing that has a horizontal scale of 1″ = 50′ and a vertical scale of 1″ = 5′ would be employing a vertical exaggeration factor of 10. For a metric example, a horizontal drawing scale of 1:500 and a vertical drawing scale of 1:50 would also achieve a vertical exaggeration of 10.

The following three profile views have a vertical exaggeration of 10, 5, and 1 from left to right. The same existing ground profile is shown as a red line in all three.

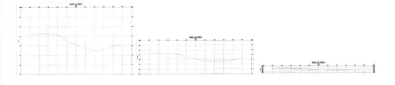

To use profile view styles to change how profile data is displayed in the drawing, complete the following steps:

1. Open the drawing named Profile View Style located in the Chapter 08 class data folder.

2. Click one of the grid lines of the Jordan Court profile view, right-click, and select Properties. Note that in the Properties window, the current profile view style is named Major Grids 10V.

3. Within the Properties window, change the style to Major & Minor Grids 10V. Note the additional grid lines that appear (Figure 8.3).

10V refers to a vertical exaggeration that is 10 times that of the horizontal.

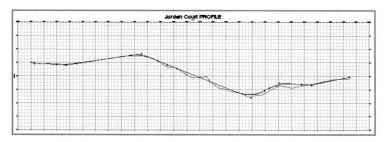

FIGURE 8.3 Additional grid lines displayed as a result of applying the Major & Minor Grids 10V profile view style

4. Change the style to Major Grids 5V. With this change, the vertical exaggeration is reduced to 5. This makes the profile appear much flatter.

5. Change the style to Major Grids 1V. This displays the profile in its true form, as it really is in the field. Think about which profile would be easier to work with. Would it be the exaggerated one where the peaks and valleys are quite obvious, or this one, which is true to scale but much more difficult to analyze?

6. Change the style of the profile view to DOT. This is an example of how the graphical standards of a client or review agency can be built into your Civil 3D standard styles, making it easy to meet the requirements of others.

7. Keep the drawing open for the next exercise.

Applying Profile View Bands

DOT stands for Department of Transportation, which is a common way in the U.S. of referring to government regulatory departments and other agencies that manage roads and other transportation infrastructure.

Earlier, you used the AutoCAD® Properties window to change the profile view style. This is another way to do it.

Profile view bands can be added to a profile view along the top or bottom axis. You can use these bands to provide additional textual or graphical information about a profile. They can be configured to provide this information at even increments or at specific locations along the profile.

To add bands to a profile view, complete the following steps (you should still have Profile View Style.dwg open from the previous exercise):

1. Click one of the grid lines of the Jordan Court profile view, and then click Profile View Properties on the contextual ribbon tab.

2. On the Information tab of the Profile View Properties dialog box, change the Object style to Major & Minor Grids 10V.

3. Click the Bands tab. Verify that Profile Data is selected as the Band Type.

Add>>

4. Under Select Band Style, choose Elevations And Stations. Then click Add.

5. In the Geometry Points To Label In Band dialog box, select Jordan Court EGCL as Profile 1, as shown in Figure 8.4. Click OK. A new entry is added to the list of bands.

You may have noticed the long list of geometry points in this dialog box. The band style you have selected does not include references to any of these points; therefore, no geometry point information will appear on the band.

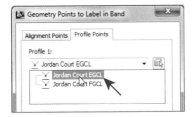

FIGURE 8.4 Assigning Jordan Court EGCL as Profile 1

6. In the Profile View Properties dialog box, scroll to the right until you see the Profile 2 column. Click the cell in this column and select Jordan Court FGCL.

7. Click OK to dismiss the Profile View Properties dialog box and return to the drawing. Across the bottom of the profile view, there is now a band that labels the station and elevation at even increments (Figure 8.5). This band is designed for two profiles, so there are two sets of elevations. The elevations on the left side of each line refer to the Jordan Court EGCL profile, and the ones on the right refer to the Jordan Court FGCL profile.

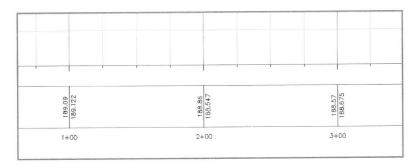

FIGURE 8.5 The newly added band showing stations, existing elevations (left), and proposed elevations (right)

8. Click the profile view and select Profile View Properties from the ribbon once again.

9. On the Bands tab, select Horizontal Geometry as the Band Type.

   10. Under Select Band Style, choose Geometry and click Add.

BAND SETS

Right after step 9, you could have clicked Save As Band Set and stored the two bands as a new band set. Then this band set could be imported into another profile view at a later time. This feature is quite handy when you repeatedly use the same list of bands, enabling you to avoid rebuilding the list each time.

11. Click OK to dismiss the dialog box and return to the drawing. The new band is a graphical representation of the alignment geometry. Upward bumps in the band represent curves to the right, and downward bumps represent curves to the left. The beginning and ending of each bump correspond with the beginning and ending of the associated curve. There are also labels that provide more specifics about the horizontal geometry.

12. Click the Jordan Court profile view; then click Profile View Properties on the ribbon. On the Bands tab, click the Horizontal Geometry band entry, and then click the red X icon to remove it.

13. Click OK to return to the drawing. The Horizontal Geometry band is removed from the bottom of the Jordan Court profile view.

Applying Profile Labels

Profile labels are similar to alignment labels. They are applied to the entire profile or a range within the profile and show up wherever they encounter the things they are supposed to label. For example, if a vertical curve label is applied to a profile that has three vertical curves, then three vertical curve labels will appear. There are two advantages to this approach. The first is that you can label multiple instances of a geometric feature with one command. This becomes quite significant when you're working on a long stretch of road with dozens of vertical curves. The other advantage is that labels appear as new geometric features are added. Continuing with using vertical curves as an example, if you apply a vertical curve label to a profile, curve labels will appear or disappear automatically whenever you create or delete vertical curves.

To apply profile labels to the profile in your drawing, follow these steps:

1. Open the drawing named `Profile Labels.dwg` located in the `Chapter 08` class data folder.

 2. Click the Jordan Court FGCL profile, and then click Edit Profile Labels on the ribbon.

3. In the Profile Labels - Jordan Court FGCL dialog box, select Crest Curves as the Type.

 4. Select Crest Only as the Profile Crest Curve Label Style, and then click Add.

5. Click OK to return to the drawing. All of the crest curves in the profile are labeled.

 6. Click the Jordan Court FGCL profile, and then click Edit Profile Labels on the ribbon once again. Add the following profile labels:

Type	Style
Sag Curves	Sag Only
Lines	Percent Grade
Grade Breaks	Station over Elevation

7. The list of labels should appear as shown in Figure 8.6. Click OK to close the Profile Labels - Jordan Court FGCL dialog box and return to the drawing. The profile is now annotated with several types of labels. Some of the label positions need to be adjusted to improve readability, which you will do in the following steps.

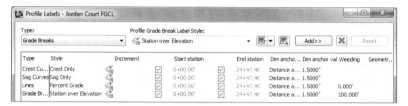

FIGURE 8.6 The list of labels to be applied to the Jordan Court FGCL profile

8. Zoom in to the third curve label from the left. Notice how the curve length dimension line is crossing through the profile.

9. Click the label to show its grips. Then click the diamond-shaped grip at the base of the dimension text, and move it up until the label is more readable.

10. Repeat step 9 for any other curve labels that need to be moved to improve readability.

Creating and Applying Profile Label Sets

In the previous exercise, you used several types of profile labels to annotate the design profile for Jordan Court. Each one had to be selected and added to the list of labels, making this a multistep process. A profile label set enables you to store a list of labels for use on another profile. The settings for each label—such as weeding, major station, minor station, and so on—can also be stored within the label set. This is quite helpful if you use the same profile labels for multiple profiles. A label set can even be stored in your company template so that it is always there for you to use.

To create a label set and apply it to another profile in your drawing, follow these steps:

1. Open the drawing named `Profile Label Set.dwg` located in the Chapter 08 class data folder.

2. Click the Jordan Court FGCL profile and click Edit Profile Labels on the ribbon.

3. In the Profile Labels - Jordan Court FGCL dialog box, click Save Label Set to open the Profile Label Set - New Profile Label Set dialog box.

4. Click the Information tab and enter **Curves-Grades-Breaks** as the Name. Click OK twice to return to the drawing.

5. Press Esc to clear the selection of the Jordan Court FGCL profile. Then click the Logan Court FGCL profile and select Edit Profile Labels on the ribbon.

6. On the Profile Labels - Logan Court FGCL dialog box, click Import Label Set.

7. Select Curve-Grades-Breaks on the Select Label Set dialog box, and then click OK. Click OK to dismiss the Profile Labels dialog box and return to the drawing. Two grade break labels and a grade label have been added to the Logan Court FGCL profile (Figure 8.7).

No curve labels appear on the profile because there are no curves. However, if a curve were added, a curve label would appear.

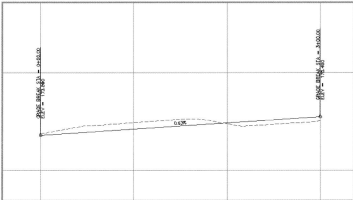

FIGURE 8.7 Logan Court FGCL profile after the newly created profile label set has been applied

Creating Profile View Labels

You have just seen how useful profile labels can be because they are applied to the entire profile and continuously watch for new geometric properties to label. However, this dynamic nature may not be ideal in certain situations, or you may need to provide annotation in your profile view that is not related to any profiles within that view. *Profile view labels* are the solution in this case.

Profile view labels are directly linked to the profile view: the grid, grid labeling, and bands that serve as the backdrop for one or more profiles. Because of this, you can use labels that are independent of any profiles. For example, you might use a station and offset label to call out the location of a pipe crossing through the profile view. Since the pipe crossing is not directly affected by any profile in the drawing, it wouldn't make sense to associate this label with a profile. Instead, you would use a profile view label that is specifically intended for the pipe crossing.

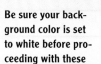

Be sure your background color is set to white before proceeding with these steps.

There are three types of profile view labels available in Civil 3D: station elevation, depth, and projection. You will work with the first two in the next exercise, and the third will be covered later in this chapter.

To create profile view labels in a profile view, complete the following steps:

1. Open the drawing named Profile View Labels.dwg located in the Chapter 08 class data folder. This drawing is zoomed in to the left end of the Jordan Court FGCL profile. At this location, there is a PVI where the new road ties to the edge of the existing road. There is also a V shape in the existing ground profile that shows the existence of a roadside drainage ditch (Figure 8.8).

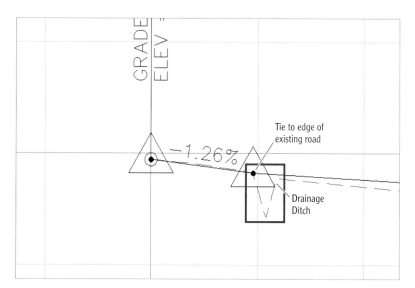

FIGURE 8.8   The beginning of the Jordan Court FGCL profile where there is a tie to the edge of the existing Emerson Road as well as a V-shaped drainage ditch

You must provide the location in two separate steps: first you specify the station (step 4), and then you specify the elevation (step 5).

2. Click one of the grid lines for the Jordan Court profile view. On the ribbon, click Add View Labels ➤ Station Elevation.

3. While holding down the Shift key, right-click, and select Endpoint from the context menu.

4. Click the center of the black-filled circle at the second PVI marker.

5. Repeat the previous two steps to specify the same point for the elevation. A new label appears, but it's overlapping the grade label to the left.

6. Press Esc twice to clear the selection of the profile view and end the command. Then click the newly created label and drag the square grip up and to the right.

 7. With the label still selected, click Edit Label Text on the ribbon. This opens the Text Component Editor.

8. In the text view window on the right, click just to the left of STA to place your cursor at that location. Press Enter to move that line of text down and provide a blank line to type on.

9. Click the blank line at the top, type **TIE TO EDGE**, and press Enter.

10. Type **OF EXIST ROAD**. The Text Component Editor dialog box should now look like Figure 8.9.

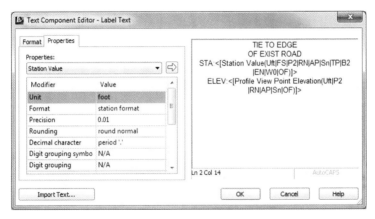

FIGURE 8.9   Additional text added to a label in the Text Component Editor dialog box

11. Click OK to return to the drawing. The label now clearly calls out the station and elevation where the new road should tie to the existing road.

 12. Press Esc to clear the current label selection. Click one of the grid lines of the profile view, and then click Add View Labels ➢ Depth.

13. Pick a point at the invert of the V-shaped ditch, and then pick a point just above it, approximating the top of the ditch.

14. Press Esc twice to end the command and clear the selection of the profile view.

Nearly all Civil 3D labels can be edited in this way.

Invert is a term referring to the lowest elevation of the ditch. It is also used to refer to the lowest elevation of a pipe or a structure such as a manhole or inlet.

15. Click the newly created depth label, and then click one of the grips at the tip of either arrow. Move the grip to a new location and note the change to the depth value displayed in the label. Both the station elevation label and the depth label can be seen in Figure 8.10.

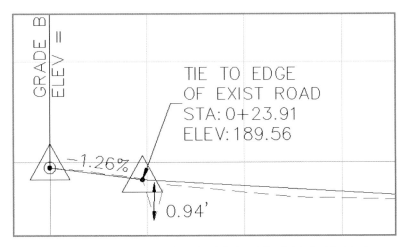

FIGURE 8.10 The station elevation label and depth label added to the Jordan Court profile view

REMEMBER EXAGGERATION?

The roughly 1-foot (0.3-meter) depth shown by the label might seem a bit small to you based on the dramatic plunge of the V in the profile. Remember that this profile view is exaggerated in the vertical aspect by a factor of 10. If you were to measure this same depth using the AutoCAD DISTANCE command, you would get about 10 feet (3 meters). Profile view labels automatically factor in the vertical exaggeration of your profile view.

Projecting Objects to Profile Views

At times, it may be necessary or helpful to show more in a profile view than just the existing and finished profiles of your design. Features such as underground pipes, overhead cables, trees, fences, and so on may be obstacles that you need to avoid or features that you need to integrate into your design. Whatever the case, Civil 3D object projection enables you to quickly represent a variety of objects within your profile view and provide the accompanying annotation.

Projecting Linear Objects

When you project an object to a profile view, different things can happen depending on the type of object you have chosen. For linear objects such as 3D polylines, feature lines, or survey figures, the projected version of the object is still linear, but it will appear distorted unless it is parallel to the alignment. This can be a bit tough to envision, but just imagine a light being shined from behind the object in the direction of the alignment. The projection of this object seen within a profile view would be somewhat like the shadow cast by the object. The parts of it that are parallel to the alignment would appear full length, and the parts that are not parallel would appear shortened.

Based on the settings you choose, the elevations that are applied to a projected linear object can vary. For linear objects that are already drawn in 3D, you can choose to use the object elevations as they are. For 2D objects that need to have elevations provided, the elevations can be derived from a surface or profile.

To project a linear object to a profile view, follow these steps:

1. Open the drawing named Object Projection.dwg located in the Chapter 08 class data folder.

2. Click one of the grid lines of the Jordan Court profile view, and then click Project Objects To Profile View on the ribbon.

3. Click the blue 3D polyline representing the water pipe that runs parallel to the eastern property line. Press Enter.

4. In the Project Objects To Profile View dialog box, verify that the Style is set to Basic and the Elevation Option is set to Use Object.

5. Click OK. The projected version of the water line is shown in the profile view (Figure 8.11). Note the strange bends in the line around station 12+00 (0+360). These are caused by the alignment turning away from the water pipe at this location, which produces some odd projection angles and distorts the projected appearance of the water pipe.

6. Keep the drawing open for the next exercise.

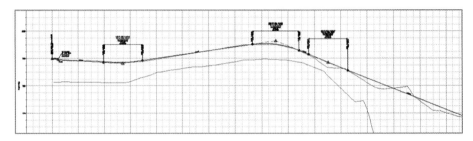

FIGURE 8.11 A 3D polyline representing a water pipe has been projected into the Jordan Court profile view.

Projecting Blocks and Points

Objects that indicate location—such as AutoCAD points, Civil 3D points, and blocks—are handled a bit differently than linear objects. They are represented with markers or as a projected version of the way that they are drawn in plan view. This can lead to a distorted view of such objects because of the common practice of applying a vertical exaggeration to the profile view. The options for assigning elevations to these types of projections are the same as the options for linear objects, with one addition: the ability to provide an elevation manually. This allows you to specify the elevation graphically or numerically, independent of a surface, a profile, or even the actual elevation of the object you've selected.

To project blocks and Civil 3D points to a profile view, follow these steps (you should still have Object Projection.dwg open from the previous exercise):

1. Select the profile view grid for Jordan Court, and click Project Objects To Profile View on the ribbon.

2. Click three of the points labeled BORE that appear along the Jordan Court alignment. Press Enter.

3. In the Project Objects To Profile View dialog box, verify that Test Bore is selected as the Style and Use Object is selected as the Elevation Option for all three points.

4. Click OK and view the projected points in the profile view. As you can see, they are inserted with a marker and a label that indicates the station and ground surface elevation of the test boring (Figure 8.12).

5. Press Esc to clear the previous selection. Zoom in near the midpoint of Logan Court and note the red test boring symbol shown there. This is an AutoCAD block, not a Civil 3D point.

> The type of style referred to here is a Civil 3D *point style*. A few steps later, you will use a different type of style for a block.

6. Click the profile view for Logan Court, and then click Project Objects To Profile View on the ribbon.

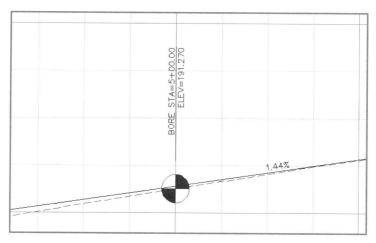

FIGURE 8.12 A Civil 3D point projected to the Jordan Court profile view

7. Click the red test boring symbol and press Enter. Verify that the Style is set to Basic, and change Elevation Options to Surface ➢ EG.

8. Click OK and examine the new projection added to the profile view. It looks similar to the projected Civil 3D points, even though the source object in this case is a block with no elevation assigned to it.

Feature lines and Civil 3D points have projection built into their styles, but for AutoCAD entities like this block, an *object projection style* is used.

THE ESSENTIALS AND BEYOND

Performing design and analysis in profile view is one of the most important capabilities in nearly every land development project. Often, the profile view is the most effective way to convey information about the existing terrain, proposed redesign of the terrain, existing and proposed underground features, and many other types of important information. And not only must this information be shown graphically, it also must be annotated so that specific information can be passed on to those responsible for reviewing the design and constructing it in the field.

In this chapter, you learned how to use profile view styles, labels, and object projection to provide details about your design in profile view. In the additional exercise, you will apply what you have learned to the design of Madison Lane. You will also add some more information to the Jordan Court and Logan Court designs.

(Continues)

THE ESSENTIALS AND BEYOND *(Continued)*

ADDITIONAL EXERCISE

Open the drawing named Profiles Beyond.dwg located in the Chapter 08 class data folder. Use the following basic guidelines to stylize, annotate, and provide object projections for the Madison Lane profile view:

1. Change the profile view style of Madison Lane and Logan Court to match Jordan Court.

2. Apply the same profile view bands to Madison Lane that have been applied to Jordan Court and Logan Court.

3. Apply the same profile label set to the Madison Lane FGCL profile that has been used for Jordan Court FGCL and Logan Court FGCL.

4. Project the test boring blocks located along the Madison Lane alignment to the Madison Lane profile view. Use the Madison Lane EGCL profile to provide elevations for these projections.

5. Project the survey figure representing the north edge of the stream to the Jordan Court profile view.

6. On the Jordan Court profile view, create a depth label showing the elevation difference between the edge of the stream and the lowest point of the curve at station 16+77.02 (0+511.15).

Visit www.sybex.com/go/civil2013essentials to download a video of the author completing this exercise. You can also download the Answers to Additional Exercises Appendix which contains even more information about completing this exercise.

CHAPTER 9

Designing in 3D Using Corridors

Long before AutoCAD® Civil 3D® objects, CAD, or even computers existed, engineers were designing roads and other linear features in three stages: alignment, profile, and cross section. I suspect that the reason for this is that it is much easier to think of a design one dimension at a time rather than all three at once. This was especially true before designs could be visualized in 3D on a computer screen. This approach to linear design has carried right through to the present day and is still quite evident, even in cutting-edge technology such as Civil 3D.

You have already learned the alignment and profile stages of this design approach. In this chapter, you will learn how assemblies are used to provide the third stage of the design process: the cross section. Then, you will combine all three elements (alignments, profiles, and assemblies) to take this three-stage design process to the next level: a dynamic three-dimensional model.

▶ **Understanding corridors**

▶ **Creating an assembly**

▶ **Creating a corridor**

▶ **Applying corridor targets**

▶ **Creating corridor surfaces**

Understanding Corridors

A corridor consists of hundreds or even thousands of individual Civil 3D objects that are dynamically linked to one another. A good way to begin understanding how corridors work is to study how these different components come together to become a 3D representation of your design.

Understanding the 3D Chain

In Chapter 5 and Chapter 6, you used alignments to design the 2D path of a linear feature, in this case a road. In Chapter 7 and Chapter 8, you designed the vertical path of the road using profiles. When combined, the alignment and profile form a three-dimensional pathway called a *3D chain*. The 3D chain serves as the backbone of your design.

3D chains can actually be seen in your drawing, but only if you view the drawing from a 3D perspective, as shown in Figure 9.1.

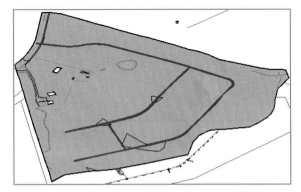

FIGURE 9.1 The blue lines represent 3D chains formed by combining alignments with profiles to form a three-dimensional pathway.

Because the 3D chain is dynamically linked to both the alignment and profile, a change to either one will automatically prompt a change to the 3D chain and subsequently update the corridor.

Understanding the Assembly

An *assembly* is a representation of the cross-sectional geometry of the feature you are designing. It establishes the overall shape of the cross section and distinguishes the areas within it. For example, a typical road cross section can have areas of asphalt pavement, base material, curbs, and sidewalks, as shown in Figure 9.2.

The parts of an assembly are called *subassemblies*. They are dynamically linked to one another and therefore have the potential to affect one another. For example, if a curb subassembly is located at the edge of a lane subassembly, the curb subassembly will automatically move outward if the lane width is increased.

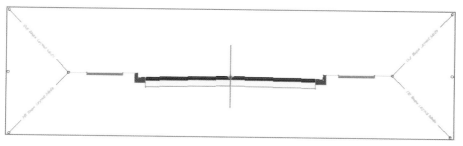

FIGURE 9.2 A Civil 3D assembly that establishes lanes, curbs, sidewalks, and grading

Understanding Assembly Insertions

To create a corridor, Civil 3D inserts instances of an assembly along a 3D chain at regular intervals. These *assembly insertions* can be thought of as the ribs of the 3D model, providing shape to the road one assembly at a time (Figure 9.3).

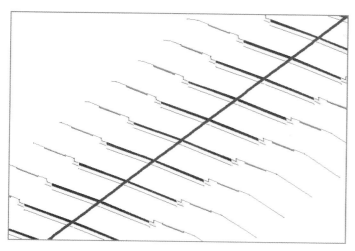

FIGURE 9.3 Assemblies inserted at intervals along a 3D chain

Because the assembly insertions are dynamically linked to the 3D chain, any change to the alignment or profile will prompt a change in the corridor. The assembly insertions are also dynamically linked to the assembly itself, so any change to the assembly will prompt an update to the corridor as well.

Understanding Corridor Feature Lines

To provide a framework in the longitudinal direction, Civil 3D draws feature lines from assembly to assembly (Figure 9.4). The feature lines employ a coding system to determine which points they are drawn through each time they cross an assembly.

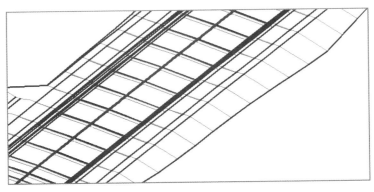

FIGURE 9.4 The red lines are feature lines that connect like points on each assembly insertion.

The feature lines are linked to the assembly insertions, which are linked to the 3D chain, and so on. I'll stop calling out relationships specifically and just cover it all by saying that everything within a corridor is essentially related.

Understanding the Corridor Surface

As you view the assembly insertions along the 3D chain previously shown in Figure 9.3, imagine this as the structural framework of a ship or an airplane. With the framework in place, now imagine the hull or fuselage being installed on the vessel. This is a great way to envision the role of a *corridor surface* (Figure 9.5).

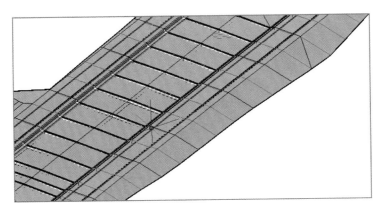

FIGURE 9.5 A corridor along with its corridor surface shown in 3D view

Although they appear in Prospector like other surfaces, corridor surfaces are built directly from the corridor and maintain a link to the corridor. They can be displayed as contours, used to create surface profiles, and perform every other function normally associated with surfaces.

Creating an Assembly

As mentioned, an assembly consists of smaller components called *subassemblies*. To create an assembly, you begin by creating an assembly baseline, which is represented by a simple vertical line in your drawing with a single base point marker at its midpoint. Then, you proceed by inserting individual subassemblies that represent elements such as lanes, curbs, ditches, and so on.

Before building an assembly, it is a good idea to have at least a sketch of the typical cross section of your design so that you have something to reference as you work. Having detailed dimensions is helpful but not critical—the subassemblies can be changed with relative ease, even after the corridor has been built.

To create an assembly that represents the cross section of a road, follow these steps:

1. Open the drawing named Creating an Assembly.dwg located in the Chapter 09 class data folder.

2. On the Home tab of the ribbon, click Assembly ➢ Create Assembly.

3. In the Create Assembly dialog box, enter **Subdivision Road** as the Name.

4. For Code Set Style, select All Codes With Hatching. Click OK.

5. Click a point within the open area on your screen to insert the assembly baseline. A vertical red line will appear in your drawing.

6. On the Home tab of the ribbon, click the Tool Palettes icon.

7. On the Tool Palettes window, right-click the gray strip labeled Tool Palettes, and select Civil Imperial (Metric) Subassemblies.

8. Click the stack of tabs at the bottom of the tool palette window, and then click Basic, as shown in Figure 9.6.

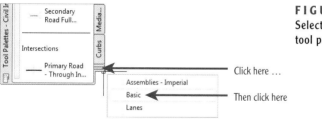

FIGURE 9.6
Selecting the Basic tool palette

9. On the Basic tool palette, click BasicLane. The Properties window will appear, and you will be prompted on the command line to select a marker point.

This is not the same Mirror command that AutoCAD® software uses for mirroring lines, arcs, and circles. This is a special command for subassemblies and must be used instead of the AutoCAD version.

▶

10. In the Properties window, verify that Side is set to Right, and then click the right side of the marker at the midpoint of the assembly baseline. A lane subassembly is attached to the assembly baseline.

11. On the Basic tool palette, click BasicCurbAndGutter.

12. In the Properties window, change the value for Curb Height to 0.50 (0.15).

13. Click the upper-right circle marker on the lane subassembly you inserted earlier. A subassembly representing curb and gutter is now attached to the lane.

14. Press Esc to end the assembly insertion command. Click the lane subassembly and the curb subassembly, and then click Mirror on the ribbon.

15. Click the vertical red assembly baseline. Both sides of the assembly now display a lane and curb subassembly.

WHAT ARE SUBASSEMBLIES MADE OF?

Subassemblies are made of three fundamental components: points, links, and shapes. A point is self-explanatory, a link is a line that is drawn between two points, and a shape is the result of three or more links forming a closed shape, as shown in the following diagram. Each point, link, and shape in a subassembly has at least one code. These codes are used to identify the purpose of a component and control its style, behavior, and relationship to other parts of the design. A collection of styles that apply to multiple codes is called a *code set style*.

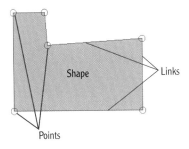

A NOTE ABOUT UNITS

Throughout this chapter, you'll notice that two values are provided for units of measurement. The first value is provided for the imperial system that is used in the United States, and the second value in parentheses is provided for the metric system that is used in many other countries. These values most often represent imperial feet and metric meters. It is important to note that generally only the numeric values are entered in the software, not terms like *feet* or *meters*. Also, you should know that the two numbers provided are not necessarily equal. In most cases, they are similar values that are rounded to work efficiently in their respective measurement systems.

Creating a Corridor

Considering the complexity and sophistication of a corridor, the process of creating one is actually quite simple. Once the alignment, profile, and assembly are in place, it's just a matter of telling these three objects that they belong together. Of course, the design is far from complete at this point, but as you'll see in the next exercise, creating the initial version of a corridor involves only a few steps.

Certification
Objective

To create a corridor from an alignment, profile, and assembly that already exist in a drawing, follow these steps:

1. Open the drawing named `Creating A Corridor.dwg` located in the Chapter 09 class data folder.

 2. On the Home tab of the ribbon, click Corridor.

3. In the Create Corridor dialog box, do the following:

    a. For Name, enter **Jordan Court**.

    b. For Alignment, select Jordan Court.

    c. For Profile, select Jordan Court FGCL.

    d. For Assembly, select Subdivision Road.

    e. Uncheck the box next to Set Baseline And Region Parameters.

    f. Click OK.

◀

The Create Corridor dialog box was redesigned in AutoCAD Civil 3D 2013 to improve the workflow of creating corridors.

4. Zoom in to the plan view and notice the corridor that has been created there.

5. Click the corridor, right-click, and select Object Viewer.

6. In the Object Viewer window, click near the bottom of the window and drag upward. The view of the corridor will rotate away from you, enabling it to be viewed from a 3D perspective. Examine the corridor by zooming and rotating the model (Figure 9.7).

FIGURE 9.7 A portion of the newly created corridor shown in a 3D perspective

Applying Corridor Targets

One thing that makes corridors so powerful is their ability to interact with other objects in the drawing. Corridors are able to morph themselves into different shapes and sizes in order to respond to existing features or components of newly designed features. This is made possible through the use of special subassemblies that can be stretched, twisted, and reconfigured as they progress along the corridor. What makes these subassemblies special is that they utilize corridor targets.

There are three types of targets that can be applied to a corridor: *surface targets*, *width or offset targets*, and *slope or elevation targets*.

Understanding Surface Targets

Surface targets are used in a number of cases where the corridor needs to interact with a surface, such as when a slope is projected from a design elevation to the point where it intercepts an existing ground surface. This is referred to as *daylighting*. For example, in a section of road design that is above existing ground, daylighting would be used to create the embankment from the elevation of the road to the original ground elevation (Figure 9.8).

F I G U R E 9 . 8 A cross-section view of a road that shows the daylighting of a 3:1 slope on either side

TYING IN PROPOSED AND EXISTING ELEVATIONS

The concept of daylighting is found throughout all types of land development. As I've mentioned, one of the fundamental activities of land development is changing the shape of the land. This means that portions of the development will have new elevations that are above or below the existing elevations. Since things such as roads and parking lots are not much good underground and are not able to simply float in midair, there must be some way of transitioning between new elevations and existing elevations. The most economical material that can be used to construct that transition is soil, but soil is not stable on steep slopes. Therefore, the transition between new and existing elevations is done with relatively mild slopes such as 3:1 (three units horizontal to one vertical) or milder. One of the most important components of your land development design will be this tie-in between proposed elevations and existing elevations.

Although daylighting is the most common example of surface targeting, there are other examples such as establishing the cross slope of an existing road, setting the top elevation of a retaining wall, setting the depth of a pipe, and many others.

Understanding Width or Offset Targets

Another type of target used in corridor design is referred to as a width or offset target. As the name suggests, this type of target is used to vary the width of an object or the distance between a point and the centerline (also known as *offset*). For example, an alignment can be used as a target that controls the outside edge of a lane. As the path of the alignment moves away from the road centerline, the lane widens. As the path of the alignment moves toward the road centerline, the lane narrows (Figure 9.9).

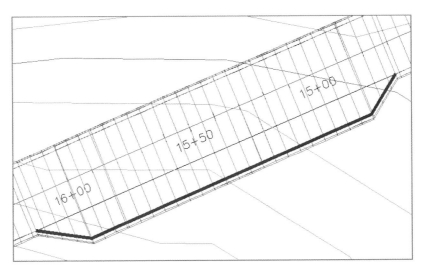

FIGURE 9.9   A width or offset target (in red) applied to a corridor to widen the lane and create a pull-off area

In addition to alignments, you can use feature lines, survey figures, and 3D polylines as width or offset targets. Lane widening is probably the most common use of a width or offset target, but there are many other uses. For example, you can use a width or offset target to control the location of a ditch, the width of a shoulder, or the distance between a shoulder and a guardrail.

Understanding Slope or Elevation Targets

Slope or elevation targets are used to control the elevations of one or more components of a corridor. For example, these targets can control the elevations of a roadside ditch to ensure that it drains to a specific point, regardless of the slope of the adjacent road (Figure 9.10). Profiles, feature lines, survey figures, and 3D polylines can be used as this type of target.

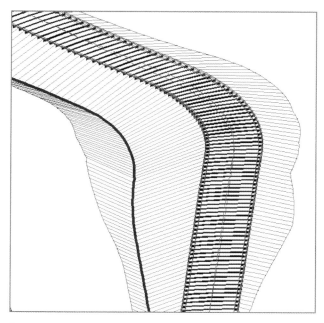

FIGURE 9.10   The use of a profile (3D chain shown in red) to control the elevations of a ditch

Applying Subassemblies That Can Use Targets

Before you can use targets within your corridor, you have to make sure that you have used subassemblies that have targeting capabilities. Civil 3D comes with hundreds of subassemblies, each designed for a different purpose or application. Some of these subassemblies can use targets and some cannot. For example, the BasicLane subassembly that you used earlier does not have the ability to target anything. So, if you would like to use a width or offset target to incorporate a turning lane, pull-off area, or some other feature into your corridor, you will have to use a different subassembly.

> **If you're having trouble locating the assembly named Subdivision Road in the drawing, you can browse to it in Prospector, right-click, and select Zoom To.**
>
>

   To modify an assembly by adding subassemblies that utilize targets, follow these steps:

1. Open the drawing named Adding Target Subassemblies.dwg located in the Chapter 09 class data folder.

2. Zoom in to the Subdivision Road assembly.

3. Open the Tool Palettes window, and click the Basic tool palette.

4. Right-click BasicLaneTransition and select Apply Tool Properties To Subassembly, as shown in Figure 9.11.

The Apply Tool Properties command is a great technique for switching out one subassembly for another. Just be aware that all of the properties are switched, which is why the subassembly is on the wrong side in this step.

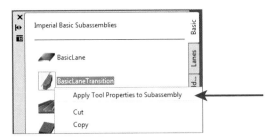

FIGURE 9.11 Selecting the Apply Tool Properties To Subassembly command

5. Select both lane subassemblies in the Subdivision Road assembly and press Enter. The assembly will appear a bit odd because everything shifts over to one side.

6. Press Esc to clear the current selection. Click the assembly baseline (the vertical line the subassemblies are attached to), and then click Assembly Properties on the ribbon.

7. In the Assembly Properties dialog box, do the following:

As the name implies, the Hold Grade, Change Offset setting will maintain the cross grade of the lane (which happens to be 2 percent) while widening or narrowing it to the specified distance.

a. Click the Construction tab. Click twice on Group (1) to edit the name. Type **Right** and press Enter. Use the same procedure to rename Group (2) to Left.

b. Under the group now named Right, rename the two subassemblies as **Right Lane** and **Right Curb**. Do the same for the Left group, naming the subassemblies **Left Lane** and **Left Curb**.

c. Click Right Lane and change the Side value to Right. Do the same for Left Lane by setting the Side value to Left.

d. For Left Lane and Right Lane, scroll down and change the value for Transition to Hold Grade, Change Offset.

Figure 9.12 shows the Assembly Properties dialog after completing all of the tasks in this step.

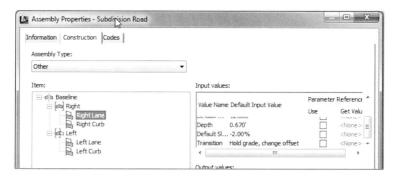

FIGURE 9.12 The Assembly Properties dialog box after the groups and subassemblies have been renamed and the properties for the lanes have been set properly

8. Click OK to close the Assembly Properties dialog box and return to the drawing. The assembly now looks the way it should.

9. On the Basic tool palette, click BasicSideSlopeCutDitch.

10. In the Properties window, verify that Side is set to Left. Click the marker in the upper-left corner of the Left Curb subassembly.

11. Click the marker in the upper-right corner of the Right Curb subassembly. The assembly should now look similar to Figure 9.13.

FIGURE 9.13 The assembly with newly added BasicSideSlopeCutDitch subassemblies on either side

Notice that this time you didn't change the Side property to Right. Civil 3D 2013 has a special feature that automatically guesses which side of the assembly you are on.

12. Press Esc to end the current command. Click the right BasicSideSlopeCutDitch subassembly, and then click Subassembly Properties on the ribbon.

13. On the Information tab of the Subassembly Properties dialog box, change the name to **Right Daylight**.

14. Repeat the previous two steps for the same subassembly on the left, this time naming it **Left Daylight**.

WHAT'S IN A NAME?

Take the time to rename your subassemblies using logical, easy-to-remember names. This not only makes it easier to keep track of these things as you continue to work on your corridor, but it also helps if you have to pass your work on to someone else.

Assigning Targets

You use the Target Mapping dialog box to assign targets within a corridor. This dialog lists the three types of targets along with subassemblies within your corridor that are able to use each type of target (Figure 9.14). Targets do not have to be used whenever they are available. In fact, for many corridors, the majority of the targets are set to <None>.

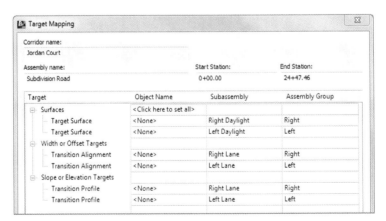

FIGURE 9.14 The Target Mapping dialog box showing the three types of corridor targets along with the subassemblies that can use each type of target

To assign a target, you click the cell within the Object Name column that corresponds to the subassembly you would like to set up. This displays a dialog box where you can select objects in the drawing graphically or by name.

To assign targets to the corridor that will provide daylighting and create a turn lane, follow these steps:

1. Open the drawing named `Applying Corridor Targets.dwg` located in the `Chapter 09` class data folder.

 2. Click the corridor in the drawing, and then click Edit Targets on the ribbon.

3. When prompted to select a region, click anywhere within the corridor. As you do, you should see a blue outline appear around the corridor.

CORRIDOR REGION

In step 3, you are prompted to select a *region* to edit. A region is essentially a part of your corridor that begins at one station and ends at another. All corridors start out with a single region that extends the full length of the corridor. This is the condition of the example corridor right now. As a design evolves, however, you will probably break up the corridor into multiple regions. This will be covered in more detail a bit later in this chapter.

4. In the Target Mapping dialog box, under Width Or Offset Targets, click <None> in the Object Name column next to the Left Lane subassembly. This will open the Set Width Or Offset Target dialog box.

5. In the Set Width Or Offset Target dialog box, under Select Object Type To Target, select Feature Lines, Survey Figures, and Polylines.

6. Click Select From Drawing. Then zoom in to the beginning of Jordan Court where it intersects with Emerson Road.

7. Click the red polyline that represents the desired path of the left lane's edge, and then press Enter. By widening the left lane in this way, you make extra room for a turning lane.

8. Click OK twice to return to the drawing. The corridor is widened near the entrance, as shown in Figure 9.15.

9. Click within the corridor to reopen the Target Mapping dialog box.

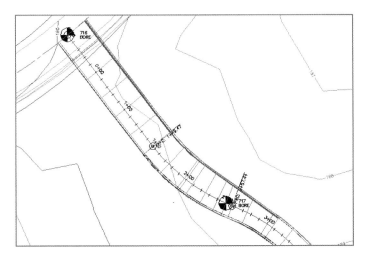

FIGURE 9.15   The corridor is wider where the lane edge polyline was targeted

10. In the Target Mapping dialog box, click the cell next to Surfaces that reads <Click Here To Set All>.

11. Select EG and click OK. Then click OK to dismiss the Target Mapping dialog box. You should now see additional geometry along the edges of the corridor (Figure 9.16). This represents the daylighting that has been applied. The daylighting geometry is noticeably wider in some areas than in others. These are areas that are below existing ground through which a ditch has been constructed. This automatic creation of ditches is a function of the BasicSideSlopeCutDitch subassembly.

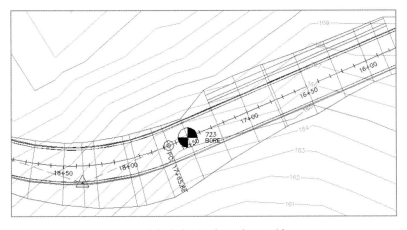

FIGURE 9.16   Areas of daylighting along the corridor

CUT AND FILL

The terms *cut* and *fill* are used quite a bit in relation to land development activities. For example, in the BasicSideSlopeCutDitch subassembly, the word *cut* refers to a condition where the road is below existing ground and therefore has to project a slope upward in order to daylight. Another way to envision this is that earth must be cut away in order to construct the road in these areas. The opposite of cut is *fill*, which refers to conditions where an area must be filled in with earth to create a design feature. Cut and fill can also be used to refer to quantities of earth, where *cut* represents the volume of earth that must be removed to build something, while *fill* represents the volume of earth that must be brought in to build something.

Creating Corridor Surfaces

In Chapter 4, you learned the benefits of using a surface to model the existing terrain. A surface provided a model of the land and enabled you to do things like display contours, label elevations, and create surface profiles. Imagine having all of those capabilities with a corridor as well. This is made possible through the creation of a corridor surface.

Corridor surfaces are unique in that they exist as a property of the corridor, although they show up in Prospector like any other Civil 3D surface. You use the Corridor Surface dialog box to create the initial corridor surface, and then you choose the data within the corridor that is to be added to this surface. You can choose links and feature lines based on the codes assigned to them. You can also click the Boundaries tab and add a boundary to the surface. You can create boundaries *automatically* based on coded feature lines within a corridor, *interactively* by selecting individual feature lines within the corridor, or *manually* by selecting a polyline that already exists in the drawing.

To create a surface for a corridor, complete the following steps:

1. Open the drawing named Creating a Corridor Surface.dwg located in the Chapter 09 class data folder.

2. Click the Jordan Court corridor, and then click Corridor Surfaces on the ribbon.

3. In the Corridor Surfaces dialog box, click the leftmost icon to create a new corridor surface.

4. Edit the name of the new surface so that it reads **Jordan Court FG**.

5. Verify that Data Type is set to Links and that Code is set to Top.

6. Click the plus sign to add the Top coded links to the surface.

7. Click OK. If the Corridor Properties – Rebuild dialog box opens, click Rebuild The Corridor. You should now see contours in the drawing; however, there is a large area in the center of the site that contains incorrect contours (Figure 9.17).

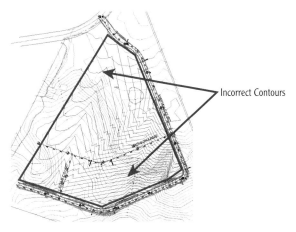

FIGURE 9.17   Contours displayed for the newly created corridor surface—note the incorrect contours in the center of the site.

8. Click the corridor in the drawing, and then click Corridor Surfaces once again.

9. Click the Boundaries tab of the Corridor Surfaces dialog box.

10. Right-click Jordan Court FG and select Corridor Extents As Outer Boundary, as shown in Figure 9.18.

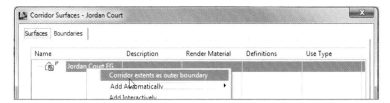

FIGURE 9.18   Selecting the corridor extents as the basis for creating a surface boundary

11. Click OK to return to the drawing. If the Corridor Properties – Rebuild dialog box opens, click Rebuild The Corridor. The surface has been contained within the extents of the corridor as it should. Now, contours appear only where valid surface data exists.

ALTERNATE CORRIDOR SURFACES

In this example, you create a surface that represents the top (finished) ground elevations of the corridor. You could have selected any one of the codes contained within the corridor, such as pave, datum, curb, and so on. While most of these codes are not particularly useful for creating surfaces, several are. The datum code, for example, is used to represent links that form the underside of the materials that make up the road. Why is this important? These links represent the trench, or *road bed*, that must be excavated to accept road materials such as stone, concrete, and asphalt. The excavation of the road bed often represents one of the most important aspects of constructing the project: earthmoving.

INTERSECTIONS

One of the most sophisticated applications of targets and regions is the design of an intersection. Here you will find multiple baselines, regions, and targets that are necessary to tie two roads together as well as provide a smooth transition between them. For this reason, Civil 3D provides the Create Intersection command, which automates the creation and management of these relationships.

Certification Objective

After launching the Create Intersection command, you will be presented with the Intersection Wizard, which contains the following series of dialog boxes that request information about the design:

► **General:** In this dialog you specify general information about the intersection such as its name, description, and associated styles. Most importantly, you choose from one of two types of intersection designs: Primary Road Crown Maintained and All Crowns Maintained, as shown here.

(Continues)

INTERSECTIONS *(Continued)*

▶ **Geometry Details:** In this dialog you will choose a profile for each alignment, which will drive the centerline elevations of each road. You will also define important horizontal geometry specifications by modifying the Curb Return Parameters and Offset Parameters. You will provide vertical design specifications by addressing the Lane Slope Parameters and Curb Return Profile Parameters. A portion of the Geometry Details dialog box is shown here.

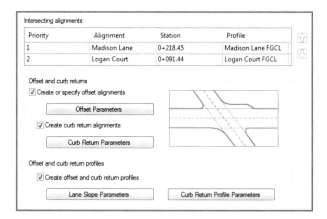

▶ **Corridor Regions:** In this dialog box you will specify the different assemblies that will be assigned to different portions of the intersection design. This group of assemblies and its assignments is called an *assembly set*. Assembly sets are typically set up by a CAD manager or lead CAD person and will most likely be provided for you, at least for your first few designs.

INTERSECTIONS *(Continued)*

After completing the Create Intersection command, your drawing will contain a full, 3D representation of the intersection, as shown in the following image. The intersection design will consist of new baselines, regions, and targets. As you make changes to your design, the relationships between the many intersection components will be honored, keeping the design in sync within itself as well as with adjacent portions of the corridor.

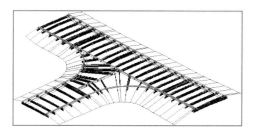

THE ESSENTIALS AND BEYOND

In this chapter, you learned how to provide the third stage of a road design: the cross section. You did this by constructing an assembly that represents the typical cross section of the road. Then you took the design of the road even further by combining the alignment, profile, and assembly to make a complete three-dimensional model of the road: a corridor. With the corridor in place, you made the model more flexible by introducing targets that enable interaction with other objects in the drawing. Now you have a model of the road that will respond to changes in the alignment, profile, assembly, existing ground surface, and other objects that have been used as targets.

ADDITIONAL EXERCISE

Open the drawing named `Corridors Beyond.dwg` located in the Chapter 09 class data folder. Use the following basic guidelines to create a corridor for Madison Lane:

▶ As a cost-cutting measure, the developer would like to omit curb and gutter from Madison Lane and Logan Court. Create a new assembly for these two roads that consists of two 12-foot (4m) lanes, a 3-foot (1m) grass strip sloped downward at 2%, and the same daylighting that was used for the Jordan Court corridor.

▶ Use the red polyline near station 3+00 (0+080) to create a pull-off area by widening the right lane to match the polyline.

(Continues)

THE ESSENTIALS AND BEYOND *(Continued)*

▶ Create a surface for the Madison Lane corridor.

▶ Use the diamond-shaped grip to move the end of the Madison Lane corridor back to station 6+00 (0+180). Use the Create Intersection command to design an intersection where Madison Lane meets Logan Court. Use the default settings of the Intersection Wizard, but be sure to investigate those settings and think about how they affect the design.

Visit www.sybex.com/go/civil2013essentials to download a video of the author completing this exercise. You can also download the Answers to Additional Exercises Appendix which contains even more information about completing this exercise.

CHAPTER 10

Creating Cross Sections of the Design

One of the requirements for a successful and efficient design process is the ability to visualize the design in many different ways. So far, you have explored how profiles can be used to augment the customary way of viewing the design: plan view. In this chapter, you will explore the utilization of cross sections to visualize and display your design in yet another way: by slicing through it in a perpendicular direction.

There are two primary AutoCAD® Civil 3D® approaches to view and document your design in cross section view. For design purposes, you use a Civil 3D feature called the Section Editor, which enables you to analyze and modify your design section by section. For documentation purposes, you use sample lines, sections, and section views. The section view, just like the profile view, is the backdrop that houses the sections while providing a grid and annotations to go with them. There are also some things that sections can do that profiles cannot, such as the ability to slice through corridors and the ability to create multiple section views at once.

▶ **Using the Section Editor**

▶ **Creating sample lines**

▶ **Creating section views**

▶ **Sampling more sources**

Using the Section Editor

To understand what the Section Editor is and how it works, let's review how a corridor is built. An alignment and profile are combined to create a 3D chain, and then an assembly is repeatedly inserted along that 3D chain to create the full model. As you construct the assembly, you are looking at a static version of the cross-sectional geometry of the road. This version does not reflect the way in which the subassemblies interact with the targets you have assigned to them. However, the Section Editor enables you to actually view each assembly insertion in cross section view, including any interactions involving targets. In addition, you can use the Section Editor to make edits to each corridor section and perfect your design down to the smallest detail.

When you click Section Editor on the ribbon, a Section Editor ribbon tab provides you with the tools you need to configure and navigate within the editor (Figure 10.1). It can be very helpful to divide your drawing area into two or three viewports so that the section viewer can be seen alongside the "normal" view of your drawing. In fact, a great feature of the tool is that it displays a marker on the alignment and profile that indicates the location of the section you are viewing. So, with three viewports available (plan, profile, and section), you can view your design from three different perspectives at once.

FIGURE 10.1 The Section Editor ribbon tab

As the name implies, you can also use the Section Editor to edit your corridor design. This is done with the Parameter Editor command found on the Section Editor ribbon tab. This command shows all of the subassemblies and their associated settings at a specific location on the corridor. These settings can be overridden one corridor section at a time, or the overrides can be applied to a range of stations. The changes you make here will be stored as overrides within the corridor.

To set up a drawing with multiple viewports and use the Section Editor to view and edit a corridor design, follow these steps:

If any of the viewports appear to be oriented to something other than plan view, click within the viewport and then click Top within the Views panel of the View ribbon tab.

1. Open the drawing named Using Section Editor.dwg located in the Chapter 10 class data folder.

2. On the View tab of the ribbon, click Viewport Configuration ≻ Three Above. This will divide the drawing window into three viewports.

3. In the top viewport, zoom in to the left end of the Jordan Court profile view. In the bottom-left viewport, zoom in to the Jordan Court alignment near the intersection with Emerson Road. Your screen should look similar to Figure 10.2.

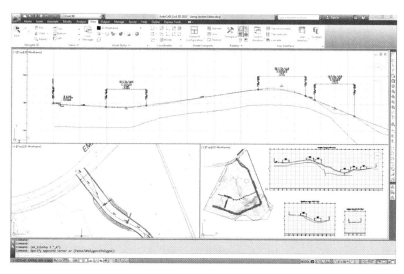

FIGURE 10.2 The drawing area divided into three viewports

4. Click the lower-right viewport and zoom in to the same area as shown in the lower-left viewport. Click one of the blue corridor lines to select the corridor, and then click Section Editor on the ribbon. The view shown in the bottom-right viewport changes to display a cross section of the corridor at the location you picked before launching the Section Editor command (Figure 10.3).

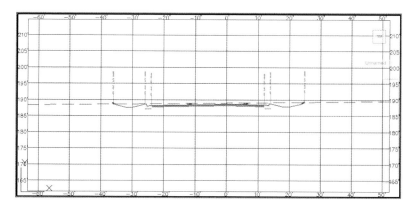

FIGURE 10.3 A section view shown by the Section Editor command

5. On the ribbon, click the Go To Next Station icon to advance to the next corridor section. Continue advancing to view several different corridor sections. Notice the line markers that indicate your location in plan and profile view.

6. On the ribbon, expand the list under Select A Station and select 1+75.00′ (0+050.00m). Zoom in to the section view and note the ditches on either side of the road. These were added automatically because the road is in a cut condition; however, the amount of cut is so small that the ditches can be omitted, a change that you will make in the next few steps.

7. Click Parameter Editor on the ribbon. This will open the Corridor Parameters window.

8. In the Corridor Parameters window, scroll down to Left Daylight and change the value for Backslope Width and Foreslope Width to 0.000.

These two values define the width of the ditch. By setting them to zero, the ditch will disappear.

9. Change the Backslope Width and Foreslope Width values for the Right Daylight subassembly to 0.000 as well.

10. Click Close on the ribbon to close the Section Editor and return the drawing to its normal state. If you zoom in to the plan view, you'll notice that the ditch has been omitted but only at one location on the corridor (Figure 10.4). You need to apply this change across a number of corridor sections.

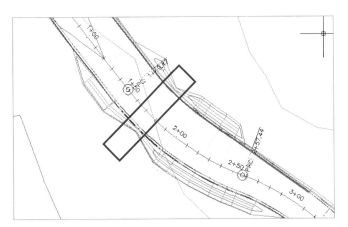

FIGURE 10.4 The ditches have been removed, but only at a single station within the corridor.

11. Click one of the blue corridor lines, and then click Section Editor on the ribbon. Select station 1+75.00′ (0+050.00m) once again.

12. On the ribbon, click Parameter Editor. This will open the Corridor Parameters window.

13. On the ribbon, click Apply To A Station Range.

14. In the Apply To A Station Range dialog box, click the Pick button next to Start Station. Pick a point just northwest of the ditches.

15. Repeat the previous step for the End Station value, this time picking a point to the southeast of the ditches.

16. Click OK to dismiss the Apply To A Station Range dialog box, and then click Close to close the Section Editor.

17. Click the corridor, and then click Rebuild Corridor on the ribbon. The ditches have been removed from the corridor, as shown in Figure 10.5.

Your start station should be around 0+80 (0+020) and your end station around 3+00 (0+090). You can type these stations in if you're not sure.

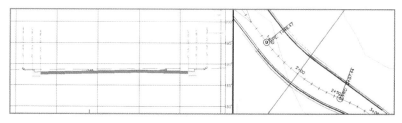

FIGURE 10.5 A section view (left) and plan view (right) of the corridor after the ditches have been removed

A NOTE ABOUT UNITS

Throughout this chapter, you'll notice that two values are provided for units of measurement. The first value is provided for the imperial system that is used in the United States, and the second value in parentheses is provided for the metric system that is used in many other countries. These values most often represent imperial feet and metric meters. It is important to note that generally only the numeric values are entered in the software, not terms like *feet* or *meters*. Also, you should know that the two numbers provided are not necessarily equal. In most cases, they are similar values that are rounded to work efficiently in their respective measurement systems.

Creating Sample Lines

With a profile, the alignment serves as the path along which the profile is cut. For a cross section, this role is assumed by the sample line. When sample lines are created, they are associated to an alignment. Multiple sample lines are typically created simultaneously, so Civil 3D requires that sample lines be placed within a sample line group. An alignment can host multiple sample line groups if necessary. So, the placement of sample lines in the alignment hierarchy is Alignment ➤ Sample Line Groups ➤ Sample Lines.

After launching the Sample Lines command on the ribbon, you will be prompted to select the parent alignment. Then you will be asked to name and stylize the sample lines and choose the sources that will be sampled to create cross sections. There are four types of objects that you can sample: surfaces, corridors, corridor surfaces, and pipe networks. Finally, you will be presented with the Sample Line Tools toolbar, which contains an array of commands for creating and modifying the sample lines within a sample line group.

On the Sample Line Tools toolbar, a pull-down menu provides several methods for placing sample lines along the alignment (Figure 10.6). A description of each method is as follows:

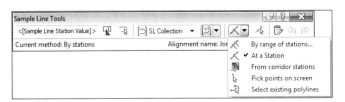

FIGURE 10.6   The Sample Line Tools toolbar showing the different methods available for sample line placement

By Range Of Stations   This method creates multiple sample lines with predetermined swath widths at a specified increment along the alignment. It is great for creating large numbers of sample lines that are evenly distributed along the alignment. These sample lines will be created perpendicular to the alignment.

At A Station   This method is probably the simplest. You supply the station value, left swath width, and right swath width for each sample line that you want to place. You can specify the station value graphically by clicking a point in the drawing or numerically by typing the value at the command line. This method is good if you only need to draw a few sample lines at odd locations. The sample lines will be drawn perpendicular to the alignment.

From Corridor Stations   This method creates a sample line wherever there is an assembly insertion on the corridor. This is a great solution when you would like to create and display cross sections for design purposes. Of course, one of the sources for your sample lines must be a corridor.

Pick Points On Screen   As the name suggests, with this method, you click points on the screen—in effect, drawing the sample line. This is ideal for irregularly shaped sample lines that have multiple vertices and/or are not perpendicular to the alignment.

Select Existing Polylines   This method yields the same result as Pick Points On Screen, but you use it when you have already drawn a polyline representing the path of the sample line.

To create sample lines in a drawing, follow these steps:

1. Open the drawing named Creating Sample Lines.dwg located in the Chapter 10 class data folder.

 2. On the Home tab of the ribbon, click Sample Lines.

3. When prompted to select an alignment, press Enter and select Jordan Court in the Select Alignment dialog box. Click OK.

4. In the Create Sample Line Group dialog box, do the following:

   ▶ For Name, enter Design.

   ▶ For Sample Line Style, verify that Road Sample Line is selected.

   ▶ For Sample Line Label Style, verify that Section Name is selected.

   ▶ Under Select Data Sources To Sample, uncheck all but the second check box.

   ▶ Verify that the settings within the dialog box match Figure 10.7 and click OK.

 5. On the Sample Line Tools toolbar, expand the button that lists creation methods and select From Corridor Stations.

6. In the Create Sample Lines - From Corridor Stations dialog box, click OK to accept the defaults and create the sample lines.

7. Press Esc to end the sample line command.

You are selecting only the Jordan Court corridor to be sampled.

The Create Sample Line Group dialog box opens because no sample line groups exist for this alignment. If one had existed, step 4 would have been skipped completely.

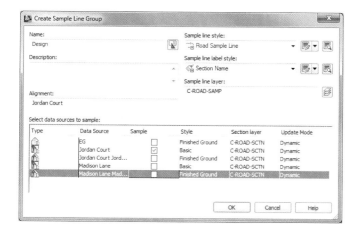

FIGURE 10.7   The Create Sample Line Group dialog box

8. Zoom in and examine the sample lines that have been created (Figure 10.8).

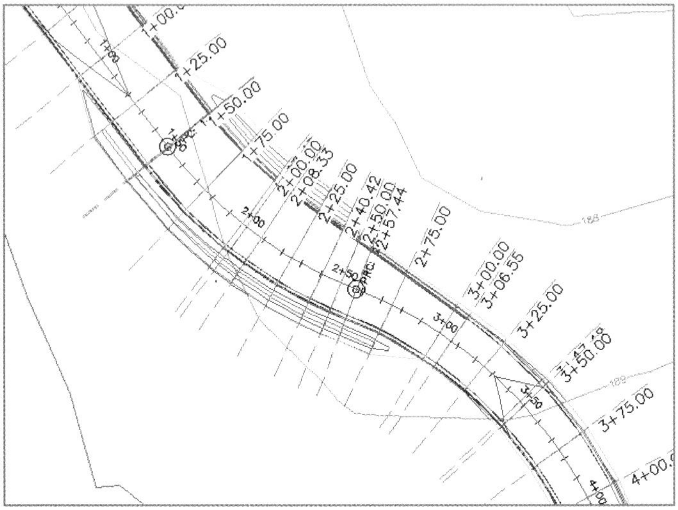

FIGURE 10.8 Sample lines created at corridor stations

Creating Section Views

Now that you have sample lines in the drawing that are able to show you cross sections of the sources you've chosen for them, you will need a means by which to display that data in your drawing. Just as a profile needs a profile view to make it visible, a cross section needs a section view. Section views are quite similar to profile views. They usually display a grid and some grid labels as a backdrop to the data that they house. The section view is dynamically linked to the sample line and associated data sources. This means, as with other Civil 3D objects, that if the sample or source data is modified, the section view will update automatically.

Creating Single-Section Views

As mentioned previously, one extra consideration with section views is that they often are created in large numbers. You will learn how to address that challenge in the next section; for now, let's focus on creating individual section views.

To create individual section views in your drawing, complete these steps:

1. Open the drawing named Creating Single Section Views.dwg located in the Chapter 10 class data folder.

2. Zoom in to the sample line labeled 13+25 (0+405). Click the sample line, and then click Create Section View ➤ Create Section View on the ribbon.

3. In the Create Section View - General dialog box, verify that the following items are selected:

   ▶ Select Alignment: Jordan Court

   ▶ Sample Line Group Name: Design

   ▶ Sample Line: 13+25 (0+405)

   ▶ Station: 13+25.00′ (0+405.00m)

4. For Section View Style, select Design.

5. Click Next to advance to the Create Section View - Offset Range dialog box. Note that you can change the width of the section view by modifying the offset range.

6. Click Next to advance to the Create Section View - Elevation Range dialog box. Note that you can change the height of the section view by modifying the minimum and maximum elevations.

7. Click Next to advance to the Section Display Options dialog box. Verify that the Style selected for the Jordan Court corridor section is Design.

8. Click Next to advance to the Data Bands dialog box. Verify that Design Offsets is selected under Select Band Set. Click Create Section View.

9. When prompted to identify the section-view origin, pick a point in the open area to the right of the project. A new section view is created in the drawing, as shown in Figure 10.9. This section view could be helpful in assessing the design at a specific location. Note how the information is displayed in a way that aids in the design of the road. Additional section views could be created at other key locations along the design of the road.

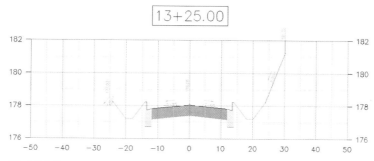

FIGURE 10.9 A newly created section view

STYLE BY DESIGN

You may have noticed that many of the styles that were selected while creating this section view had the word *design* in their names. The significance of this is that the styles you chose were set up to aid the designer during the design process but may not be appropriate for final documents such as construction drawings. For example, the elevation and slope labels on the section would be much too small to read if this drawing were plotted. For design, however, they come in quite handy—enabling the designer to zoom in and quickly get information about key geometry. Leveraging styles by having some for design and others for documentation can be very useful.

Creating Multiple-Section Views

For some projects, you may be required to provide documentation of cross sections at regular intervals along your design. This is especially common for road design projects, because a cross-section view is traditionally used to construct the road. Although newer techniques and technologies have replaced the use of cross sections to some extent, the creation of cross-section sheets is still a common practice for these types of designs.

For most projects, there are too many section views to fit on a single sheet, so multiple sheets are required. This means that the section views must be created in groups that each fit efficiently within the printable area of a typical sheet. This "per sheet" arrangement is handled through a *group plot style*.

To create a new sample line group configured for section sheets and then create multiple sheets containing section views, complete the following steps:

1. Open the drawing named Creating Multiple Section Views.dwg located in the Chapter 10 class data folder. This drawing contains a new sample line group named Section Sheets, which distributes the sample lines along the alignment at a consistent interval.

 2. On the Home tab of the ribbon, click Section Views ➤ Create Multiple Views. This launches the Create Multiple Section Views Wizard with the General dialog box being the first in a series of dialog boxes.

3. In the Create Multiple Section Views - General dialog box, select Section Sheets as the Sample Group Name. Click Next.

WHY MORE SAMPLE LINES?

As you may recall, the first sample line group you created used the From Corridor Stations method to create the sample lines. This creates a sample line and the potential for a section view at each assembly insertion of the corridor. This configuration is specifically for design purposes so that the designer can see a section view at any key point in the design if desired. Now, you need to create section views that meet the requirements for construction drawings. For this application, you are often required to show cross sections at regular intervals. Here the intent is related not to the design process but to documentation. Since you can create multiple sample line groups for any given alignment, you could set up one sample line group for design purposes and one for documentation purposes. In fact, if you use Prospector to browse to the sample line groups of Jordan Court in this example, you will find that the Design sample line group still exists but the styles have been set to hide the sample lines and their labels.

4. In the Create Multiple Section Views - Section Placement dialog box, select Production under Placement Options.

5. Click the ellipsis next to the path to open the Select Layout As Sheet Template dialog box.

6. Click the ellipsis on the Select Layout As Sheet Template dialog box to browse for a template file.

7. Browse to the Chapter 10 class data folder, select Sections.dwt, and click Open.

8. Select ARCH D Section 20 Scale (ISO A0 Section 1 to 200) and click OK.

9. Verify that Group Plot Style is set to Plot By Page.

10. Click Next for each of the remaining dialogs in the Create Multiple Section Views Wizard, and examine the settings for each one. Click Create Section Views.

11. Click a point in the open area to the north of the project. Three new section sheets should be created (Figure 10.10).

This is an important step because it configures the layout of the section views by telling how big a sheet is, how much space should be allowed between section views, and so on.

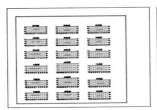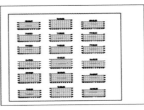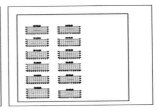

FIGURE 10.10 Newly created section views configured by sheet

Sampling More Sources

So far, you have seen that corridors can be sampled and shown in a cross-section view, but what about other sources of data? It turns out that sample lines can also slice through surfaces and pipe networks. In this section, you will learn how to sample and display data from these sources. In addition, you will learn how to add more sources of data to an established set of sample lines and section views so that you don't have to start all over when new data becomes available.

To add more data sources to your drawing, sample them, and show them in section views, follow these steps:

1. Open the drawing named Sampling More Sources.dwg located in the Chapter 10 class data folder. After opening the file, type **REGEN** on the command line and press Enter.

2. Click one of the section views in the drawing, and then click Sample More Sources on the ribbon.

3. In the Section Sources dialog box, click EG under Available Sources. Then click Add.

4. Under Sampled Sources, verify that the style for EG is set to Existing Ground.

5. Verify that the Section Sources dialog box looks like Figure 10.11, and then click OK. After a pause, a red dashed line is added to each section view. This line represents the surface of the existing ground. In addition, a default label set has been applied to the existing ground line, which is not appropriate for this application. You will remove the labels in the next several steps.

You may notice that the sections and section views are misaligned when you open the drawing. The REGEN command refreshes the drawing graphics and realigns them.

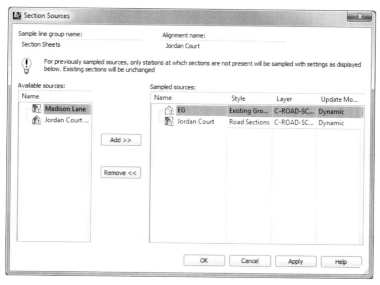

FIGURE 10.11 Sampling additional sources using the Section Sources dialog box

6. With the section view still selected, click View Group Properties on the ribbon. This opens the Section View Group Properties dialog box.

7. On the Sections tab, click <Edit> in the Change Labels column next to EG.

8. Select _No Labels and click OK. Click OK again to close the Section View Group Properties dialog box and return to the drawing. The labels should be removed.

9. Zoom in to the first section view at 0+50 (0+010) in the lower-left corner of the first sheet. Pan upward and examine each section view. When you get to the top of the column, move to the bottom of the next column and pan upward to continue viewing the sections in order. As you do this, try to visualize traveling down the road and experiencing the changes in the road geometry that you see from section to section.

10. On the Insert tab of the ribbon, click LandXML.

11. Browse to the Chapter 10 class data folder and select Preliminary Waterline.XML. Click Open.

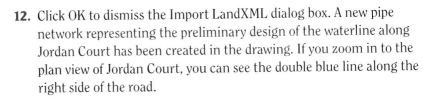

The scenario here may be that an engineer has asked you to check his waterline design against your road design to see if there are any problems.

12. Click OK to dismiss the Import LandXML dialog box. A new pipe network representing the preliminary design of the waterline along Jordan Court has been created in the drawing. If you zoom in to the plan view of Jordan Court, you can see the double blue line along the right side of the road.

13. Click one of the section views, and then click Sample More Sources on the ribbon.

14. In the Selection Sources dialog box, click Preliminary Waterline and then click Add. Click OK to close the dialog box.

15. Press Esc to clear the selection of the section view. Zoom in and examine the section views to verify that the waterline is being shown. As you look at the section views, do you see any problems with the location of the waterline?

16. Use the LandXML command to import Subsurface Rock.xml.

17. Use the Sample More Sources command to add this new surface to the section views. Set its style to Rock.

18. Once again, you need to clear away the labels. Click a section view, and then click View Group Properties on the ribbon.

19. Click <Edit> in the Change Labels column next to Rock. Select _No Labels and click OK. Click OK again to return to the drawing.

WHAT DO YOU SEE?

As you pan from section view to section view, what story are you being told about the construction of this road? Which section views do you feel represent areas that require more time, effort, and money to build as opposed to others? In the first section views, you can see that the road cross section is much wider on the left side to account for the turning lane that you built into the corridor. As you progress further, you see sections that are very close to existing ground elevations, sections that are some distance above existing ground (a fill condition), and sections that are some distance below existing ground (a cut condition). How will the relationship of the road elevation to the existing ground elevation affect drainage for the homes that will be built along the road? Did you notice that ditches have been created in places where the road is in a cut condition? The amount of information and the number of additional questions generated by these simple pictures of the design is quite remarkable. The following images show some of the highlights of the design.

WHAT DO YOU SEE? *(Continued)*

Station 1+50 (0+050) showing the widened left lane

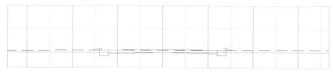

Station 4+50 (0+140) which is in an area that is very close to existing ground

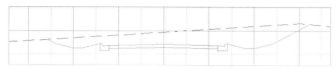

Station 13+50 (0+410) is in an area that is in cut. Note the ditches that are created.

Station 19+50 (0+600) is in an area that is in fill.
Note that no ditches are created in this condition.

20. Study the section views again. In a real-life situation, you may need to inform the engineer that the waterline design requires the excavation of a significant amount of rock. Also notice that around station 9+00 (0+270), the rock layer is very close to the surface—you may want to consider raising the road a bit in this area to avoid costly rock excavation.

THE ESSENTIALS AND BEYOND

In this chapter, you were introduced to the concept of using a cross section view for various purposes within your design process. You began by using the Section Editor to view and modify the corridor. You then studied the use of sections and section views to display cross sections of your design in a more permanent form. You also used styles to refine the appearance of the sections and section views to best meet your needs as they relate to design or to documentation.

(Continues)

THE ESSENTIALS AND BEYOND   *(Continued)*

ADDITIONAL EXERCISE

Open the drawing named `Sections Beyond.dwg` located in the Chapter 10 class data folder. Use the following basic guidelines to make edits, create sample lines, and create section views for Madison Lane:

1. Divide the screen into three viewports: one showing the plan view, another showing the profile view, and another showing the Section Editor view.

2. Remove the ditch on the left side of Madison Lane between stations 1+50 and 2+50 (0+040 and 0+080).

3. Create a Design sample line group that locates a sample line at every corridor section. Create several section views that are stylized for design purposes.

4. Create a sample line group intended for section sheets that locates the sample lines at 50′ (10m) increments. Create section views for this sample line group that are arranged within individual sheets. The section views and sheets should look similar to the ones you created for Jordan Court earlier in this chapter.

5. Add the Jordan Court FG surface as a sampled source for the Design sample line group. Create a section view at the beginning of the Madison Lane alignment where it intersects Jordan Court. When you look at the relationship between the elevations of Madison Lane and Jordan Court in the same section view (shown here), what story does it tell?

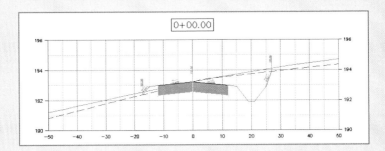

Visit `www.sybex.com/go/civil2013essentials` to download a video of the author completing this exercise. You can also download the Answers to Additional Exercises Appendix which contains even more information about completing this exercise.

CHAPTER 11

Displaying and Annotating Sections

As you have learned by now, creating a design is only part of the story—you also have to display and annotate it in ways that effectively represent your design for its intended purpose. This applies to sections also. As you will see in this chapter, there are styles that control the appearance of the sections themselves as well as the section views that house them. There are labels that attach themselves to the sections and labels that can float within the section views. In fact, the methods that you used to stylize and annotate sections and section views are very similar to those used for profiles and profile views.

Of course, there are also differences. For instance, you have to address the stylization and labeling of a corridor section, which you don't need to do with profile views. Another difference is that section views are typically created in bulk, so their arrangement and grouping into sheets must be managed as well.

▶ **Applying section styles**

▶ **Applying section labels**

▶ **Controlling section display with code set styles**

▶ **Applying labels with code set styles**

▶ **Applying section view styles**

▶ **Applying section view bands**

▶ **Applying group plot styles**

▶ **Creating section view labels**

Applying Section Styles

Certification
Objective

Before I jump into section styles, I'll discuss the difference between sections and corridor sections. Sections are derived from surfaces and can be thought of as a very close relative to surface profiles. Like surface profiles, they are typically represented by a single line and can be annotated using a label set. Corridor sections are something quite different. You can think of a corridor section as an assembly superimposed on a section view. It consists of subassemblies, points, links, and shapes. Because of the differences between sections and corridor sections, the methods you use to stylize and label them are also quite different.

With that out of the way, let's look at section styles. Section styles are used to change the appearance of a section either directly or by displaying it on a different layer. The most common application of a section style is the differentiation between sections that represent existing and proposed ground surfaces. Section styles can also be used to show point markers at each vertex in the section line.

To apply section styles to vary the display of different types of sections, follow these steps:

1. Open the drawing named Applying Section Styles.dwg located in the Chapter 11 class data folder. Here, you see three section views that were plotted to investigate the shallow rock layer. The section views show a corridor section, existing ground surface section, and rock section.

2. Click the lowest section in the 8+50.00 (0+260.00) section view, and then click Section Properties on the ribbon.

3. On the Information tab of the Section Properties dialog box, change Object Style to Rock. Click OK to close the dialog box. Press Esc to clear the selection. The rock section now appears as a gray dashed line.

Using the Section Properties command to change the style is only one of three ways you can do this. You'll try out the other two later in this exercise.

4. Repeat the previous two steps for the section that appears above the rock layer, this time assigning a style of Existing Ground. Press Esc to clear the selection. The section representing existing ground now appears as a red dashed line along with the rock section from the previous step (Figure 11.1).

5. Click the lower section in the 9+00.00 (0+270.00) section view, right-click, and select Properties.

6. In the Properties window, change Style to Rock. Keep the Properties window open.

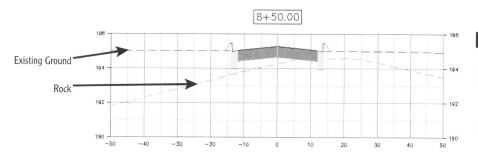

Existing Ground

Rock

If the red dashed line is obscured by the section view grid, select it, right-click, and select Display Order ➤ Bring to Front.

FIGURE 11.1   The sections have been stylized to differentiate between rock and existing ground.

7. Press Esc to clear the selection of the rock section. Click the existing ground section and use the Properties window to change its style to Existing Ground.

8. Click one of the grid lines for the 9+25.00 (0+280.00) section view. Click Section View Properties on the ribbon.

9. On the Sections tab of the Section View Properties dialog box, in the Style column, change the style of the section named EG to Existing Ground and for the section named Rock change the style to Rock. Click OK. All three section views should now properly display the existing ground and rock sections.

Using the Properties window to change the style is the second of three methods available to you. This method is a bit quicker because both sections can be changed within the same window.

Using the Section View Properties command to change the style is the third of three methods available to you. This method shows all of the sections that are present in the section view.

A NOTE ABOUT UNITS

Throughout this chapter, you'll notice that two values are provided for units of measurement. The first value is provided for the imperial system that is used in the United States, and the second value in parentheses is provided for the metric system that is used in many other countries. These values most often represent imperial feet and metric meters. It is important to note that generally only the numeric values are entered in the software, not terms like *feet* or *meters*. Also, you should know that the two numbers provided are not necessarily equal. In most cases, they are similar values that are rounded to work efficiently in their respective measurement systems.

Applying Section Labels

Certification
Objective
At times, you may need to annotate sections with information about their elevations, slopes, offsets, and so on. As you learned in Chapter 8, label sets enable you to apply multiple labels at once as well as apply important configuration settings to the labels such as increment, weeding, and so on. The AutoCAD® Civil 3D® software environment provides the following four types of labels that can be compiled into a label set.

► Major offset labels: These labels are placed at constant increments along the section. You can use this label type to label offset, elevation, instantaneous grade, and many other properties.

► Minor offset labels: These are the same as major offset labels except they are created at a smaller increment and must exist as a child of the major offset labels.

► Segment labels: You use this label type to label the grade, length, and other properties of the line segments that make up the section.

► Grade break labels: You use this label type to label the offset, elevation, and other properties of grade breaks: the locations where segments meet.

The first two types are created at increments, so they are spaced evenly across the section. The last two are created at individual components of the section, so they are placed wherever these components exist. Because sections can sometimes have many short segments, you can configure the label sets to skip points that are close together to prevent labels from overlapping.

To apply section labels to a section, follow these steps:

1. Open the drawing named Applying Section Labels.dwg located in the Chapter 11 class data folder. Here, you see the same three section views from the previous exercise. The section view styles have been modified a bit to create some extra space beneath the sections.

2. Click the rock section on the lowest section view, and then click Edit Section Labels on the ribbon.

3. In the Section Labels – Rock dialog box, do the following:

   a. For Type, select Grade Breaks.

   b. For Section Grade Break Label Style, select Rock.

    c. Click Add.

    d. For Dim Anchor Opt, select Graph View Bottom.

    e. For Dim Anchor Val, enter 0.

    f. Click OK.

ANCHORS AWEIGH

In the previous step, you adjusted two settings relating to anchors. The concept of anchors is unique to certain types of labels that appear in section views and profile views. As a label style is composed, certain key points can be located at an anchor point whose location will be determined at the time the label is applied. This gives you some additional control over the placement of the labels. For example, in the previous steps, you specified that the labels should be aligned to the bottom of the grid by assigning Graph View Bottom as the Dim Anchor Opt. The Dim Anchor Val setting is an offset from the anchor point, which enables you to fine-tune the position of the label even more. An easy way to find out whether a label style you have selected can respond to anchors is to look for a second grip. When initially created, this grip will be located where the anchor options specify. The grip can be moved to a location of your choice, providing even more flexibility with label placement.

---

4. With the options you have selected, only three labels appear. It would be better to increase the number of labels to include more points along the section. In the next two steps you will adjust the Weeding setting to provide more labels.

5. Press Esc to clear the selection from the previous step. Click one of the labels, and then click Edit Label Group on the ribbon.

6. In the Weeding column, change the value to 5′ (2m). Click OK. As shown in Figure 11.2, more labels appear because the weeding setting allows the space between the labels to be as small as 5 feet (2 meters) rather than 100 feet (25 meters).

7. Apply the same labels to the rock section in the other two section views.

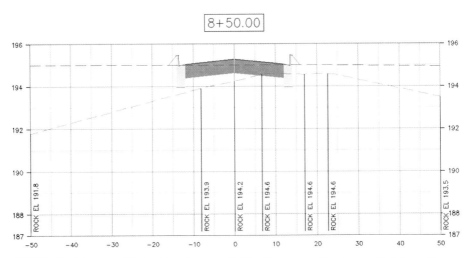

FIGURE 11.2 A label set has been applied to the rock section to provide information about the elevations of the rock layer.

Controlling Section Display with Code Set Styles

You have already seen how section styles can be used to change the appearance of sections, but what about corridor sections? As stated earlier, the way this is handled is quite different and is done through the use of a *code set style*. The setup of code set styles is quite complicated and often left to the expertise of a CAD manager or very experienced Civil 3D user. However, once code set styles are created and made available to you, the task of assigning them to a corridor section is fairly simple.

CODE SET STYLES

Let's take a closer look at code set styles. First, it will be easier if you think of a corridor section as an assembly. You have already learned that assemblies are made up of smaller parts called subassemblies. You have also learned that subassemblies are made up of smaller parts called points, links, and shapes. Points, links, and shapes all have at least one *code* assigned to them, and this little string of text is the key to how code set styles work.

CODE SET STYLES *(Continued)*

For example, one code that is used quite often is Pave. The BasicLaneTransition subassembly in your corridor uses a rectangular shape to represent the lane itself, and the Pave code is assigned to this shape as a property of the subassembly.

Shapes have styles just like all the other Civil 3D objects that you have learned about. For example, you can create a shape style called Hatched Pavement that displays the outline of the shape and fills it with a dot hatch to represent the pavement material. Another shape style might be Basic Pavement, which just shows an outline and no hatching.

Even for a simple assembly, the number of codes that are involved can grow quickly. And the number of styles can grow quickly as well—for example, you may want to apply a different style to each code to visually differentiate pavement from curbing from sidewalk, among other things. One job of a code set style is to match up multiple codes with multiple styles and store them all under one name. So, for example, you may have a code set style called Basic that uses the Basic Pavement style for any shape coded Pave. This might be only one of several or even dozens of matchups between style and code within this code set style. Then, in another code set style named Detailed, you may decide to use the Hatched Pavement style for any instances of the Pave shape code. Again, this might be one of many code-style matchups.

Now, with both code set styles in place, you can quickly change the appearance of your corridor section to take on either a *Basic* or *Detailed* appearance by simply switching the code set style, as shown in the following diagrams.

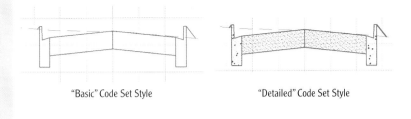

"Basic" Code Set Style   "Detailed" Code Set Style

To change the appearance of corridor sections by assigning different code set styles, follow these steps:

1. Open the drawing named Applying Code Set Styles.dwg located in the Chapter 11 class data folder. The drawing is zoomed in to the same three section views from the previous exercise.

2. Click the corridor section in the bottom section view, and then click Section Properties on the ribbon.

3. On the Information tab of the Corridor Section Properties dialog box, change the Object Style to Road Sections and click OK. The appearance of the corridor section changes to a more basic outline.

4. Using the same procedure, change the style to Road Sections – Top Highlighted.

5. Turn the lineweight display on for the drawing by clicking the Lineweight icon on the status bar at the bottom of your screen. You will now see the top surface of the corridor section highlighted in red.

6. Change the style of the corridor section to Presentation. With this style, the pavement is hatched with a different pattern than the curbs.

7. Press Esc to clear the previous selection. Zoom out and pan to the north where the sheets of section views are located. Click one of the section views and select View Group Properties on the ribbon. This opens the Section View Group Properties dialog box.

8. Click the Sections tab. In the Style column, change the style for Jordan Court to Presentation.

9. Click OK to dismiss the Section View Group Properties dialog box and return to the drawing. Zoom in and study the change to the section views. As you can see, the code set style has been assigned throughout the entire section view group (Figure 11.3).

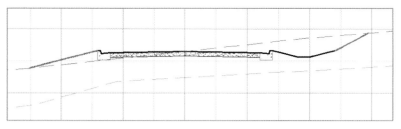

FIGURE 11.3 The Jordan Court corridor section with the Presentation code set style applied

Applying Labels with Code Set Styles

As you have seen, code set styles are very effective at assigning styles based on point, link, and shape codes. They can also be used to apply labels to corridor sections, and just as with styles, codes are the key to automating the placement of labels.

To apply labels to a corridor section using a code set style, follow these steps:

1. Open the drawing named Labeling with Code Set Styles.dwg located in the Chapter 11 class data folder. Once again, the drawing is zoomed in to the design section views from the previous exercises.

2. Click the corridor section in the bottom section view, and then select Section Properties on the ribbon.

3. Change Object Style to Design With Labels and click OK. The corridor section now includes labels for slopes, elevations, and shape codes. Next, you will modify the code set style to add an elevation label at the crown of the road.

4. Open the Tool Palettes window by clicking the Tool Palettes icon on the Home tab of the ribbon. Click the Basic tab of the Tool Palettes window to make the Basic palette come to the forefront.

5. Right-click BasicLaneTransition and select Help. You will be taken directly to the help window for this subassembly.

6. Scroll to the bottom of the help page and study the coding diagram. Note that point P1 is coded Crown (Figure 11.4). This is the code that you will use.

Point, Link, or Shape	Codes	Description
P1	Crown	Crown of road on finish grade
P2	ETW	Edge-of-traveled-way on finish grade
P3	Crown_Subbase	Crown of road on subbase
P4	ETW_Subbase	Edge-of-traveled-way on subbase
L1	Top, Pave	Paved finish grade
L3	Datum, Subbase	Subbase
S1	Pave1	

Coding Diagram

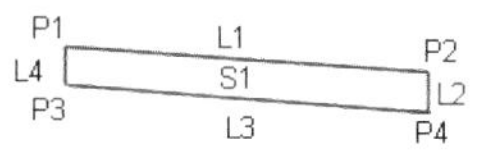

FIGURE 11.4   Coding diagram for the BasicLaneTransition subassembly

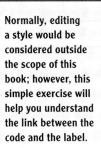

**Normally, editing
a style would be
considered outside
the scope of this
book; however, this
simple exercise will
help you understand
the link between the
code and the label.**

7. Close the Help window. Click the corridor section, and then click Section Properties ➤ Edit Code Set Style on the ribbon.

8. On the Codes tab of the Code Set Style dialog box, scroll down to the Point section and locate the Crown code.

9. Click the icon to the right of <none> in the Label Style column across from Crown. Select Crown Elev and click OK.

10. Click OK to dismiss the Code Set Style dialog box. A marker and label are now displayed at the crown of the road. The code set style recognized the use of the Crown code within the corridor section and applied the label accordingly (Figure 11.5).

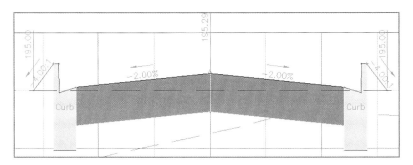

FIGURE 11.5 A code set style has been applied to the Jordan Court corridor section that includes labels.

Applying Section View Styles

Certification
Objective

Now that you have studied the display and annotation of sections, let's take a look at the appearance of the section view that provides the backdrop for the sections. Once again, there are many similarities between section views and profile views. Both have the capability to display a grid, both can apply a vertical exaggeration, and both can use bands to provide supplemental information along the bottom or the top of the view. In fact, the only significant difference between profile views and section views is that profile views display stations (read along the alignment), whereas section views display offsets (read perpendicular to the alignment).

To change the appearance of section views by applying different styles, complete the following steps:

1. Open the drawing named Applying Section View Styles.dwg located in the Chapter 11 class data folder. Once again, you are

viewing the three design cross sections that you have been working with in previous exercises.

2. Click the lowest section view, and then click Section View Properties on the ribbon.

3. On the Information tab of the Section View Properties dialog box, change the style to Design 10V Major And Minor – No Padding. Click OK. One way you might use this section view style is for close inspection and detailed editing of the section since the grid lines appear very frequently and the vertical dimensions of the sections are exaggerated even more.

ALL THAT WITH ONE STYLE?

When you changed the section view style from Design 5V Major And Minor to Design 10V Major And Minor – No Padding, the following changes were made to the section view:

► The vertical exaggeration changed from 5 to 10, causing the elevation changes within the sections to be much more dramatic.

► The elevation grid interval changed to increase the frequency of both the major grids and minor grids, along with their associated labels.

► The space beneath the sections (padding) was removed.

► The minor interval of the offset grid lines was increased.

This is a classic example of the power of styles. To make all of those changes manually would have taken several minutes to figure out, even for an experienced user. Instead, all you have to do is assign a different style, and all of these changes are applied instantaneously.

4. Use the Section View Properties command to change the style to Design 1V Major and Minor – No Padding. This view is similar to the previous one but this time there is no vertical exaggeration.

5. Use the Section View Properties command to change the style to Design 1V – No Grid. Because this section view style excludes the grid and labels, you might use it to create illustrations for a report.

6. Use the Section View Properties command to change the style to Design 5V Major Only. This view is similar to the other views immediately above it except that the minor grids are not displayed.

7. Press Esc to clear the previous selection. Zoom out and pan north to the three sheets of section views. Click one of the section views and select View Group Properties on the ribbon. This opens the Section View Group Properties dialog box.

8. On the Section Views tab, click in the Style column in the first row across from Section View Group – 1.

9. Select Road Section Type 2 and click OK. Click OK again to dismiss the Section View Group Properties dialog box. The new section view style applies a vertical exaggeration of 2, so the section views take up more space top to bottom. In the next step, you'll rearrange the views within the sheet so they're easier to read.

10. With one of the section views still selected, click Update Group Layout on the ribbon. The sections are rearranged, and the new layout must include a fourth sheet to accommodate the extra space that is now taken up by the section views (Figure 11.6).

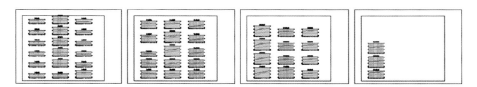

FIGURE 11.6   A fourth sheet is created as a result of changing the section view style applied to the section view group.

Applying Section View Bands

You may need to display additional information about the sections to accompany what is conveyed by the section view. Bands can be a useful tool for this purpose, enabling you to display information both graphically and textually. There are two types of section view bands, as described here:

Section Data Bands   You use this type of band for labeling offset and elevation data at regular increments along the profile view.

Section Segment Bands   You use this type of band to label length and slope information about the individual segments. Since the individual labels are created segment by segment, they are not evenly spaced across the band like you see in a section data band. Weeding can be applied to improve situations where segments are short and labels overlap.

To apply section view bands to section views, follow these steps:

1. Open the drawing named Applying Section View Bands.dwg located in the Chapter 11 class data folder.

2. Click the grid of the bottom section view and select Section View Properties on the ribbon.

3. On the Bands tab of the Section View Properties dialog box, do the following:

    a. For Band Type, verify that Section Data is selected.

    b. Under Select Band Style, select Design – EG Elev.

    c. Click Add.

    d. Change the Gap value for the newly added band to 0.

    e. Scroll right and select EG in the Section1 column.

    f. Click OK.

4. The band is added, but there are values with lines through them at either end of the band. With the section view still selected, click Section View Properties on the ribbon once again.

5. On the Bands tab of the Section View Properties dialog box, uncheck the boxes in the Label Start Offset and Label End Offset columns. Click OK. The labels at either end of the band are now omitted.

6. Add a band showing the depth of the rock surface beneath the existing ground surface by applying these settings:

    ▶ Type: Section Data

    ▶ Style: Rock Depth

    ▶ Gap: 0

    ▶ Label Start Offset: Unchecked

    ▶ Label End Offset: Unchecked

    ▶ Section1: EG

    ▶ Section2: Rock

7. Add a band showing offset values by applying these settings:

   ▶ Type: Section Data

   ▶ Style: Design – Offsets

   ▶ Gap: 0

   ▶ Label Start Offset: Checked

   ▶ Label End Offset: Checked

8. Access the Bands tab of the Section View Properties dialog box once again. Click Save As Band Set.

9. Enter **Sta-Elev-Rock Depth** in the Name field and click OK. Click OK to close the Section View Properties dialog box.

 10. Press Esc to clear the previous selection. Click the section view to the north, and then click Section View Properties on the ribbon.

11. On the Bands tab of the Section View Properties dialog box, click Import Band Set. Select Sta-Elev-Rock Depth and click OK.

12. Select EG for Section1 of the first two bands. Select Rock as Section2 of the second band. Click OK. The bands for this section view now match the bands of the section view that you modified in steps 1–7 (Figure 11.7).

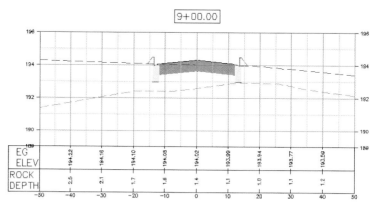

FIGURE 11.7   A section view with bands added for existing ground elevations, rock depth, and offsets

13. Repeat steps 10–12 to add the same band set to the third design section view.

14. Press Esc to clear the previous selection. Zoom out and pan north to the sheets of section views. Click one of the section views, and then click View Group Properties on the ribbon.

15. On the Section Views tab, click the ellipsis in the first row of the Change Band Set column.

16. Click Import Band Set and select Section Sheets. Click OK until you have dismissed all dialog boxes and returned to the drawing. The bands have been added to the section views, but the section views must now be rearranged to account for the additional space they occupy. You will address this in the next step.

17. With one of the section views still selected, click Update Group Layout on the ribbon. Civil 3D automatically creates a fourth sheet as a result of this update (Figure 11.8).

FIGURE 11.8 A fourth sheet is created to accommodate the extra area taken up by the section view bands.

Applying Group Plot Styles

Throughout this chapter, you have been working with several sheets worth of section views all neatly arranged within predefined sheet borders. You may be wondering what controls this behavior, and if you guessed that it's some sort of style, you are correct. The arrangement of multiple section views is accomplished by a *group plot style*.

A group plot style uses an assortment of settings to configure the layout of multiple section views. When section view groups are created, there are two placement options: *Production* and *Draft*. When a section view group is created using the Production placement option, the layout of section views is made to fit within individual sheets. The size and shape of the individual sheets comes from a template (.dwt) file. When the Draft placement option is used, the section views are laid out as a single group and are not bound within a given area.

Certification
Objective

Another function of group plot styles is to overlay a grid on the sections. With this approach to sheet creation, the section views do not typically have their own grid but are superimposed on a grid that covers the entire sheet.

To use group plot styles to change the arrangement of multiple section views, follow these steps:

1. Open the drawing named Applying Group Plot Styles.dwg located in the Chapter 11 class data folder.

2. Click one of the section views displayed within the three sheets, and then click View Group Properties on the ribbon. The Section View Group Properties dialog box opens.

3. On the Section Views tab, click on the first row within the Group Plot Style column (Figure 11.9).

Click here

FIGURE 11.9 Where to click to change the group plot style for the section view group

4. Select Left To Right – Top Down and click OK.

5. Click OK to dismiss the Section View Group Properties dialog box. Notice that the section views shift toward the top left of the sheet and that they are arranged with the stations increasing from left to right.

6. Click one of the section views and click View Group Properties once again. This time do the following:

   a. Click the top row in the Group Plot Style column and select Bottom Up – Left To Right With Grid.

   b. Click the top row in the Style column and select Design 1V – No Grid.

   c. Click the ellipsis in the Change Band Set column.

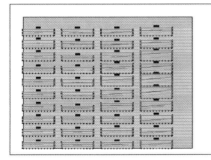

d. Select the Section Data band listed in the Section View Group Bands dialog box, and then click the red X to remove it. Click OK.

e. Click OK to close the Section View Group Properties dialog box.

7. Zoom in and study the newly configured sheets. With this config-uration, the section views are superimposed on a grid provided by the sheets. Since the grid is already there, the section view styles do not show the individual grids. These styles also have their own offset labels across the bottom, so the section view bands were removed as well.

8. Click one of the section views, and then click Update Group Layout on the ribbon. With the newly applied section view styles and group plot style, the section views can now all fit on two sheets (Figure 11.10).

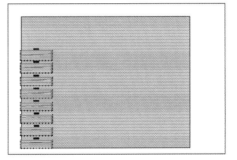

FIGURE 11.10 A section view group with a new group plot style applied

Creating Section View Labels

So far in this chapter, you have seen how to create many different types of annotations. There are label sets that are applied to sections, labels applied to corridor sections through code set styles, labels applied to the section views and bands, and even labels attached to objects that have been projected to the sec-tion views. One limitation of these labels is that they're all connected to some-thing and therefore get their information and location from another object. What if you need to create a basic, all-purpose label that can be used to convey offset and elevation on a section view? To do this, you use a section view label.

Section view labels are attached to the section view itself. They can be placed anywhere within the section view and used to label just about anything.

To create section view labels, complete the following steps:

1. Open the drawing named `Creating Section View labels.dwg` located in the Chapter 11 class data folder. The drawing is zoomed in to the first section view on Jordan Court where the road is widened to accommodate a turn lane. The scenario for this exercise is that you have been asked to include offset and elevation information for the curb flowline so that the contractor knows exactly where to place the curb in the widened area.

2. On the Annotate tab of the ribbon, click Add Labels.

3. In the Add Labels dialog box, do the following:

   a. For Feature, select Section View.

   b. For Label Type, select Offset Elevation.

   c. For Offset Elevation Label Style, select Offset Over Elevation.

   d. For Marker Style, select Basic.

   e. Click Add.

4. Click one of the grid lines of the section view.

5. Right-click while holding down the Shift key, and then select Endpoint. Click the flowline of the left curb.

6. Press Esc to clear the current command. Click the newly created label and drag its square grip up and to the left to improve its readability.

7. Click the label, and then click Edit Label Text on the ribbon. This opens the Text Component Editor dialog box.

8. In the window on the right, click just to the left of the word *Offset* to place your cursor in the position just before it. Click the blank line at the top, type **CURB FLOWLINE**, and press Enter. The result should look like Figure 11.11.

9. Click OK to dismiss the Text Component Editor dialog box. The label now includes the identification of the point to go along with the offset and elevation (Figure 11.12).

The flowline is located at the bottom of the vertical curb face. This is where the flow of water is concentrated during a rainfall event.

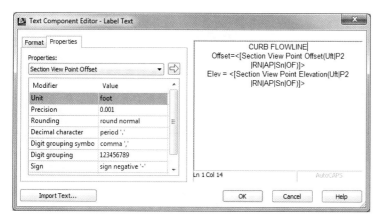

FIGURE 11.11   Adding text to a label using the Text Component Editor

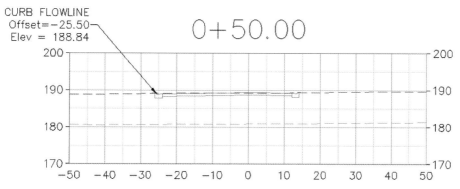

FIGURE 11.12   A label has been added that indicates the offset and elevation of the curb flowline.

BE CAREFUL

Although this label is pointing to the curb, it is not attached to it. If a change in the design causes the curb to move, the label might not be pointing to the right spot and will need to be updated manually. This is not a difficult thing to do, but it's something that could easily be overlooked. A more permanent solution would be to incorporate the label into a code set style.

THE ESSENTIALS AND BEYOND

In this chapter, you used styles to control the appearance of sections and section views. You learned the difference between "regular" sections and corridor sections as well as the different ways in which they are stylized and annotated. You saw how to use group plot styles to arrange large numbers of section views into individual sheets. Finally, you used section view labels to provide even more detail to your section views.

In the following exercise, you will apply what you have learned about displaying and annotating sections and section views to the Madison Lane road design.

ADDITIONAL EXERCISE

Open the drawing named Section Views Beyond.dwg located in the Chapter 11 class data folder. Use the following basic guidelines to change the display of the sections and section views contained within the section sheets.

1. Assign the following styles to the section view group:

   a. Arrange the section views using the Bottom Up – Left To Right With Grid group plot style.

   b. Apply the Design 1V – No Grid section view style to all section views.

   c. Apply the _No Bands band set to all section views.

   d. Apply the label set named Rock to the rock sections.

   e. Apply the Presentation code set style to the Madison Lane corridor section.

2. Update the group layout after you've made the preceding changes.

3. Create section view labels for any section views that fall within the bus pull-off at station 3+00 (0+090). The labels should call out the offset and elevation of the right edge of pavement.

Visit www.sybex.com/go/civil2013essentials to download a video of the author completing this exercise. You can also download the Answers to Additional Exercises Appendix which contains even more information about completing this exercise.

CHAPTER 12

Designing and Analyzing Boundaries Using Parcels

In the previous chapter, you completed the road design portion of the example project by creating and displaying cross sections. With the roads in place, it is now time to look at another aspect of the design: the layout of real estate lots. Although the road design and lot layout are very different types of design, they are still dependent on one another since the roads determine the front boundaries of the lots. In the example project, you will not return to road design, but in a real project, there are often adjustments to the road layout that can affect the parcels as well as other design aspects.

As the designer in this project, you will be asked to design the layout of the lots to be sold as well as open space areas, community areas, utility easements, and so on. The developer makes money by selling the lots, so the more lots there are to sell, the more profit that can be had. So, why not just make a thousand tiny little lots? Well, of course, if a lot is too small to fit a house, then it will be nearly useless and will not sell. But in addition to that, other aspects will set minimum size requirements for the lots, such as the market the developer is targeting and/or the zoning laws. Your job as the designer will be to create as many lots as possible while meeting these minimum size requirements.

▶ **Understanding parcels**

▶ **Creating parcels from objects**

▶ **Creating parcels by layout**

▶ **Editing parcels**

Understanding Parcels

Quite often, a land development project involves the purchase, consolidation, or subdivision of a piece of real estate. Even if this is not the case, the boundary of the developed property must be accurately depicted in the design drawings. It must also be marked in the field to ensure that neighboring properties are not encroached upon. Yet another potential aspect of a land development project is accurately determining the location of rights-of-way and easements, whether existing or proposed. Through parcel objects and their associated commands and annotations, the AutoCAD® Civil 3D® software environment provides you with tools for creating, analyzing, and displaying legal boundaries efficiently and accurately.

Understanding Parcel Objects

As you have seen with other Civil 3D features, Civil 3D makes use of specialized objects to perform specific tasks. Creating parcels is no different. It involves the use of specialized objects whose behavior makes the process of creating and modifying parcels as efficient as possible. The objects that are applied in this case are called *parcel segments*. You can think of parcel segments as just lines and curves that have been identified as sides of a parcel. They can be drawn from scratch using a special toolbar, or they can be created by converting lines, arcs, and polylines. Parcel segments must be assigned to a site so that Civil 3D understands that they should react to one another. When parcel segments in the same site form a closed shape, that shape becomes a *parcel object*. This is a rather unique arrangement because you cannot directly create a parcel object; instead, you create other objects to form a closed area, and then Civil 3D creates the parcel object for you (Figure 12.1).

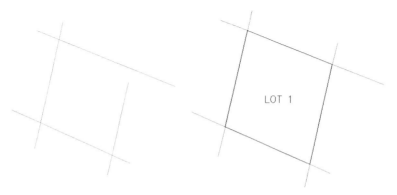

FIGURE 12.1 The four parcel segments on the left do not form a closed shape; therefore, no parcel is created. On the right, a parcel object is created automatically, as shown by the black outline and the LOT 1 label.

In the same manner, any modifications to the fundamental objects that make up a parcel will result in an automatic update to the parcel itself. This is most evident when the parcels are labeled with area, bearing, and distance information.

Understanding Sites

Placing objects within the same *site* is how you tell Civil 3D that you want these objects to "see" each other and interact. You can also prevent objects from interacting by placing them in different sites. The sites are listed in Prospector, and you can create as many as you need within a given drawing (Figure 12.2).

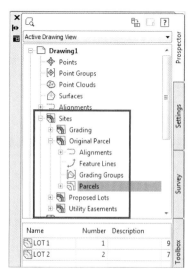

F I G U R E   1 2 . 2   Sites listed in Prospector with the contents of one site expanded

When parcel segments are placed in the same site in such a way that they create one or more closed shapes, the closed shapes will automatically become parcels. Alignments, feature lines, grading groups, and survey figures can also occupy sites. These objects are able to interact with parcels and with one another. For example, if an alignment crosses through a parcel, it will automatically subdivide it to create two parcels. For this to take place, the parcel and the alignment must be in the same site. By the same token, you can prevent the alignment from subdividing the parcel by placing it in a different site. In the left image of Figure 12.3, the alignment and parcel are in different sites and therefore do not interact to create two parcels from one. In the right image of Figure 12.3, the alignment has been moved to the same site as the parcel, causing it to be subdivided automatically.

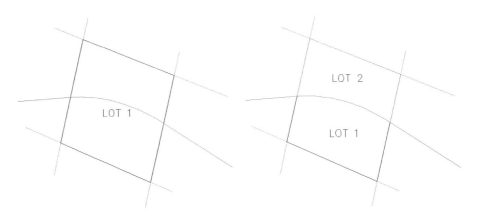

FIGURE 12.3 The effect of sites on the interaction between an alignment and a parcel

Creating Parcels from Objects

One way you can create parcels is to use lines, arcs, and polylines that already exist in your drawing and convert them into parcel segments. This technique is often used when the parcel geometry is especially complex or must be drawn based on other geometry in the drawing. Civil 3D provides a few tools for drawing parcel segments directly, but there are many more drawing and editing commands available within the AutoCAD® part of Civil 3D. For this reason, you may find it easier to create the necessary geometry using the AutoCAD drafting commands rather than the Civil 3D commands.

Converting basic AutoCAD entities to parcel segments is relatively simple. You launch the command from the ribbon; select the lines, arcs, and/or circles you would like to convert; and then provide some information about the parcel segments you are about to create. If the selected objects intersect to create closed shapes, Civil 3D will take care of the rest. You will know that the parcels have been created when the labels appear in the drawing area and the parcels are listed in Prospector.

To create parcels by converting basic AutoCAD entities, complete the following steps:

1. Open the drawing named `Creating Parcels from Objects.dwg` located in the `Chapter 12` class data folder.

2. On the Home tab of the ribbon, click Parcel ➢ Create Parcel From Objects.

3. Click the green polyline representing the overall parcel boundary.

4. Click the magenta polyline representing the southern right-of-way of Emerson Road. Press Enter.

5. In the Create Parcels From Objects dialog box, click OK to accept the default settings. The area is hatched and a parcel label appears near the center of the property, indicating that a new parcel has been created.

The hatching is a function of the parcel style that has been applied by default.

6. Open Prospector and expand Sites ➤ Lot Layout. Right-click Parcels and select Refresh. A plus sign should appear next to Parcels, and a parcel named Basic : 1 should be listed in the item view area of Prospector (Figure 12.4).

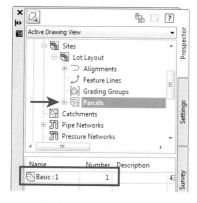

FIGURE 12.4 The newly created parcel shown in Prospector

7. If the item preview icon at the top left of Prospector is not depressed, click it.

8. Right-click Parcels, and verify that there is a check mark next to Show Preview. If there is not, click Show Preview.

9. Expand Parcels, and then click Basic : 1 listed beneath it. A preview of the shape of the parcel is shown in the item view area.

10. Click one of the red polylines in the drawing, right-click, and select Select Similar.

11. On the Home tab of the ribbon, click Parcel ➤ Create Parcel From Objects.

12. In the Create Parcels – From Objects dialog box, change the Parcel Style to Property and click OK. Two new parcels are created, as shown by the areas where the hatching has been carved away.

The red polylines represent the backs of the parcels. Selecting them will subdivide the property into several large pieces. These pieces will be subdivided further to create individual lots.

13. In Prospector, right-click Parcels and select Refresh. Preview the parcels in the item view window as you did earlier with the Basic : 1 parcel.

14. Click one of the dashed right-of-way lines, right-click, and then pick Select Similar.

15. Once again, on the Home tab of the ribbon, click Parcel ➤ Create Parcel From Objects. Click OK to dismiss the Create Parcel – From Objects dialog box with default settings.

You will be skipping over the Create Parcel – From Objects dialog box settings in this chapter. These settings are discussed in detail in the next chapter.

16. Refresh and preview the parcels in Prospector once again. Now there are seven parcels in all (Figure 12.5).

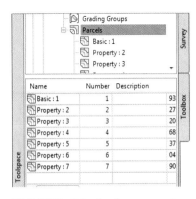

FIGURE 12.5 Seven parcels are now listed in the Prospector item view.

A NOTE ABOUT UNITS

Throughout this chapter, you'll notice that two values are provided for units of measurement. The first value is provided for the imperial system that is used in the United States, and the second value in parentheses is provided for the metric system that is used in many other countries. These values most often represent imperial feet and metric meters. It is important to note that generally only the numeric values are entered in the software, not terms like *feet* or *meters*. Also, you should know that the two numbers provided are not necessarily equal. In most cases, they are similar values that are rounded to work efficiently in their respective measurement systems.

Creating Parcels by Layout

Earlier in this chapter, you read about the advantage of using basic AutoCAD drafting commands to produce parcel geometry. As mentioned, these commands are great for drawing lines and curves based on general geometric principles. But what if you need to create parcels that occupy a certain area, parcel segments that are perpendicular to a road frontage, or parcels that meet a minimum depth requirement based on zoning laws? These are all criteria that are specific to property boundaries, and they are all built into the Civil 3D *Parcel Layout Tools*. When you launch the Parcel Layout Tools from the ribbon, they appear on a specialized toolbar similar to what you have seen for alignments and profiles.

Certification Objective

PARCEL TERMINOLOGY

Certain terms are unique to property boundary design. Here are a few you will want to become familiar with:

Parcel or Lot   This is a piece of land delineated by a legal boundary.

Bearing   This is a horizontal direction expressed in degrees east or west of a north or south direction. For example, N 25° E would mean to face north and then rotate to the right 25 degrees. Bearings are often combined with distances to mathematically define a parcel line.

Right-of-way   This is a strip of land utilized for transportation purposes. It is commonly expressed as a constant width on either side of a road centerline.

Frontage   For lots along a road, this is the length of the front line that is coincident with the edge of the right-of-way. Increased frontage typically increases the value of a piece of land.

Setback   This is the required distance between a property line and a building. Often the front, rear, and side setbacks are expressed separately.

Easement   This is a strip of land that someone is given the right to use for a certain purpose but not to own. For example, a utility easement might give a utility company the right to install and maintain a utility line within a certain area of another person's property.

Zoning   Zoning is a way of dividing large areas of land into zones and dictating different land use requirements for each zone. For example, in one zone, the minimum lot size might be 5 acres (2 hectares), while in another, it might be 0.25 acres (0.10 hectares). Zoning boundaries and regulations are typically determined by a local government entity.

Using the Lot Line Tools

The first few buttons on the Parcel Layout Tools toolbar are used for basic parcel segment drafting that is similar to basic AutoCAD line and curve commands, as shown in Table 12.1. You can use these tools to draw parcels freehand or to retrace geometry that already exists in the drawing.

TABLE 12.1   Important lot line tools

Icon	Tool
	Add Fixed Line – Two Points
	Add Fixed Curve (Three Point)
	Add Fixed Curve (Two Points And Radius)
	Draw Tangent – Tangent With No Curves

To use the lot line tools to create parcels in a drawing, complete the following steps:

1. Open the drawing named Using the Lot Line Tools.dwg located in the Chapter 12 class data folder.

2. On the Home tab of the ribbon, click Parcel ➢ Parcel Creation Tools.

3. On the Parcel Layout Tools toolbar, click Add Fixed Line – Two Points.

4. Click OK to accept the defaults in the Create Parcels – Layout dialog box.

5. Zoom in to Jordan Court near station 4+00 (0+100). Hold down the Shift key and right-click to open the Object Snap shortcut menu.

6. Click Endpoint. Then click the end of the magenta curve at station 4+20.38 (0+128.13), as shown in Figure 12.6.

7. Hold down the Shift key and right-click. Select Perpendicular.

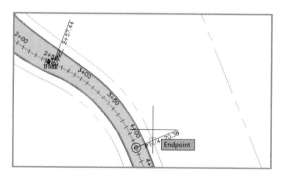

FIGURE 12.6   Snapping to the end of the curve to begin creating a new parcel line

8. Click the magenta back lot line, as shown in Figure 12.7. Press Esc twice to end the command. You have created a new parcel near the front entrance that will be used for a community clubhouse and administrative offices.

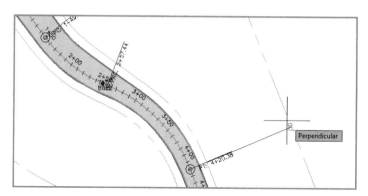

FIGURE 12.7   Snapping to a location that is perpendicular to the eastern lot line

9. Click Parcel ➤ Parcel Creation Tools on the Home tab of the ribbon.

10. Click Draw Tangent – Tangent With No Curves, and then click OK to dismiss the Create Parcels – Layout dialog box.

11. Using the Endpoint object snap, trace the fence line that surrounds the existing farm buildings. Begin at the north end of the fence and work toward the south and west.

12. Once you have selected the last point on the fence, use the Perpendicular object snap to select the western boundary line, as shown in Figure 12.8.

FIGURE 12.8 Completing the farm property boundary by clicking a point perpendicular to the west property boundary

13. Press Esc twice to exit the Parcel command. You have created a new parcel that will remain the property of the original landowner.

Using the Parcel Sizing Tools

The next set of Parcel Layout Tools that you will learn about is by far the most powerful: the Parcel Sizing Tools. These tools enable you to lay out multiple lots within a predetermined area, with each lot meeting the size parameters that you specify. These tools will create the bulk of the lots in a residential land development design such as the example project you have been working on.

You can use the following three tools to create new lots based on size:

Slide Line – Create   This tool creates one or more lots by sliding a line along the frontage until all size and dimension requirements are met.

Swing Line – Create   This tool creates one or more lots by rotating a line around a fixed swing point and intersecting it with a lot line across from the swing point. The result is one or more lots that radiate outward from the swing point.

Free Form Create   This tool creates a lot by attaching one end of a line to a parcel segment and extending that line along a specified angle (usually perpendicular) until it intersects another parcel segment.

In an actual project, to delineate this boundary properly, you would probably offset it a short distance behind the fence so that the fence is entirely on the landowner's property.

To create lots using the parcel sizing tools, complete these steps:

1. Open the drawing named Using the Parcel Sizing Tools.dwg located in the Chapter 12 class data folder.

2. On the Home tab of the ribbon, click Parcel ➤ Parcel Creation Tools.

3. On the Parcel Layout Tools toolbar, expand the button containing the parcel sizing tools and click Slide Line – Create.

4. Click OK to dismiss the Create Parcels – Layout dialog box.

5. When you're prompted to select a parcel, click the label that reads "Property : 25" at the southwest end of the project.

6. When you're prompted to select the first point on the frontage, click the western endpoint of the lot line you previously created at station 4+20.38 (0+128.13), as shown in Figure 12.9.

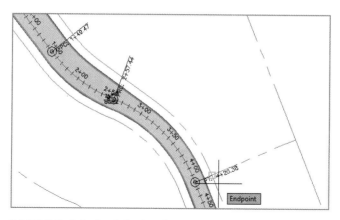

FIGURE 12.9   Selecting the beginning point of the frontage

This "highlighter" is called a *jig line* and it serves as a visual cue that your cursor is graphically linked to something; in this case, it's a parcel segment.

7. Move your cursor in a southeastern direction along the frontage line. Note the orange "highlighter" that follows your cursor. Snap to the endpoint of the curve at station 11+83.29 (0+360.67), as shown in Figure 12.10.

8. When you're prompted to specify the angle, type **90** at the command line and press Enter. A preview of the new parcel will appear near the start point of the frontage.

Since 90 degrees is the default, you could have simply pressed Enter when prompted for the angle.

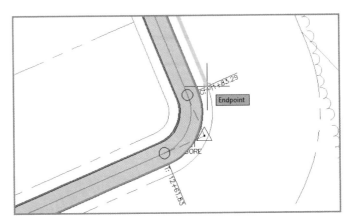

FIGURE 12.10   Selecting the endpoint of the frontage

9. Press Enter to accept the current sizing parameters and create the parcel.

10. Press Esc to exit the current command but keep the Parcel Layout Tools toolbar open.

11. Click Swing Line – Create and click the label that reads "Property : 2" near the southeastern corner of the project.

12. When you're prompted for the start point of the frontage, snap to the northern endpoint of the Property : 2 parcel, as shown in Figure 12.11.

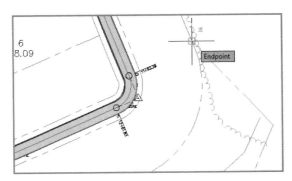

FIGURE 12.11   Selecting the beginning point of the frontage

13. When you're prompted for the endpoint of the frontage, move your cursor in a westerly direction along the property line and snap to the western endpoint of the same parcel (Figure 12.12).

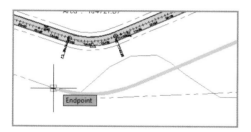

FIGURE 12.12 Selecting the ending point of the frontage

14. When you're prompted for the swing point, use an Endpoint object snap to select the property corner just south of the Property : 2 label. A preview of the parcel will be displayed using the current Minimum Area setting of 10890 Sq. Ft. (1500sq.m.).

To use an Endpoint object snap, hold down the Shift key and right-click; then select Endpoint.

15. If the chevron at the right end of the Parcel Layout Tools toolbar is pointing downward, click it. If not, skip to the next step.

16. Type **1acre (0.4hectare)** for the Minimum Area value and press Enter. The preview is updated to reflect the new area.

You can type a number followed by the unit (without a space), and that number will be converted to the current units.

17. Press Enter to create the parcel. One scenario where this type of parcel might be used would be if an environmental agency requested a 1 acre (0.4 hectare) preservation area to mitigate environmental impacts elsewhere on the site.

18. Press Esc to clear the current command. On the Parcel Layout Tools toolbar, click Free Form Create.

19. Move your cursor along the property line to the east of the Property : 25 label. Note how the line preview attaches itself to the parcel segment and extends outward until it intersects another parcel segment.

20. With your cursor on the west side of the line, snap to the midpoint of the parcel segment.

To use a Midpoint object snap, hold down your Shift key and right-click; then select Midpoint.

21. When you're prompted for a direction, press Enter to specify perpendicular. A new parcel line and a new parcel are created.

22. Press Esc twice to clear the current command and close the Parcel Layout Tools toolbar.

Using Parcel Sizing and Layout Parameters

The Parcel Layout Tools toolbar includes commands for creating new parcel geometry as well as editing it. The toolbar expands downward to reveal parameters that determine the dimensions of the lots that are created. This enables you to include size requirements in your parcel design that may have been requested by the developer or dictated by zoning laws.

The layout parameters available to you are listed here. The image next to each parameter matches the schematic preview shown in the bottom of the Parcel Layout Tools toolbar as you click each parameter.

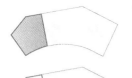

Minimum Area   This is the minimum area occupied by the lot. Minimum area is a common requirement that designers must meet to satisfy zoning requirements.

Minimum Frontage   This is the minimum length of the lines or arcs that make up the side of the lot that is coincident with a road right-of-way. This is also a common parameter that designers must meet to satisfy zoning requirements.

Use Minimum Frontage At Offset   Some zoning regulations allow the frontage to be measured at the building setback line rather than at the frontage line itself. This would enable you to create a larger number of smaller lots, especially when creating lots along the outside of a curve.

Frontage Offset   This parameter is typically used to define the building setback line.

Minimum Width   This is the minimum width allowed for the resulting parcel.

Minimum Depth   This is the minimum depth allowed for the parcel, measured perpendicular to the frontage at its midpoint.

Use Maximum Depth   This parameter prevents the development of exceedingly deep lots, potentially enabling the area to be subdivided more efficiently.

Maximum Depth   This is the maximum depth allowed for the parcel, measured perpendicular to the frontage at its midpoint.

Multiple Solution Preference – Use Shortest Frontage   When multiple solutions are possible, the one that produces the shortest frontage is selected.

Multiple Solution Preference – Use Smallest Area   When multiple solutions are possible, the one that produces the smallest area is selected.

In addition to the parcel sizing parameters, there are also parcel layout parameters that affect the creation of multiple parcels. The first is Automatic Mode, which determines whether parcels are created individually or all at once, as follows:

Automatic Mode – On   Multiple parcels are created within the selected area based on the parameters that have been specified.

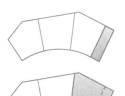

Automatic Mode – Off   Parcels are created one at a time, and you are prompted for information for each parcel.

The second parcel layout parameter is Remainder Distribution, which determines what is done with the "leftover" area after all parcels that meet the size requirements have been created. The Remainder Distribution options are as follows:

Create Parcel From Remainder   A new parcel is created that is smaller than the specified sizing parameters.

Place Remainder In Last Parcel   The last parcel is oversized by adding the remainder to it.

Redistribute Remainder   All parcels are oversized by a small amount so that the leftover area is spread across all parcels.

To use the parcel sizing and parcel layout parameters to create multiple lots, complete the following steps:

1. Open the drawing named Using Parcel Sizing Parameters.dwg located in the Chapter 12 class data folder.

2. On the Home tab of the ribbon, click Parcel ➤ Parcel Creation Tools.

3. On the Parcel Layout Tools toolbar, change Automatic Mode to On.

4. Click Slide Line – Create, and then click OK to dismiss the Create Parcels – Layout dialog box.

5. When you're prompted to select a parcel, click the label that reads "Property : 30."

Automatic Mode will subdivide the area into as many parcels as possible while maintaining the current parcel size requirements.

6. When you're prompted for the start point of the frontage, snap to the endpoint of the right-of-way line at the entrance of Jordan Court, as shown in Figure 12.13.

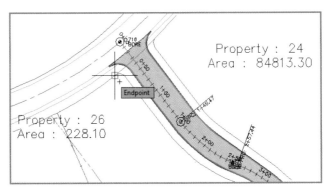

FIGURE 12.13   Selecting the beginning point of the frontage

How you move your cursor will control the path taken by the orange jig line. If the jig line takes a wrong turn, move your cursor back to the frontage start point and start over.

7. When you're prompted for the endpoint of the frontage, move your cursor along the west right-of-way line of Jordan Court and then along the north right-of-way line of Madison Lane. Move your cursor around the Madison Lane cul-de-sac and snap to the endpoint of the right-of-way line at the intersection of Madison Lane and Logan Court, as shown in Figure 12.14.

8. When you're prompted to specify an angle, press Enter. A preview of the parcels is shown.

9. On the Parcel Layout Tools toolbar, type **0.333acres** (or **0.135hectares**) for Minimum Area and press Enter. The preview updates.

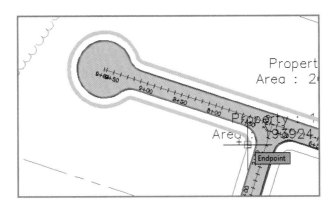

FIGURE 12.14   Selecting the ending point of the frontage

10. Change the following settings (noting how the preview updates after each):

Minimum Frontage	100 (35)
Frontage Offset	25 (8)
Remainder Distribution	Redistribute Remainder
Multiple Solution Preference	Use Smallest Area

11. Press Enter to create the parcels. Press Esc twice to end the command.

Editing Parcels

As you have seen with other design elements, the ability to edit parcels is even more important than their initial layout. Civil 3D provides you with three fundamental tools to edit your parcel geometry: grips, Edit Geometry commands, and Parcel Layout Tools.

Editing Parcels Using Grips

Graphically editing parcels is fairly simple when compared to editing alignments or profiles. There are only two types of grips to learn: the square grip and the diamond-shaped grip. The square grip is simply the standard grip that allows movement in any direction with no restriction. The diamond-shaped grip is displayed on parcel lines that have been created using the Parcel Layout Tools. These grips slide one parcel line along another parcel line or curve while maintaining the angle (usually perpendicular) between the two lines.

To perform some graphical editing of parcels, complete the following steps:

1. Open the drawing named `Editing Parcels Using Grips.dwg` located in the `Chapter 12` class data folder.

2. Zoom in to the parcel labeled "Property : 28." Click the northern side of this parcel and notice the square grips that appear on either end of the line.

3. Click the eastern square grip to select it. Move your cursor around the screen and notice the behavior of this grip. You can move it in any direction.

4. Hold down the Shift key and right-click to reveal the object snap context menu. Select Nearest.

5. Pick a point somewhere along the property line that forms the eastern side of the lot. Notice that the value for the area of this parcel changes.

6. Click the line that forms the southern boundary of this parcel. Notice that a single diamond-shaped grip appears.

7. Click the diamond-shaped grip and slide it along the parcel line it is attached to. Slide it north to the curved areas and notice how it stays perpendicular to the parcel segments it is attached to (Figure 12.15).

8. Pick a new location for the line and note the change to the parcel label.

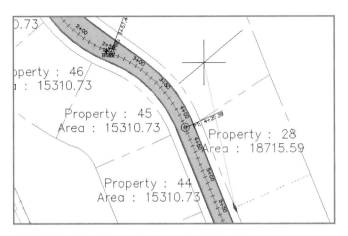

FIGURE 12.15 As it is moved with the diamond-shaped grip, the parcel line stays perpendicular to the parcel segments it is associated with.

Editing Parcels Using the Edit Geometry Commands

When you need to modify the parcel lines and curves themselves, you can use the commands found on the Edit Geometry panel of the Parcel ribbon tab. The commands included on this panel are as follows:

Insert PI   Inserts an angle point into a parcel line segment.

Delete PI   Removes an angle point from a parcel line segment.

Break   Creates a gap in a parcel segment.

Trim   Shortens a parcel segment using some other entity as a cutting edge.

Join   Joins two parcel segments together.

Reverse Direction   Changes the direction of the parcel segment.

Edit Curve   Allows you to change the radius of a parcel curve segment.

If the line is not sliding along smoothly, it might be because you have running object snaps turned on. Try pressing F3 to turn them off.

Fillet   Replaces an angle point with a parcel curve segment that is tangent at either end.

Fit Curve   Replaces a series of parcel line segments with a parcel curve segment.

Stepped Offset   Similar to the AutoCAD offset command except that it prompts you for an elevation; the resulting entity is a polyline, not a parcel segment.

To perform some graphical editing using a few of these commands, follow these steps:

1. Open the drawing named Editing Parcels Using Edit Commands.dwg located in the Chapter 12 class data folder.

2. Zoom in to the area of the farm buildings and notice the small triangular parcel labeled Property : 26. This parcel was created when the new parcel segments were added along the fence line.

3. Click the Property : 26 label. If the Edit Geometry panel is not visible on the ribbon, click Edit Geometry.

4. Click Trim on the Edit Geometry panel of the contextual ribbon. When you're prompted for the cutting edge, select the parcel segment that is drawn along the fence. Press Enter.

5. When you're prompted for the objects to trim, click the west side of the small triangular parcel. The Property : 26 parcel disappears and the area of Property : 27 is updated (Figure 12.16).

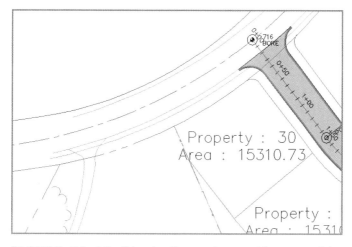

FIGURE 12.16   Trimming the parcel segment has removed the small triangular parcel.

6. Press Esc to clear the current command. Pan southward and click the Property : 7 parcel label. Click Edit Curve on the ribbon.

7. Click the curve just north of the Property : 7 label.

8. On the Edit Feature Line Curve dialog box, enter **250 (85)** for the radius value and click OK. The parcel is updated.

FEATURE LINE OR PARCEL?

You may have noticed that the dialog box that appears when you're editing the curve refers to the entity as a feature line. Parcel segments are close relatives of feature lines, and many of the feature line commands can be used on them. In fact, all of the Edit Geometry commands in this section work for feature lines too.

---

9. Press Esc twice to clear the current command and the current selection. Zoom in to the western end of the Property : 2 parcel. Notice that there is a very narrow section of Property : 2 that is not wide enough to be useable.

10. Click the north boundary of the Property : 2 parcel to reveal its grips. Click the western-most grip and snap it to the center of the red circle.

11. With the parcel segments still selected, click Delete PI on the ribbon. Then click the triangle marker to the right of the red circle. The parcel geometry for Property : 2 has been improved (Figure 12.17).

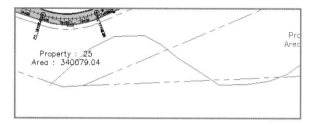

FIGURE 12.17 The western end of the parcel has been simplified.

Editing Parcels Using the Parcel Layout Tools

For the most advanced parcel editing, you can look to the Parcel Layout Tools toolbar. This toolbar includes some of the same tools as on the Edit Geometry panel of the Parcel ribbon tab, such as Insert PI and Delete PI. You will also find editing versions of the parcel sizing commands you used earlier to create parcels. The Slide Line – Edit and Swing Line – Edit commands work much like their Create counterparts, but instead of creating new parcel lines, they slide or rotate existing parcel lines to meet new size requirements. In addition, you can create a parcel union that combines multiple parcels into a single identity. There is also a command that will dissolve this union, returning the component parcels to their individual status.

To use a few of the Parcel Layout Tools to edit parcels, follow these steps:

1. Open the drawing named `Editing Parcels Using the Layout Tools.dwg` located in the `Chapter 12` class data folder.

2. Click the Property : 28 parcel label, and then click Parcel Layout Tools on the ribbon.

3. On the Parcel Layout Tools toolbar, type **0.5acres** (or **0.20hectares**) for the Minimum Area and press Enter.

4. Expand the parcel sizing tools and click Slide Line – Edit. Click OK to dismiss the Create Parcels – Layout dialog box.

5. When you're prompted to select a lot line, click the southern boundary line of Property : 28.

6. When you're prompted to select a parcel to adjust, click somewhere within the Property : 28 parcel.

7. When you're prompted for the start point of the frontage, snap to the northwest corner of the Property : 28 parcel.

8. Move your cursor southward along the right-of-way line and click somewhere near station 7+00 (0+210), as shown in Figure 12.18.

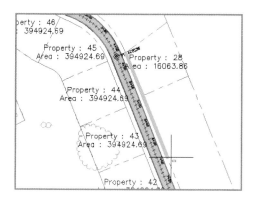

F I G U R E 1 2 . 1 8 Defining the frontage for the parcel editing command

9. When you're prompted to specify the angle, press Enter. A preview of the resized parcel is shown.

10. Press Enter to complete the command and resize the parcel.

11. Press Esc three times to clear the current command and clear the current selection. Click the Property : 27 label, and then click Parcel Layout Tools on the ribbon.

12. On the Parcel Layout Tools toolbar, click Parcel Union.

13. When you're prompted for the destination parcel, click the Property : 3 label. The Property : 27 label disappears and the area of Property : 3 is updated.

14. Expand the Parcel Union icon and select Dissolve Parcel Union.

15. Click the Property : 3 label. Two new parcels are created to replace the original parcels 3 and 27.

The Essentials and Beyond

In this chapter, you learned how to create parcels from existing geometry and from scratch using the layout tools. You also learned how to use the sizing parameters to incorporate various design criteria into your layout. Finally, you learned about the various editing techniques and commands that you can use to adjust your initial layout to meet the specific needs of the project.

In the following exercise, you will apply what you've learned about creating and editing parcels to design an alternate parcel layout for the project.

Additional Exercise

Open the drawing named Parcels Beyond.dwg located in the Chapter 12 class data folder. This drawing contains a road layout that is different from the one you have been working with. Create a new parcel layout based on this road layout.

Visit www.sybex.com/go/civil2013essentials to download a video of the author completing this exercise. You can also download the Answers to Additional Exercises Appendix which contains even more information about completing this exercise.

CHAPTER 13

Displaying and Annotating Parcels

In the previous chapter, you used AutoCAD® Civil 3D® software to design a layout for subdividing the original project parcel into many smaller parcels. The reason for this was to create pieces of land that were the right size and shape for selling to prospective homeowners. However, before any sales can take place, that subdivision plan typically has to be reviewed and approved by an agency that oversees planning for that region. In many places, it must also be presented as an official legal document to be recorded at the local courthouse. Because of the need to create documentation of your layout, you must now address the appearance of the layout as well as the annotation needed to convey important information about it. In this chapter, you will study the use of parcel styles, parcel labels, and tables to effectively display and annotate your parcel layout.

▶ **Applying parcel styles**

▶ **Applying parcel area labels**

▶ **Creating parcel segment labels**

▶ **Editing parcel segment labels**

▶ **Creating parcel tables**

Applying Parcel Styles

Parcels can represent individually owned lots, public areas, road rights-of-way, easements, and so on. When different types of parcels are shown on the same plan, there must be some way of visually differentiating them. When using Civil 3D, this is best handled through parcel styles.

Using Parcel Styles to Control Appearance

Using a parcel style, you can control the appearance of the edges of the parcel as well as any hatching that is applied to the area. The hatching can be applied through the entire area or as a strip along the edges. Using these capabilities, you can graphically differentiate one type of parcel from another.

To use parcel styles to control the appearance of parcels in your drawing, follow these steps:

One way to select a parcel is to click its label. You cannot select a parcel by clicking one of its segments.

1. Open the drawing named Applying Parcel Styles.dwg located in the Chapter 13 class data folder. The drawing contains a complete parcel layout, and all of the parcels have been assigned a style of Standard.

2. Click the Standard : 3 label located near the center of the area containing the farm buildings. On the ribbon, click Parcel Properties.

3. On the Information tab of the Parcel Properties dialog box, change Object Style to Adjoiner. Click OK. The linetype of the parcel segments changes to a double-dash pattern. Also, the label changes and now reads "Adjoiner : 3."

This parcel is renamed automatically because of a setting within the style that combines its style name with a number.

4. Press Esc to clear the previous selection. Click the Standard : 6 label located within the cul-de-sac of Madison Lane. Right-click and select Properties.

5. Using the Properties window, change the Style to ROW. The right-of-way area is now outlined by a dashed line and has been hatched with a dot pattern.

6. Use either the Parcel Properties command or the Properties window to change the large parcels at the northeast and southeast corners of the site (Standard : 7 and Standard : 4) to a style of Open Space. These parcels are now outlined in green and hatched with a green crossing pattern.

Using the Properties window is faster, because you can change both parcels at once.

7. Zoom in to the 90-degree bend on Jordan Court and note the narrow Standard : 1 parcel located there. This is a drainage easement for installing a storm pipe that leads to the creek.

8. Change the style of the Standard : 1 parcel to Easement. The area is hatched with a diagonal stripe pattern.

9. Click one of the remaining parcels that is still labeled Standard and change its style to Lot. The color of the parcel outline changes to blue and displays with a smaller dashed pattern.

10. Go to Prospector and expand Sites ➢ Lot Layout. Click Parcels to display all of the parcels in the item view at the bottom of Prospector.

11. Scroll to the right until you can see the Style column. Click the Style column heading to sort the parcels by style.

12. Click the first parcel with a style of Standard. Then press and hold the Shift key, scroll down, and select the last parcel with a style of Standard. This will select all parcels that have a style of Standard assigned to them.

13. Right-click the Style column heading and select Edit.

14. In the Select Style dialog box, select Lot and click OK. There will be a pause as all of the parcels in the drawing are updated. Now all of the parcels you selected in Prospector have been assigned the Lot style (Figure 13.1).

Within the Prospector item view area, you can make multiple edits by selecting multiple rows, right-clicking a column heading, and selecting Edit.

FIGURE 13.1 A view of the project after all parcels have been assigned the appropriate styles

A NOTE ABOUT UNITS

Throughout this chapter, you'll notice that two values are provided for units of measurement. The first value is provided for the imperial system that is used in the United States, and the second value in parentheses is provided for the metric system that is used in many other countries. These values most often represent imperial feet and metric meters. It is important to note that generally only the numeric values are entered in the software, not terms like *feet* or *meters*. Also, you should know that the two numbers provided are not necessarily equal. In most cases, they are similar values that are rounded to work efficiently in their respective measurement systems.

Applying Parcel Style Display Order

It is quite common for adjacent parcels to share one or more segments. If the adjacent parcels have different styles assigned to them, you can control which style is used for the shared segments via the Site Parcel Properties dialog box. To access this dialog box, right-click Parcels from within Prospector and select Properties. The Parcel Style Display Order is displayed on the Composition tab, as shown in Figure 13.2. When two different styles are used for adjacent parcels, the style that is higher in this list will be assigned to the shared segments. You can control the result for the shared segments by using the arrow keys or dragging and dropping the style names to change the order of the list.

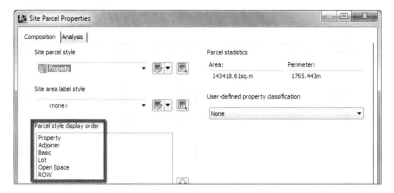

FIGURE 13.2 Parcel Style Display Order shown within the Site Parcel Properties dialog box

Typically you will want certain types of parcel line styles to always override others. For example, right-of-way lines are considered one of the most important boundaries in the drawing, so their style is often placed at the top of the list. As a result, the color and linetype of the right-of-way lines are uninterrupted throughout the drawing. On the other hand, the lot lines are considered one of the least important, so their styles are typically placed at the bottom of the list.

To apply parcel style display order to your drawing, follow these steps:

1. Open the drawing named Applying Parcel Style Display Order.dwg located in the Chapter 13 class data folder. The drawing is zoomed in to Lot : 23, where the entire lot is outlined in blue.

2. On Prospector, expand Sites ➢ Lot Layout.

3. Right-click Parcels and select Properties.

4. On the Composition tab of the Site Parcel Properties dialog box, click ROW under Parcel Style Display Order.

5. Click the upward-pointing arrow icon until ROW is at the top of the list.

6. Click OK. Lot : 23 is now bounded by a black line on the south and east sides and a blue line on the north and west sides. The ROW parcel style is being displayed "on top of" the Lot style as dictated by Parcel Style Display Order (Figure 13.3).

F I G U R E 1 3 . 3 Parcel style display order at work

7. In Prospector, right-click Parcels and select Properties.

8. Arrange the styles under Parcel Style Display Order as follows: ROW, Adjoiner, Open Space, Lot, Property, Basic. Click OK.

9. Zoom in to the drawing and study the different areas where parcels of different styles are adjacent to one another. For example, the back line of lots 48–50 is green because the Open Space style has been placed above the Lot style in Parcel Style Display Order.

Applying Parcel Area Labels

The labels that you have seen at the center of each parcel are known as *parcel area labels*. They do not have to contain information about the area of the parcel; however, they often do. You can create parcel area labels by using the Add Labels command as you have done before to create other labels. One unique capability of parcel area labels is that they can also be assigned through the Parcel Properties command. Like all other labels you have learned about, the appearance and content of parcel area labels are controlled by styles.

  To see how parcel area labels are used to provide information about parcels in your drawing, follow these steps:

1. Open the drawing named Applying Parcel Area Labels.dwg located in the Chapter 13 class data folder.

2. Click the Adjoiner : 3 label, and then click Parcel Properties on the ribbon.

3. Click the Composition tab of the Parcel Properties dialog box. For the Area Selection Label Style, select Existing Description And Area.

4. Click the Information tab. In the Description box, enter **JOHN SMITH** on the first line and **DBV 1234, PG 567** on the second line, as shown in Figure 13.4. Click OK and press Esc to clear the selection. The appearance and content of the label changes dramatically. This is a possible format for labeling a parcel that is not part of the main project but is adjacent or nearby. It includes the owner's name plus the deed book and page where the official documentation of the parcel is recorded. Notice how this label style combines the hand-entered Description value with the calculated area value.

FIGURE 13.4 Entering a description for the Adjoiner : 3 parcel

5. Click the ROW : 6 label located within the cul-de-sac at the end of Madison Lane, and then click Parcel Properties on the ribbon.

6. On the Composition tab of the Parcel Properties dialog box, change the Area Selection Label Style to <none>. Click OK. This removes the label from the parcel.

7. Click the parcel area labels for both open space parcels hatched in green. Right-click and select Properties.

8. Use the Properties window to change the Parcel Area Label Style value to Proposed Description And Area. The labels now display the lot description and area using a different text style and color.

9. Press Esc to clear the selection from the previous command. On the Annotate tab of the ribbon, click Add Labels.

10. In the Add Labels dialog box, do the following:

   a. For Feature, select Parcel.

   b. For Label Type, select Replace Area.

   c. For Area Label Style, select Lot Number.

   d. Click Add.

11. Click several parcels labeled as Lot and press Enter. The labels are updated and appear simply as a number within a circle.

12. On Prospector, expand Sites ➤ Lot Layout. Click Parcels to list all of the parcels in the item view.

13. Click the Area Label Style column to sort the list of parcels by this value.

Now that there is no parcel area label, the only way to select this parcel is by right-clicking it in Prospector and then clicking Select.

The descriptions of COMMON AREA and RESOURCE PROTECTION AREA were already entered for you.

14. Click the first item in the list with an area label style of Standard. Then hold down the Shift key and select the last item with an area label style of Standard.

15. Right-click the Area Label Style column heading and select Edit.

16. In the Select Label Style dialog box, select Lot Number and click OK. After a pause, all of the lot area labels are updated to appear as a number within a circle. Now all of the parcel area labels have the desired style.

Creating Parcel Segment Labels

The most common use of parcel segment labels is to provide numerical information that defines the geometry of property boundaries. This numerical information appears as bearings and distances for line segments, and curve data for curve segments. When an adequate numerical description of a parcel is provided, the parcel can be re-created either on paper or in the field.

CURVE DATA

There are many geometric properties that can be used to define a curve. The most common properties are shown in the following drawing and then described.

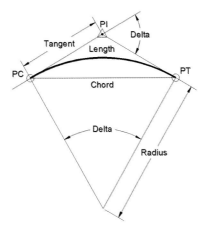

▶ Length: The length of the curve measured along its arc.

▶ Radius: The distance from the center point of the curve to a point on the curve.

CURVE DATA *(Continued)*

▶ Chord: The straight line from the beginning point of the curve to the ending point of the curve. The bearing and distance of this line can be labeled.

▶ Delta: The change in direction between a line tangent to the curve at its beginning point and a line tangent to the curve at its ending point.

▶ Tangent: The distance between the point of curvature (PC) and the point of intersection (PI) or between the point of tangency (PT) and the PI.

Depending on the requirements, you may need to include different combinations of these curve dimensions. Typically, you must create multiple curve dimension labels in order to provide enough information to reconstruct the curve.

To add labels to parcel segments, you use the Add Labels command. You can label the segments one by one, or you can provide labels for all the segments that make up a parcel.

To use parcel segment labels to provide bearings, distances, and curve data in your drawing, complete the following steps:

1. Open the drawing named Creating Parcel Segment Labels.dwg located in the Chapter 13 class data folder.

2. Zoom in to lots 32 and 33 near the center of the project.

 3. On the Annotate tab of the ribbon, click Add Labels.

4. In the Add Labels dialog box, select Parcel as the Feature. Click Add.

5. Click the north side of lot 33. A new bearing and distance label is added.

6. Click the east and west sides of lot 33. Two more bearing and distance labels are created.

7. Pan south to lot 69 and click the curve that makes up the south boundary of lot 69. A curve label is created that displays the delta, length, and radius.

The labels will be created at the location you click, so you should click near the midpoint of the line.

8. In the Add Labels dialog box, select Multiple Segment as the Label Type, and then click Add.

9. Click the parcel area label for lot 32. When you're prompted to select a direction, press Enter to accept the default direction of Clockwise. All segments for lot 32 are labeled simultaneously.

LABELING LINES AND CURVES

Thus far in this chapter, you've learned how to label parcel segments, but what about plain old lines, arcs, and polylines? Do these entities have to be converted to parcel segments in order to be labeled? The answer is no. Civil 3D enables you to label basic AutoCAD® entities using the same Add Labels command that you used for labeling parcel segments. Just remember that you need to choose Line And Curve as the Feature in the Add Labels dialog box, as shown here.

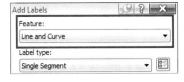

Editing Parcel Segment Labels

Once you have placed parcel segment labels in the drawing, you usually need to do some work to change their position, style, orientation, and whatever else is necessary to create a readable, professional-looking legal document. Fortunately, Civil 3D provides a number of ways for you to do this.

Applying Segment Label Styles

You can use parcel segment label styles to change the appearance, content, and behavior of the segment labels. For example, when labeling an existing property line, you could assign a different style that displays the bearing and distance text slanted—a common practice for differentiating text that refers to existing features. In another part of the drawing, you might assign a different style to a curve label so that the appropriate combination of dimensions is shown according to local requirements.

To apply different segment label styles to segment labels in your drawing, complete the following steps:

1. Open the drawing named Applying Parcel Segment Label Styles.dwg located in the Chapter 13 class data folder.

2. Zoom in to the bearing and distance labels along the west side of the project. Currently, these labels are all shown in a proposed style with both bearing and distance. This side of the project is actually a mixture of existing and proposed geometry, and the display of the same bearing multiple times is redundant.

3. Click on the label for the west side of the John Smith property, and then click Label Properties on the ribbon.

4. In the Properties window, change the Line Label Style to (Span) Bearing And Distance With Crows Feet [Existing]. The color and text style of the label are changed, and the label now reflects the full length of the line.

5. On the Annotate tab of the ribbon, click Add Labels.

6. In the Add Labels dialog box, do the following:

   a. For Feature, select Parcel.

   b. For Label Type, select Single Segment.

   c. For Line Label Style, select Distance [Existing].

   d. Click Add.

7. Click the west side of the John Smith property. A new label is created that reflects the distance associated with just the John Smith property, not the overall distance.

8. Close the Add Labels dialog box. Pan to the south to view the labels for lots 36, 37, 60, and 59.

9. Click these four labels, and then click Label Properties on the ribbon.

10. In the Properties window, change the Line Label Style to Distance. The text of each label changes to include only the inside distance of the associated parcel. The bearing for the individual segments can be omitted, because the bearing on the opposite side of the line provides that information.

Label styles can be set up to *span* across the outside of multiple end-to-end segments and display the overall length. *Crows feet* are the curved tick marks at either end of the line that indicate the extents of the distance that is being labeled.

Editing Parcel Segment Labels Graphically

You can use a number of methods to graphically edit parcel segment labels. The labels are equipped with special grips that enable you to move them easily. You can also capitalize on their built-in dragged state in areas where there is not enough room for the label to be placed right on the line or curve. In addition, you can flip labels to change which side of a line or curve they are placed on, and you can reverse labels to change a NE bearing to SW and vice versa.

To employ several graphical editing techniques on parcel segment labels in your drawing, follow these steps:

1. Open the drawing named Editing Labels Graphically.dwg located in the Chapter 13 class data folder. The drawing is zoomed in to lot 68.

2. Notice the bearing and distance labels for the west sides of lots 68 and 62. The bearing is listed twice, which is redundant. Click the label on the west side of lot 68, and then click Label Properties on the ribbon.

3. In the Properties window, change the Line Label Style to Bearing. Close the Properties window.

4. With the label still selected, click Flip Label on the ribbon. The label is now displayed on the west side of the line.

5. Click the diamond-shaped grip of the label and slide it south to the line that is shared between lots 68 and 62. This bearing will now serve both lots.

6. Notice that this is a NE bearing, while those to the east are SW bearings. With the label still selected, click Reverse Label on the ribbon. The bearing now reflects a SW orientation.

7. Repeat steps 2–4 for the label on the west side of lot 62 using a label style of Distance. The label should now show only the distance and should be located on the east side of the line.

8. Use the Add Labels command to add a new distance label to the west side of lot 68. Don't forget to flip the label so that it is shown on the inside of the lot.

9. Click the curve label at the northwest corner of lot 68. Click the square grip and drag it to the south and east. Place it in the open space between the lot 68 area label and the northwest corner of the

lot. The label is reoriented and a leader appears that points back to the curve (Figure 13.5).

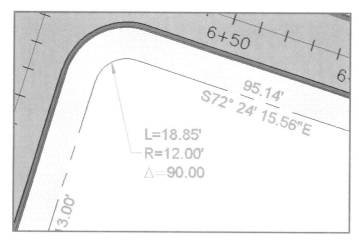

FIGURE 13.5 A curve label that has been dragged away from the curve to reveal its dragged state

10. Continue moving, flipping, and reversing labels to improve the readability of the drawing and remove redundant bearings. Assign new styles where applicable.

Creating Parcel Tables

As you can guess, property drawings can become quite cluttered with many labels for areas, bearings, distances, and curve dimensions. As the drawing becomes more complex, it might make sense to put all that information in a table instead of trying to place it directly on the lines and curves. Line labels can be replaced with tags such as L1, L2, and so on, and the same can be done for curves. These abbreviated labels take up much less space than the full bearing and distance labels, making the drawing appear less cluttered and easier to read. Of course, the trade-off is that now the person viewing the drawing will have to scan back and forth between the drawing and the table to obtain all of the information that pertains to a given parcel. This is why not all drawings use tables to store parcel information. A drawing can be read more easily, and information obtained from it more efficiently, if the labels are placed directly on the lines and curves. However, for some drawings you simply cannot show the information directly on the lines and curves and you must use a table.

Creating Area Tables

You can use area tables to display information about each parcel in the drawing. Depending on the table style that you use, you can vary the amount of information as well as the formatting.

One thing you will probably need to do prior to creating an area table is renumber the lots. You do this by using the Renumber/Rename command on the ribbon.

To renumber the lots in your drawing and list their areas in a table, follow these steps:

1. Open the drawing named Creating An Area Table.dwg located in the Chapter 13 class data folder.

2. Click one of the lot number labels, and then click Renumber/Rename on the ribbon.

3. In the Renumber/Rename Parcels dialog box, check the box next to Use Name Template In Parcel Style. Click OK.

4. When you're prompted to specify a start point, click near the center of lot 24. Then to select the parcels in the correct order, draw the line segments indicated by the red arrows in Figure 13.6.

This setting will cause the parcels to be automatically renamed to reflect their new numbers.

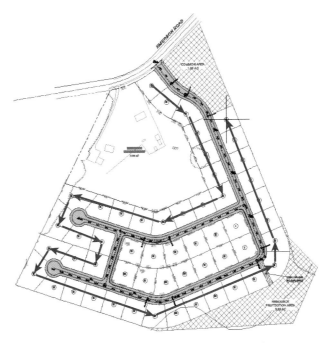

FIGURE 13.6 Selecting parcels in the order they are to be renumbered

5. Press Enter twice to end the command and update the numbers. The numbers should now start at 1 and end at 40 along the same path that you selected.

6. Press Esc to clear the previous selection. Zoom to the lots in the center of the project. Select one of the lot labels, and then click Renumber/Rename on the ribbon.

7. In the Renumber/Rename Parcels dialog box, check the box next to Use Name Template In Parcel Style. Click OK.

8. Draw lines through the parcels as you did before, beginning at lot 68, drawing in a clockwise fashion, and ending at lot 62. Press Enter twice to end the command. These lots should now be numbered from 41 to 53.

9. Press Esc to clear the previous selection. Click one of the lot labels, and then click Add Tables ➣ Add Area on the ribbon.

10. In the Table Creation dialog box, do the following:

   a. For Table Style, select Area Only.

   b. Under Select By Label Or Style, check the Lot Number box in the Apply column.

   c. Click OK.

11. Click a point in an open area of the drawing to insert the tables. A new set of tables is inserted.

Notice that the starting number is 41. The command remembered that you stopped at 40 during the previous renumbering process.

You may need to resize the dialog box or scroll to the right to see the Apply column where the box can be checked.

Creating Parcel Segment Tables

The process of creating parcel segment tables is similar to the way you create area tables. You can select the segments that are listed in the table based on their label style or select each segment individually. When a segment is listed in the table, its label is transformed into a tag that simply assigns a number to the segment. Usually you will want to renumber these tags to follow a sequential order that matches how they are laid out in the drawing. You can do this using the Renumber Tags command on the ribbon.

There are three types of segment tables you can create: line, curve, and segment. The last type (segment) is simply a combination of line and curve data in the same table.

To create a parcel segment table in your drawing and then renumber the tags, complete the following steps:

1. Open the drawing named `Creating a Segment Table.dwg` located in the Chapter 13 class data folder. The drawing is zoomed in to the central portion of the project where the interior lots have been labeled. There are many short curves in this layout, and in many cases, the labels don't fit on the curves. To improve the clarity of the drawing, you are going to put all curve data in a table.

2. On the Annotate tab of the ribbon, click Add Table ➢ Parcel ➢ Add Curve.

3. In the Table Creation dialog box, do the following:

    a. For Table Style, verify that Length Radius & Delta is selected.

    b. Under Label Style Name, scroll down and check the box in the Apply column next to Parcel Curve: Delta Over Length And Radius.

    c. Click OK.

4. Pick a point in an open area of the drawing to insert the table.

5. Click the curve label at the northwest corner of lot 41, and click the circular grip to reset the label and place it back on the curve.

6. With the label still selected, click Renumber Tags on the ribbon. The label now reads "C1."

7. Continue working in a clockwise direction until all of the tags have been renumbered.

8. On the Annotate tab of the ribbon, click Add Labels.

9. In the Add Labels dialog box, select Parcel as the Feature and select Multiple Segment as the Label Type. Click Add.

10. Click the lot 17 label and press Enter to accept the default direction of Clockwise. Do the same for the lot 18 label. New line and curve labels are placed in the drawing.

11. Renumber the new curve tags so that they continue the numbering sequence.

You can click each label and press Enter to repeat the Renumber Tags command. This makes the process go a little quicker.

▶

12. Click the table, then click Add Items on the ribbon. In the Add Selection dialog box, check the box next to Parcel Curve: Delta over Length and Radius. Click OK.

13. Pan over to the table and note that information was automatically added (Figure 13.7).

Curve Table					
Curve #	Length	Radius	Delta	Chord Direction	Chord Length
C1	18.85	12.00	90.00	N62° 35' 44"E	16.97
C2	10.75	225.00	2.74	S73° 46' 23"E	10.75
C3	97.34	225.00	24.79	S87° 32' 06"E	96.58
C4	49.56	225.00	12.62	N73° 45' 41"E	49.46
C5	18.85	12.00	90.00	S67° 32' 57"E	16.97
C6	39.27	25.00	90.00	S22° 27' 03"W	35.36
C7	96.39	175.00	31.56	S83° 13' 45"W	95.17
C8	26.23	175.00	8.59	N76° 41' 54"W	26.21
C9	18.85	12.00	90.00	N27° 24' 16"W	16.97
C10	12.79	350.00	2.09	N73° 27' 03"W	12.79
C11	3.94	350.00	0.64	N74° 49' 11"W	3.94
C12	99.69	350.00	16.32	N83° 18' 05"W	99.35
C13	51.72	350.00	8.47	S84° 18' 20"W	51.68
C14	17.24	350.00	2.82	S78° 39' 40"W	17.23
C15	59.86	350.00	9.80	S72° 21' 02"W	59.79
C16	18.85	12.00	90.00	S27° 24' 16"E	16.97
C17	18.85	12.00	90.00	S62° 35' 44"W	16.97

FIGURE 13.7 New lines added to a curve table

THE ESSENTIALS AND BEYOND

In this chapter, you learned how to use styles to create visual differentiation between different types of parcels. You also learned how to use parcel style display order to control the display of adjacent parcels.

In addition, you learned how to provide annotation for each parcel, as well as annotation for all of the segments that make up the parcels. You now know how to use styles to control the appearance and content of the labels to meet various requirements. Finally, you practiced using tables as an alternate way of organizing and displaying this information.

(Continues)

THE ESSENTIALS AND BEYOND *(Continued)*

ADDITIONAL EXERCISE

Open the drawing named Parcel Display and Labeling Beyond.dwg located in the Chapter 13 class data folder. This drawing contains an alternate road and parcel layout where parcel styles and labeling have not been addressed. Using the prior exercises in this chapter as a guide, create a professional-looking legal document that conveys the same types of information in the same ways.

Visit www.sybex.com/go/civil2013essentials to download a video of the author completing this exercise. You can also download the Answers to Additional Exercises Appendix which contains even more information about completing this exercise.

CHAPTER 14

Designing Pipe Networks

With the completion of parcel design, you are ready to move on to another major area of design: pipe design. As a designer, one type of pipe design that you must address is the safe and efficient collection and conveyance of water that falls on the site during a rainstorm. This type of pipe design is part of a larger design process called *stormwater management*. Because the development of land often involves turning absorbent surfaces (soft grassy soil, trees, and forest floors) into impervious surfaces (pavement, concrete, and asphalt rooftops), rain that falls on the site will travel farther and much faster before it is absorbed. This water on the move can cause erosion or flooding, so it must be safely collected and placed in surface channels or underground pipes. The pipes and channels then carry the water to a safe place where it can be discharged without doing harm.

Other types of pipes are used to provide conveyance to and from the buildings that will occupy the site. Water and gas lines provide valuable utility services to the new residents, while sanitary sewer pipes carry waste away from them. All of these underground piping systems undergo a detailed design to ensure that they function as intended and integrate well with surrounding features, whether new or existing.

▶ **Understanding gravity pipe networks**

▶ **Creating gravity pipe networks**

▶ **Editing gravity pipe networks**

▶ **Understanding pressure pipe networks**

▶ **Creating pressure pipe networks**

▶ **Editing pressure pipe networks**

Understanding Gravity Pipe Networks

AutoCAD® Civil 3D® pipe network design is divided into two types: gravity networks and pressure networks. Because the performance requirements for these two types of systems are so different, the approach to designing and constructing them is also quite different. In this chapter, we'll begin with gravity pipe network design.

For a gravity pipe network design to be a success, it must meet the following basic requirements:

- ▶ The pipes must be sloped enough for water to flow through them.

- ▶ The pipes must be large enough to allow the expected amount of water to pass.

- ▶ The pipes must be far enough underground to avoid being damaged by freezing or by activities on the site.

- ▶ The pipes must not be so far underground that it is cost-prohibitive to install them.

- ▶ Structures must be provided that allow people to access the pipes to perform maintenance.

- ▶ In the case of stormwater management, structures must be provided that allow surface water to enter the pipes.

These requirements relate to two basic types of gravity pipe design components: structures and pipes. This chapter describes these components as well as their relationship to each other when represented within a Civil 3D pipe network.

Understanding Structures

Structures provide access to the pipes underground. This access can be for people, or it can be for rainwater that is flowing across the surface of the ground, also known as *runoff*. In the case of stormwater management design, structures called *inlets* or *catch basins* are placed on the site at locations that are best for collecting runoff. Typically, the runoff falls through a grate into a concrete chamber and then out through a pipe toward its final destination. For other types of pipelines, manholes and cleanouts are placed at predetermined increments so that workers can access the pipes to perform maintenance. Manholes are also used to create a bend in a pipeline when one pipe enters in one direction and a second pipe exits in another. Whatever the case, the placement of these structures is part of the pipe network design process and is not done arbitrarily.

Understanding Pipes

Pipes are used to safely convey water to a predetermined destination. In the case of stormwater pipes, collected runoff commonly passes through one or more forms of onsite treatment and then empties into a nearby stream or ditch. In the case of a sanitary sewer, the journey can be much longer—connecting to a local sewer main and then merging with any number of larger and larger mains until the water reaches a treatment plant. In some cases, the length of that journey can be quite a few miles.

In these systems, the flow of water depends on gravity. This means part of your job as the designer will be to ensure that all of the pipes are pointing downhill. That may sound like an easy task by itself, but when you introduce other design requirements, it can become quite challenging. For example, you also need to ensure that the pipes are at a depth that is neither too shallow nor too deep. Another part of the design is to ensure that the pipes are large enough to convey the amount of water that is expected. This part is usually handled by a licensed engineer or trained designer and is beyond the scope of this book.

Exploring the Pipe Network

Civil 3D enables you to create objects that represent structures and pipes. It also establishes relationships between the structures and pipes as well as other important design elements such as surfaces, alignments, profiles, and profile views. The pipes, structures, and their associated relationships are referred to as a Civil 3D *pipe network*. In Figure 14.1, a plan view of a few pipes and structures is shown on the left, and the same pipes and structures are shown in profile view on the right.

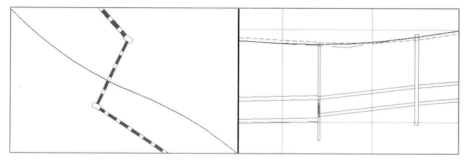

FIGURE 14.1 A pipe network shown in plan view (left) and profile view (right)

In Prospector, gravity systems are listed under Pipe Networks, and pressure systems (covered later in this chapter) are listed under Pressure Networks.

Each component of a pipe network is shown in Prospector. From here, you can right-click each component to access various context commands for it. You can also use the item view at the bottom of Prospector to edit information about each component. Figure 14.2 shows the contents of a pipe network in Prospector.

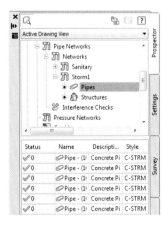

FIGURE 14.2 A pipe network shown in Prospector

The shape, dimensions, and behavior of a pipe network component are determined by the *part* that represents it. Parts are stored in a *parts list*, which is a kind of library from which you can select parts for the different components in your pipe network. Most companies have several parts lists, each one containing parts for a certain type of system such as storm, sanitary, or water. Parts lists can be stored in a template file so that they are available in each new drawing that is created from that template. Figure 14.3 shows an example of a very basic parts list that would be used for storm sewer design.

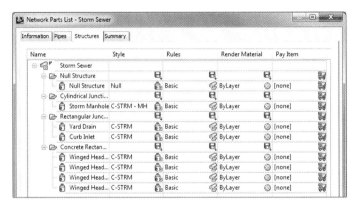

FIGURE 14.3 A parts list configured for storm sewer design

Creating Gravity Pipe Networks

Gravity pipe networks can be created in two basic ways. The first is to create a pipe network from one or more objects that have been drawn beforehand, such as lines, arcs, or a polyline. With this approach, all of the pipes and structures are created at once. The other approach is to create the pipes and structures one by one. This is referred to as creating a pipe network by layout.

Certification
Objective

Creating a Pipe Network from Objects

At times, you will find it easier to start with AutoCAD® commands to sketch your pipe network using basic entities. This approach works quite well because Civil 3D provides a command that will convert these basic entities to pipe networks: the Create Pipe Network From Object command. This command will create pipe networks from Civil 3D alignments and feature lines as well. One disadvantage to this method is that the same parts are used for pipes and structures throughout the entire network.

To create a pipe network from an object in your drawing, complete the following steps:

1. Open the drawing named `Creating Pipe Networks From Objects.dwg` located in the `Chapter 14` class data folder.

2. Zoom in to the beginning of the Jordan Court alignment at the north end of the project. Note the heavy green polyline marked SAN that has been sketched in to represent the location of a new sanitary sewer pipeline.

3. On the Home tab of the ribbon, click Pipe Network ➤ Create Pipe Network From Object.

4. Click the green polyline with the SAN labeling on it. Some black arrows should appear that point toward the south. These arrows indicate the assumed flow direction of the pipes.

5. Press Enter to accept the current flow direction.

6. In the Create Pipe Network From Object dialog box, do the following:

    a. For Network Name, enter **Sanitary**.

    b. For Network Parts List, select Sanitary Sewer.

    c. For Surface Name, select Road FG.

Make sure that your screen background color is set to white before continuing this exercise.

This surface will be used to automatically set the top elevations of the structures.

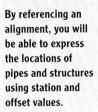

By referencing an alignment, you will be able to express the locations of pipes and structures using station and offset values.

    d. For Alignment Name, select Jordan Court.

    e. Select the Erase Existing Entity box.

    f. Click OK.

A new pipe network is created in place of the polyline. The entities look rather simple, but as you'll see in the next few steps, they are actually 3D pipe and structure objects.

7. Click the manhole symbol and connected pipe at the beginning of the pipeline. Right-click and select Object Viewer.

8. Click near the bottom of the Object Viewer window and drag upward to rotate the model away from you. Then roll the mouse wheel forward to zoom in. As you can see, the structure is shown differently depending on the perspective of the viewer. In plan view, it appears as a symbol, but in 3D view, it appears as a 3D representation of the actual structure, as shown in Figure 14.4.

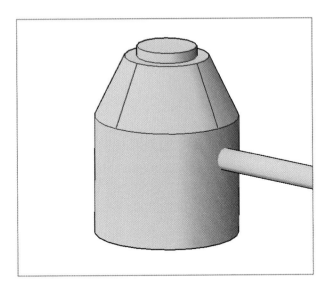

FIGURE 14.4 A 3D view of a pipe object and structure object

9. Close the Object Viewer window. Pan southward until you can see Madison Lane. Note the green polyline that starts near Madison Lane station 2+50 (0+080) and ends near Jordan Court station 21+50 (0+650).

10. On the Home tab of the ribbon, click Pipe Network ➤ Create Pipe Network From Object.

11. Click the green polyline somewhere along Madison Lane. Some black arrows should appear that point toward the south. These arrows indicate the assumed flow direction of the pipes.

12. Press Enter to accept the flow direction indicated by the black arrows.

13. In the Create Pipe Network From Object dialog box, do the following:

    a. For Network Name, enter **Sanitary-2**.

    b. For Network Parts List, select Sanitary Sewer.

    c. For Surface Name, select Road FG.

    d. For Alignment Name, select Madison Lane.

    e. Check the box next to Erase Existing Entity.

    f. Click OK.

14. Repeat steps 10–13 with the remaining polyline that begins at the Madison Lane cul-de-sac. This time use a Network Name of **Sanitary-3**. Now all of the sketch polylines have been converted to sanitary sewer pipes and structures.

15. Select one pipe and one structure. Right-click, and then click Select Similar.

16. Right-click and select Object Viewer. Rotate the view as you did in step 8 to reveal a 3D view of all pipes and structures in the drawing.

Notice that one of the pipes is located at a much lower elevation than the others. This will be addressed later in this chapter.

A NOTE ABOUT UNITS

Throughout this chapter, you'll notice that two values are provided for units of measurement. The first value is provided for the imperial system that is used in the United States, and the second value in parentheses is provided for the metric system that is used in many other countries. These values most often represent imperial feet and metric meters. It is important to note that generally only the numeric values are entered in the software, not terms like *feet* or *meters*. Also, you should know that the two numbers provided are not necessarily equal. In most cases, they are similar values that are rounded to work efficiently in their respective measurement systems.

Creating a Pipe Network by Layout

If you haven't sketched the pipe design or when you want more control of the design as you go, the best choice is to create a pipe network by layout. This is done by using the Pipe Network Creation Tools command. After you launch this command and enter some information about the pipe network, you will be presented with the Network Layout Tools toolbar (Figure 14.5). This is similar to the toolbars you have used for other layout designs, such as creating alignments by layout or profiles by layout.

FIGURE 14.5 The Network Layout Tools toolbar

From the Network Layout Tools toolbar, you can choose pipes and structures from a parts list and then use commands on the toolbar to insert those parts into the drawing. You can change parts at any time and apply different types and sizes as you go. As you draw pipes and structures, special icons next to the cursor inform you when you are connecting parts to one another. For example, Figure 14.6 shows a pipe being drawn between two inlets. The yellow icon indicates that the pipe will be connected to the inlet when the user clicks the mouse.

New pipe drawn between inlets

Icon indicating a connection

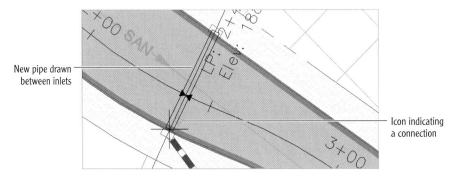

FIGURE 14.6 Icon indicating a connection between a pipe and structure

To create a pipe network by layout, follow these steps:

1. Open the drawing named Creating Pipe Networks by Layout
   .dwg located in the Chapter 14 class data folder. In this drawing, red circles have been provided that indicate the locations of inlets. If you study the placement of these inlets, you will notice that some of them have been placed at low points, as indicated by the alignment labels. To prevent the inlets at the low points from being overloaded,

additional inlets have been placed between low points and high points to collect some of the runoff. Figure 14.7 further illustrates inlet placement within the drawing.

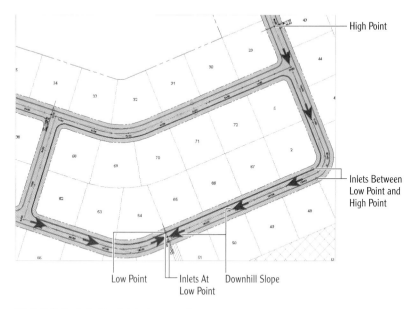

FIGURE 14.7 Inlet placement

2. On the Home tab of the ribbon, click Pipe Network ➤ Pipe Network Creation Tools.

3. In the Create Pipe Network dialog box, do the following:

   a. For Network Name, enter **Storm1**.

   b. For Network Parts List, select Storm Sewer.

   c. For Surface Name, select Road FG.

   d. For Alignment Name, select Jordan Court.

   e. Click OK.

4. You are prompted to specify a structure insertion point. Zoom in to the red circles at Jordan Court station 5+50 (0+170). On the Network Layout Tools toolbar, do the following (Figure 14.8):

   ▶ To choose a structure, select Rectangular Junction Structure NF (SI) ➤ Curb Inlet from the first drop-down list.

   ▶ To choose a pipe, select Concrete Pipe (SI) ➤ 15 Inch (400mm) Concrete Pipe from the second drop-down list.

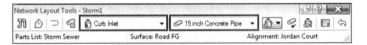

FIGURE 14.8 The Network Layout Tools toolbar after selecting the structure and pipe

5. Right-click the Osnap icon at the bottom of the screen, and then click Settings.

6. On the Object Snap tab of the Drafting Settings dialog box, do the following:

   a. Check the box next to Object Snap On (F3).

   b. Click Clear All.

   c. Select the Center box.

   d. Click OK.

7. Click the center of the red circle to the east of station 5+50 (0+170).

8. Click the center of the red circle to the west of station 5+50 (0+170).

9. Pan northward until you can see the two red circles at the low point of station 2+40.42 (0+073.28). Click the circle to the south of the road.

10. On the Network Layout Tools toolbar, choose the pipe Concrete Pipe (SI) ➤ 18 Inch (450mm) Concrete Pipe.

11. Click the center of the red circle located north of station 2+40.42 (0+073.28).

12. On the Network Layout Tools toolbar, do the following:

    a. Choose the structure Cylindrical Junction Structure NF (SI) ➤ Storm Manhole.

    b. Choose the pipe Concrete Pipe (SI) ➤ 24 Inch (600mm) Concrete Pipe.

13. Click the red circle located at the western corner of the Common Area.

14. On the Network Layout Tools toolbar, choose a structure of Concrete Rectangular Winged Headwall (SI) ➤ Winged Headwall for 24″ (600mm) Pipe.

15. Click the red circle on the opposite side of Emerson Road.

16. Press Esc to end the command. You have created a storm sewer network that discharges at a location across Emerson Road (Figure 14.9).

> These settings will cause the Center object snap to be used each time you click a point in the drawing. This will help you do the next few steps a bit quicker.

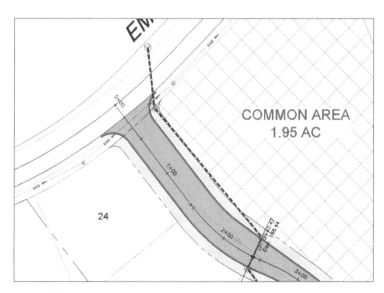

FIGURE 14.9 A portion of the newly created storm pipe network

Drawing a Pipe Network in a Profile View

Viewing a pipe network within a profile view is critical to performing an accurate design. The depths, slopes, and elevations of an underground pipe system are every bit as important as the horizontal location of each component on the plan. Civil 3D enables you to represent a pipe network in profile view, which is the ideal way to visualize and modify the vertical aspect of a pipe network design.

You can use the Draw Parts In Profile command to draw an entire network in profile view or to draw select parts. When this is done, the pipes and structures shown in plan view are the same pipes and structures shown in profile view. Any change or addition to the pipe network will be visible in both views.

To draw the pipe network within a profile view, complete the following steps:

1. Open the drawing named `Drawing Pipe Networks in Profile View.dwg` located in the `Chapter 14` class data folder.

2. On the View tab of the ribbon, click Viewport Configuration ➤ Two Vertical.

3. In the left viewport, zoom in to the plan view of the beginning of Jordan Court.

4. In the right viewport, zoom in to the profile view of the beginning of Jordan Court.

5. Select the new storm manhole near the western corner of the Common Area, and then click Draw Parts In Profile on the ribbon.

If either of the viewports displays as something other than plan view, click within the viewport and click Top on the Views panel of the ribbon.

6. Click one of the grid lines of the Jordan Court profile view. The manhole is drawn within the profile view.

7. Press Esc to clear the selection of the manhole, and then click the pipe that connects to the manhole from the southeast.

 8. Click Draw Parts In Profile on the ribbon, and then click the grid of the Jordan Court profile view.

9. Repeat steps 7 and 8 for the inlet located north of station 2+40.42 (0+073.28).

10. Repeat steps 7 and 8 for the pipe that begins at station 2+40.42 (0+073.28) and ends at station 5+50 (0+170).

11. Repeat steps 7 and 8 for the inlet located to the west of station 5+50 (0+170). Now, there are two pipes and three structures drawn in the profile view (Figure 14.10).

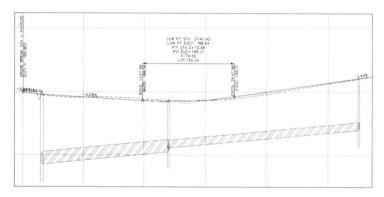

FIGURE 14.10   Two pipes and three structures drawn in a profile view

Editing Gravity Pipe Networks

As you might guess, the tools for editing pipe networks are even more extensive than the tools used to create them. This is one reason that the recommended way to approach your pipe design is to perform a rough layout and then use the editing tools to perfect the design. As you are about to learn, Civil 3D provides many ways to edit pipe networks. In this section, the ways to edit pipe networks are presented in four groups: grips, editing tools, properties, and the Pipe Network Vistas.

Editing Pipe Networks Using Grips

Grips are a great tool for making quick and simple graphical edits. Civil 3D provides the following specialized grips for pipes and structures:

Structure – Square Grip – Plan View   This grip changes the location of the structure without changing its rotation. As a structure is moved, the ends of any pipes that connect to it will move with it.

Structure – Circular Grip – Plan View   This grip changes the rotation of the structure without changing its location.

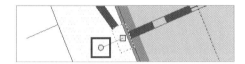

Structure – Top Triangular Grip – Profile View   This grip changes the elevation of the top of the structure. Use caution when editing the top of a structure because, depending on its properties, the software may automatically reset it to match a surface.

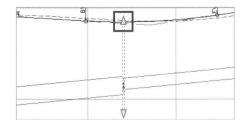

Structure – Bottom Triangular Grip – Profile View   This grip changes the elevation of the *sump* (inside floor) of the structure. This elevation cannot be placed above the *invert* (bottom of the inside wall) of the lowest incoming pipe.

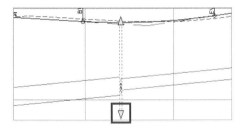

Pipe Midpoint – Triangle Grip – Plan View   This grip is used to change the diameter of a pipe. Dragging it away from the pipe increases the diameter, and dragging it toward the pipe decreases the diameter. This grip can be used in conjunction with the AutoCAD Dynamic Input feature to view the diameter or even type it in.

Pipe Midpoint – Square Grip – Plan View   This grip moves the pipe to a new location without changing its angle or its slope.

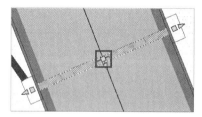

Pipe Endpoint – Square Grip – Plan View   This grip moves the location of one end of the pipe while keeping the other end fixed. In profile view, it maintains the current elevation of that end of the pipe.

Pipe Endpoint – Triangular Grip – Plan View   This grip changes the length of the pipe while maintaining the angle of the pipe and the location of the opposite end.

Pipe Endpoint Grips – Profile View   These grips change the elevation of a pipe at its endpoint. The diamond-shaped grip at the top sets the crown (top of the inside wall) elevation. The diamond-shaped grip at the bottom sets the invert (bottom of the inside wall) elevation. The triangular grip sets the centerline elevation. These grips can be used in conjunction with the AutoCAD Dynamic Input feature to view the elevation or even type it in. They do not change the horizontal location of the pipe's endpoint.

Pipe Midpoint – Square Grip – Profile View   This grip changes the elevation of the pipe without changing its slope. It does not affect the location of the pipe in plan view.

You should note that when you change the location of the endpoint of a pipe in plan view, the structure connected to it does not move with it. To place the structure at the end of the pipe, you must move the structure as a separate action. If you do not update the location of the structure, the pipe may reset to match the structure at some point in the future.

To use grips to edit the pipes and structures in your drawing, follow these steps:

1. Open the drawing named Editing Pipe Networks Using Grips.dwg located in the Chapter 14 class data folder.

2. In the plan view on the left, zoom in to the inlets located at station 5+50 (0+170).

3. Click both inlets to select them, and then click the circular grip on the inlet to the east.

4. Click the square grip of the west inlet. This will rotate the east inlet to align it with the west inlet, which also aligns the east inlet with the curb.

Step 4 will be easier if you press F3 to turn off running object snaps.

5. If it is not already turned on, click the Dynamic Input icon at the bottom of your screen to turn it on.

6. Zoom in to the pipe at station 5+50 (0+170) and select it. Click the triangular grip at the midpoint of the pipe.

7. Drag the grip away from the pipe and click when the dynamic input text box reads 1.5 (0.450). Or you can just type **1.5 (0.450)** in the box, as shown in Figure 14.11. This changes the diameter of the pipe to 18 inches (450mm).

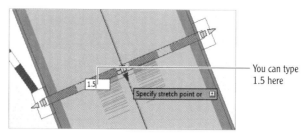

You can type 1.5 here

FIGURE 14.11 Using Dynamic Input to enter a pipe diameter value

8. Pan to the north until you can see the manhole located near the western corner of the Common Area. Click the manhole, and then click the square grip at its center.

9. If your Osnap icon is turned off, click it to turn it on.

10. Click the center of the red circle west of the manhole. If you watch carefully, you'll see the position of the manhole change slightly in the profile view.

11. Click within the right viewport, and then click the pipe within the Jordan Court profile view that is farthest to the left.

12. Click the bottom diamond-shaped grip on the left end of the pipe, and then zoom out until you can see the dynamic view dimension and text box. Type **180 (54.864)** in the text box, and press Enter.

13. Click the Dynamic Input icon to turn off that feature, and then click the structure farthest to the left within the Jordan Court profile view.

14. Click the triangle grip at the bottom of the structure and drag it upward until a symbol appears that is a red circle with a slash through it (Figure 14.12). Click while this symbol is visible. The sump elevation of the structure is raised slightly, but Civil 3D will not allow the sump to be placed above the lowest connecting pipe.

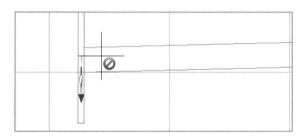

FIGURE 14.12 Editing the sump elevation of a
structure using grips

Editing Pipe Networks Using Editing Tools

Another way to edit a pipe network is to use the Network Layout Tools toolbar,
which is the same toolbar that you used initially to create the pipe network. To
launch the toolbar in editing mode instead of creation mode, you use the Edit
Pipe Network command.

In addition to the Network Layout Tools toolbar, there are several commands
located on the ribbon and within a context menu that give you even more functionality. These include the following:

Swap Part   This command calls up the current parts list and enables you
to select a part and replace it with any part in the list.

Disconnect Part   This command disconnects a pipe from a structure,
enabling you to connect it to a different part or move it independently of
other parts.

Connect Part   This command connects a pipe to a structure to reestablish
the dynamic behavior of connected parts.

Split Network   This command divides a network into two separate
networks.

Merge Networks   This command combines two or more networks into a
single network.

To use the ribbon commands and Network Layout Tools toolbar to edit a pipe
network in your drawing, follow these steps:

1. Open the drawing named Editing Pipe Networks Using Editing
   Tools.dwg located in the Chapter 14 class data folder.

2. Click any storm pipe or structure in the drawing, and then click Edit
   Pipe Network on the ribbon. This opens the Network Layout Tools
   toolbar.

3. On the Network Layout Tools toolbar, do the following:

   a. Choose a structure of Cylindrical Junction Structure NF (SI) ➤ Storm Manhole.

   b. Click the small black triangle to expand the button to the right of the pipe drop-down list. Select Structures Only.

4. If your Osnap icon is turned on, click it to turn it off.

5. Click near the midpoint of the pipe that begins at station 2+40.42 (0+073.280) and ends at station 5+50 (0+170). A new manhole is inserted along the pipe.

6. Press Esc to clear the current command. Click the newly created structure, and then click the square grip at its center.

7. Snap to the center of the red circle located near Jordan Court station 3+50 (0+110).

8. Press Esc to clear the previous selection. Click the pipe that enters the new manhole from the south. Click Swap Part on the ribbon.

9. In the Swap Part Size dialog box, click Concrete Pipe (SI) ➤ 18 Inch (450mm) Concrete Pipe, then click OK.

10. Repeat steps 8 and 9 for the pipe that exits the new manhole to the north. You have now inserted a new manhole and resized the pipes that connect to it (Figure 14.13).

11. Close the Network Layout Tools toolbar and press Esc to clear the previous selection. Click one of the sanitary sewer pipes in the drawing, and then click Merge Networks on the ribbon.

12. In the first dialog box, click Sanitary-2 and then click OK. Here, you are selecting a network that will be merged into another. When the process is complete, a network of this name will no longer exist.

13. In the second dialog box, click Sanitary and then click OK. Here, you are selecting the network that is having Sanitary-2 merged into it.

14. In Prospector, expand Pipe Networks ➤ Networks. Note that the Sanitary-2 network is no longer listed.

15. Repeat steps 11–13, this time selecting Sanitary-3 in the first dialog box. All sanitary sewer networks have been merged into one; therefore, only one sanitary sewer network is listed in Prospector.

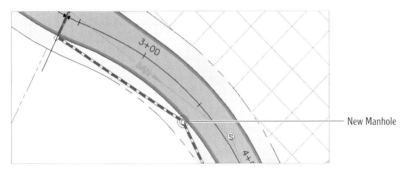

FIGURE 14.13 Newly created manhole and resized connecting pipes

Editing Pipe Networks Using Properties

Many of the values that you need to change when editing pipes and structures can be found within their *properties*. There are two ways to access the properties of a pipe or structure: the Civil 3D method or the AutoCAD method. To use the Civil 3D method, you select a pipe or structure and then click Pipe Properties or Structure Properties on the ribbon. This method provides extensive information about the pipe or structure, much of which can be edited to change the design. The one disadvantage of this method is that you must launch the Pipe Properties or Structure Properties command separately for each pipe or structure that you want to edit.

With the AutoCAD method, you select the pipe or structure and then use the Properties command from the ribbon or the context menu. Here, you are given access to a limited number of properties, but the advantage is that you can modify multiple pipes or structures simultaneously.

To use properties to modify a pipe network design in your drawing, follow these steps:

1. Open the drawing named `Editing Pipe Networks Using Properties`
   `.dwg` located in the `Chapter 14` class data folder. In this exercise, you will focus on the sanitary sewer pipes that lie within Madison Lane. In the profile view on the right, notice that the pipe beginning at the intersection with Logan Court and ending at the Madison Lane cul-de-sac has been incorrectly placed at a very low elevation.

2. Zoom in to the Madison Lane profile and note the label at the right end that reads "ELEV = 180.972 (55.160)." This elevation corresponds with the center point of the cul-de-sac, which is also the location of the manhole.

The problem with the incorrect pipe elevation was brought to your attention during the first exercise in this chapter, when the sanitary sewer pipe networks were first created.

3. Click within the left viewport, and then zoom in and click the manhole located at the center of the Madison Lane cul-de-sac. Click Structure Properties on the ribbon.

4. On the Part Properties tab of the Structure Properties dialog box, do the following:

   a. For Automatic Surface Adjustment, select False.

   b. For Insertion Rim Elevation, enter 180.972 (55.160).

   c. Click OK.

5. This corrects the top elevation of the structure, but the pipe still requires some editing. Press Esc to clear the selection of the manhole. Then in the plan view, select the pipe that begins at the Madison Lane cul-de-sac. Right-click and select Properties.

6. In the Properties window, change the Start Invert Elevation to 176.972 (53.941).

7. With the pipe still selected, click Pipe Properties on the ribbon.

8. On the Part Properties tab of the Pipe Properties dialog box, enter -1.5 for Pipe Slope (Hold Start). Click OK. The pipe is corrected, but the sump of the manhole at the cul-de-sac is still incorrect.

9. Press Esc to clear the selection of the pipe. Click the manhole at the center of the Madison Lane cul-de-sac, right-click, and select Structure Properties.

10. Although it is already set to 2.000 (0.600), type 2 (0.6) for Sump Depth and press Enter. Click OK. If you're zoomed in closely to the profile view, it may seem as though it has disappeared. Actually, the profile view has become much shorter because it no longer needs to accommodate the excessively tall manhole (Figure 14.14). The manhole depth is updated because the apparent change to the sump depth triggered a recalculation of the manhole dimensions.

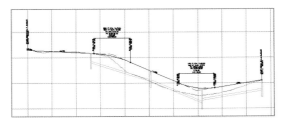

FIGURE 14.14 The sanitary pipe network in profile view after correcting several elevations

Editing Pipe Networks Using the Pipe Network Vistas

The pipe network editing methods you've learned about thus far in this chapter are great for working with individual pipes and structures, but what if you want see the entire network or make edits to multiple parts simultaneously? Luckily, you can do these things with the Pipe Network Vistas command, which opens Panorama and displays two tabs: Structures and Pipes. Each of these tabs displays all pipes or structures in the entire network in a spreadsheet format, enabling you to view and edit the properties of multiple components at once.

The Pipe Network Vistas button is located near the right end of the Network Layout Tools toolbar (Figure 14.15).

FIGURE 14.15   The Pipe Network Vistas button highlighted in the Network Layout Tools toolbar

To use the Pipe Network Vistas to edit a pipe network in your drawing, follow these steps:

1. Open the drawing named Editing Pipe Networks Using the Pipe Network Vistas.dwg located in the Chapter 14 class data folder.

2. Click any storm pipe or structure in the drawing, and then click Edit Pipe Network on the ribbon.

3. On the Network Layout Tools toolbar, click Pipe Network Vistas. Panorama will open, displaying the Pipes and Structures tabs.

4. Click the Structures tab. While holding down the Ctrl key, click the four rows that currently have Rectangular Junction Structure NF (SI) as the Description (Figure 14.16).

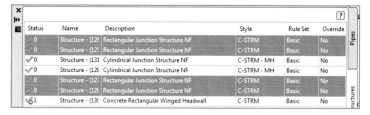

FIGURE 14.16   Selecting multiple rows within the Structures tab of Panorama

5. Right-click the Description column heading and select Edit.

6. Type **INLET** and press Enter. All four Description values should change to INLET.

7. In the Description column, change any instances of Cylindrical Junction Structure NF (SI) to **MANHOLE**.

8. Change the Description for the last structure to **ENDWALL**.

9. Click the Pipes tab. While holding down the Shift key, click the first and last rows. All rows should now be selected.

10. Right-click the Style column and select Edit.

11. In the Select Pipe Style dialog box, select C-STRM – Walls In Profile. Click OK. The appearance of the pipes in profile view changes so that the inside and outside pipe walls are shown (Figure 14.17).

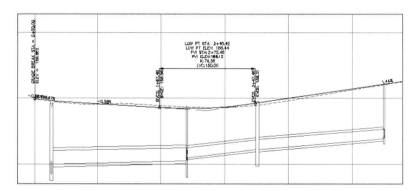

FIGURE 14.17   Pipes in profile view shown with inside and outside walls

Understanding Pressure Pipe Networks

As mentioned earlier, gravity system designs and pressure system designs are quite different and must be addressed using different tools. For a pressure pipe network design to be a success, it must meet the following basic requirements:

▶ The bends and curves must be constructed according to industry standard fittings and allowable joint deflections.

▶ The pipes must be sized according to specific flows and pressures.

▶ The pipes must be far enough underground to avoid being damaged by freezing or by activities on the site.

▶ The pipes must not be so far underground that it is cost-prohibitive to install them.

These requirements relate to two basic types of pressure pipe design components: fittings and pipes. This chapter describes these components as well as their relationship to each other when represented within a Civil 3D pressure network.

Pressure networks can also contain appurtenances which are not addressed in detail in this book.

Understanding Fittings and Angles

Pressure pipe fittings serve two purposes. The first, like structures in gravity systems, is to enable two or more pipes to connect together. For example, a tee or wye fitting provides a connection for three pipes, while a crossing fitting provides a connection for four. The second purpose of a fitting is to create a bend in the direction of the pipeline, the angle of which is typically dictated by manufacturing standards. For example, elbows are commonly available in 90, 45, 22.5, and 11.25 versions. For this reason, bend angles are a big part of pressure pipe design.

In addition to bend angles, a slight amount of deflection is also allowed within connections. This deflection angle varies depending on how the pipes or fittings have been manufactured and is also part of the design. This allowable deflection also enables a series of pipes to form a curve by providing a little deflection at each joint. Therefore, pressure pipes can be laid out on a curve with the radius determined by the allowable deflection.

Because of available fittings and allowable deflection angles, each bend in a pressure pipe is a design in itself. As a designer, you will be required to choose the right combination of fitting and deflection angle to make each bend in the pipeline.

Understanding Pressure Pipes

Like gravity pipes, pressure pipes are used to convey a substance, but the main difference, of course, is that the substance is moved by pressure rather than gravity. For this reason, elevations are not nearly as important to ensure adequate flow. They are important, however, to ensure that the pipeline has adequate cover to prevent freezing or physical damage and that it avoids underground obstacles, including other pipes. In the event of a conflict, because pressure pipe flow is not dependent on elevation, a pressure pipe will usually bend to avoid a gravity pipe. As discussed previously, the required bends will be a design challenge because of the available fittings and deflection angles.

Exploring the Pressure Network

Civil 3D enables you to create objects that represent fittings and pipes. It also establishes relationships between the fittings and pipes as well as other important design elements such as surfaces, alignments, profiles, and profile views. The pipes, fittings, appurtenances, and their associated relationships are referred to as a Civil 3D *pressure network*. In Figure 14.18, a plan view of a few pipes and fittings representing a water line is shown on the left, and the same pipes and structures are shown in profile view and model view on the center and right, respectively.

Each component of a pressure network is shown in Prospector beneath the Pressure Networks node. From here, you can right-click each component to access various context commands for it. You can also use the item view at the bottom of Prospector to edit information about each component. Figure 14.19 shows the contents of a pressure network in Prospector.

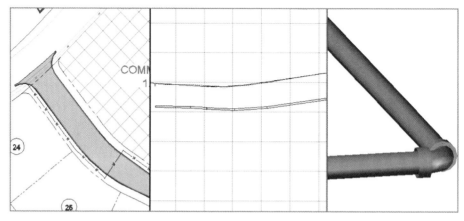

FIGURE 14.18 A pressure network shown in plan view (left), profile view (center), and model view (right)

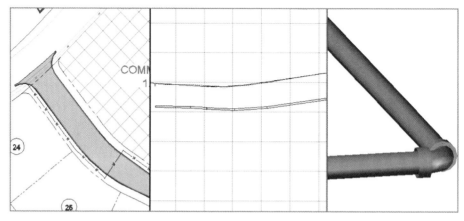

FIGURE 14.19 A pressure network shown in Prospector

Just like gravity networks, the shape, dimensions, and behavior of a pressure network component are determined by the *part* that represents it. Pressure networks have their own parts lists, separate from gravity networks. Most companies have several parts lists, each one containing parts for a certain type of system such as water, sanitary, or natural gas.

Creating Pressure Pipe Networks

Unlike gravity networks, pressure networks cannot be created from objects in Civil 3D. You do, however, have a robust set of layout tools that can be used to create a pressure network by layout. Also different from gravity networks, the layout tools for pressure networks are housed in the ribbon rather than on a toolbar. The specialized ribbon tab (Figure 14.20) is launched by using the Pressure Network Creation Tools command.

Certification
Objective

FIGURE 14.20   The specialized ribbon for pressure network layout

From this specialized ribbon tab, you can choose the pipes, fittings, and appurtenances from the parts list and use the commands on the ribbon to insert those parts into the drawing. You can change parts at any time and apply different types and sizes as you go. To guide your design, Civil 3D provides a *compass* (Figure 14.21), which displays the bend angles and deflections available at a given point based on information stored within the parts list. The compass will automatically "snap" your cursor to an available bend angle to prevent you from laying out a nonstandard bend in the pipeline.

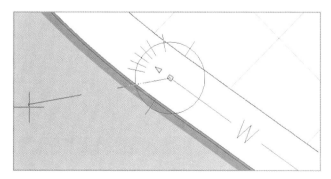

FIGURE 14.21   The compass (the red circle) shows the available bend angles and deflections

Another fundamental difference with pressure network layout is that you provide a value for *cover*, and Civil 3D will automatically set the elevation at each end of a pipe according to that value. You can change the Cover value as you design.

To create a pressure network, follow these steps:

1. Open the drawing named Creating Pressure Networks.dwg located in the Chapter 14 class data folder. In this drawing, red circles have been provided that indicate the locations of bends.

 2. On the Home tab of the ribbon, click Pipe Network ➤ Pressure Network Creation Tools.

3. In the Create Pressure Pipe Network dialog box, do the following:

    a. For Network Name, enter **Water Main**.

    b. For Parts List, select Water Supply.

    c. For Surface Name, select Road FG.

    d. For Alignment Name, select Jordan Court.

    e. Click OK.

4. The Pressure Network Plan Layout ribbon tab opens. Do the following:

    a. On the Network Settings panel, enter **4.5 (1.5)** for Cover.

    b. Under Select A Size And Material, select 6 INCH (150mm) DUCTILE IRON.

5. Click Pipes Only. Snap to the center of the circle marked A; then snap to the center of the circle marked B. Notice the compass that appears at point B that shows the allowable deflection at the pipe joint and restricts the ability to draw the next pipe to stay within that allowable deflection.

6. At the command line, type **C** and press Enter to apply the Curve option. Snap to the center of the circle marked C.

7. At the command line, type **S** and press Enter to apply the Straight option. Snap to the center of the circle marked D.

 8. On the ribbon, to the right of Add Fitting, select 6 INCH (150mm) ELBOW 90 DEG. Click Add Fitting. Snap to the end of the last pipe that you drew. A new 90 ° fitting should be placed at the end of the pipe but it curves in the wrong direction.

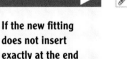
If the new fitting does not insert exactly at the end of the pipe, delete it and repeat step 8.

9. Press Esc to end the current command. Click the new fitting, then click the northward-pointing arrow grip to flip the fitting so that it curves toward the southwest. Press Esc to clear the selection of the fitting.

10. Click Pipes & Bends on the ribbon. Click the 90 ° elbow and then snap to the center of the circle marked E. Notice the difference in the compass, which now shows available bend angles rather than deflections. The available angles are based on the fittings listed in the parts list.

11. On the command line, type **C** and press Enter to apply the Curve option. Click a point somewhere between circles E and F; then snap to the center of circle F. Press Esc to end the command. A new 90 ° elbow has been inserted, and a curved section of pipe has been drawn from circle E to circle F (Figure 14.22).

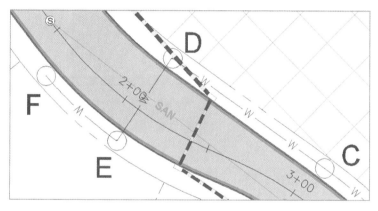

FIGURE 14.22   The newly drawn water line including the 90 ° elbow at circle E and the curved section of pipe between circles E and F

Editing Pressure Pipe Networks

Before editing a pressure network, it is best to display it in profile view so that you can analyze your design from more than one perspective. This is done using the Draw Parts In Profile View command, much like you did with gravity networks. And just like gravity networks, pressure networks can be edited using four basic approaches: grips, layout tools, properties, and Pipe Network Vistas. Of these four approaches, the grips and layout tools approaches differ considerably from how they are applied in gravity systems. The next two sections explain the details of how these two approaches are applied to pressure networks.

Editing Pressure Networks Using Grips

Grips are a great tool for making quick and simple graphical edits. Civil 3D provides the following specialized grips for pressure pipes and fittings:

Fitting – Square Grip – Plan View   This grip changes the location of the fitting without changing its rotation. As the fitting is moved, the ends of any pipes that connect to it will move with it.

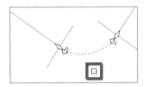

Fitting – Arrow Grip – Plan View   This grip changes the direction of the fitting by flipping it around the axis of the connecting pipe.

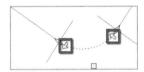

Fitting – Diamond Grip – Plan View   This grip slides the fitting along the pipe that it is connected to without changing the rotation angle of the fitting.

Fitting – Plus Grip – Plan View   This grip creates a new pipe projecting from the end of the fitting with the angle restricted to the allowable deflection at the joint. This grip does not appear in a location where a pipe is already connected.

Fitting – Diamond Grip – Profile View   This grip changes the elevation of the fitting.

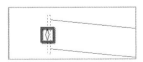

Pipe Endpoint – Square Grip – Plan View   This grip changes the location of one end of the pipe without changing the location of the other. It is only available if neither end of the pipe is connected to a fitting.

Pipe Endpoint – Diamond Grip – Plan View   This grip swings the pipe around a fitting at the opposite end. A graphic will display the allowable deflection but will not restrict movement to stay within it. This grip will not change the length of the pipe.

Pipe Endpoint – Plus Grip – Plan View   This grip creates a new fitting and pipe projecting from the end of the pipe you've selected. The angle of the new pipe will be restricted to the allowable angles as per the fittings in the parts list. This grip does not appear in a location where a fitting is already connected.

Pipe Endpoint – Triangular Grip – Plan View   This grip changes the length of the pipe while maintaining the angle of the pipe and the location of the opposite end. If the pipe is curved, it will maintain the radius of the pipe while extending it along its own curvature.

Pipe Midpoint Grip – Plan View   For a straight pipe, this grip changes the location of the pipe without changing its rotation. It will disconnect the pipe from any fittings it is attached to. For a curved pipe with a connection at both ends, this grip changes the radius of the curve without changing the location of either endpoint. If one or both of the ends is not connected, it will work the same as if it is a straight pipe.

Pipe Endpoint Grips – Profile View   These grips change the elevation of a pipe at its endpoint. The diamond-shaped grip at the top sets the crown (top of the inside wall) elevation. The diamond-shaped grip at the bottom sets the invert (bottom of the inside wall) elevation. The triangular grip sets the centerline elevation. These grips can be used in conjunction with the AutoCAD

Dynamic Input feature to view the elevation or even type it in. They do not change the horizontal location of the pipe's endpoint.

Pipe Endpoint – Triangle Grip – Profile View　　This grip changes the length of the pipe while holding its slope. This grip does change the length of the pipe in plan view.

Pipe Midpoint – Square Grip – Profile View　　This grip changes the elevation of the pipe without changing its slope. It does not affect the location of the pipe in plan view. It will disconnect the pipe from any fittings or appurtenances it is connected to.

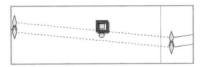

Pipe Midpoint – Circular Grip – Profile View　　This grip curves the pipe by holding the endpoints and forcing it to pass through the new location that you select for the grip. Movement is not restricted based on allowable deflections.

To use grips to edit the pipes and fittings in your drawing, follow these steps:

1. Open the drawing named `Editing Pressure Networks Using Grips` `.dwg` located in the `Chapter 14` class data folder.

2. Zoom in to the circle marked D1 and click the 90 elbow fitting near its center. Click the fitting, and then click the square grip.

3. Snap to the center of the circle marked D2. The fitting moves to the new location along with the ends of the two pipes that are connected to it. The geometry of the fitting looks a bit odd at the moment, because the fitting should be changed to a 45 elbow. This will be addressed in a later exercise.

4. Click the curved pipe between E and F1; then click the triangular grip at circle F1. Snap to the center of circle F2.

5. Press Esc to end the current layout command. Select the water pipe between E and F2; then click Network Properties on the ribbon. On the Layout Settings tab select EG for Surface Name; then click OK.

6. Click the plus sign grip at circle F2. On the ribbon, change the Cover value to **4.5 (1.5)** and select 6 INCH (150mm) DUCTILE IRON as the pipe size. Snap to the center of circle G.

7. Press Esc to end the current command and clear any selections in the drawing. Click the pipe between E and F2, then click Draw Parts In Profile on the Pipe Networks: Water Main ribbon tab.

8. Click one of the grid lines of the Jordan Court profile view. The water pipe should appear in the profile view.

9. Press Esc to clear the current selection. Select all pipes and fittings from circle E to circle A; then use the Draw Parts In Profile command to add them to the profile view. The water line should now appear in the profile view, as shown in Figure 14.23.

◀ The location of the next fitting will be outside the area covered by the Road FG surface and will therefore be based on EG surface elevations.

FIGURE 14.23 The Water Main pressure pipes and fittings shown in profile view

10. In the profile view, click the second fitting from the left located near station 2+75 (0+080). Click the diamond-shaped grip. If Dynamic Input is turned off, turn it on by clicking the icon at the bottom of your screen.

11. Zoom out until you can see the Dynamic Input elevation value for the grip. Type **184 (55.45)** and press Enter.

12. Pan to the right and click the long pipe at the right end of the water main. Click the circular grip; then click a point slightly above the pipe. The pipe will curve upward so that it passes through the point you selected.

Editing Pressure Networks Using Editing Tools

Another way to edit a pressure network is to use the Pressure Network Plan Layout ribbon tab, which is the same one that you used initially to create the pressure network. To launch the ribbon in editing mode instead of creation mode, you select a component of the pressure network and then click Edit Network ➢ Plan Layout Tools (Figure 14.24).

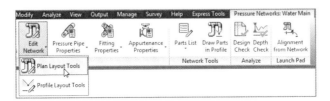

FIGURE 14.24 Launching the Pressure Network Plan Layout ribbon tab by clicking the Plan Layout Tools command

As you may have noticed in Figure 14.24, there is also a *Profile* Layout Tools command. The editing capabilities of pressure networks in profile view are a bit more numerous when compared to gravity networks. For example, with pressure networks you can add new pipes, add fittings, extend pipes, and perform several other functions that are not possible with gravity pipes. When you click the Profile Layout Tools command, the Pressure Network Profile Layout ribbon tab opens (Figure 14.25), which provides many useful editing commands that are carried out in profile view.

FIGURE 14.25 The Pressure Network Profile Layout ribbon tab.

To use the specialized ribbon commands to edit a pressure network in your drawing, follow these steps:

1. Open the drawing named Editing Pressure Networks Using Editing Tools.dwg located in the Chapter 14 class data folder.

2. Zoom in to circle D2 and delete the 90 elbow located there.

3. Click one of the pipes to display the Pressure Networks ribbon tab. Then click Edit Network ➢ Plan Layout Tools.

4. On the Pressure Network Plan Layout ribbon tab, do the following:

   a. Verify that Road FG is the selected surface.

   b. For Cover, enter 4.5 (1.5).

    c. Select 6 INCH (150mm) DUCTILE IRON as the pipe size.

    d. Select 6 INCH (150mm) ELBOW 45 DEG as the fitting.

5. Click Add Fitting; then click the end of either pipe within the D2 circle. Press Esc twice to end the command and clear the selection. If the fitting is turned the wrong way, click it and use the arrow grip to flip it in right direction.

◀

If the new fitting does not insert exactly at the end of the pipe, delete it and repeat step 5.

6. Click the pipe that is not connected to display its grips. Click the diamond-shaped grip; then click the new fitting to connect the pipe to the fitting. Press Esc to clear the selection of the pipe.

7. Delete the 90 fitting at circle E and repeat steps 5 and 6 to replace it with a 45 fitting.

8. On the ribbon, select 6 INCH (150mm) TEE as the current fitting.

9. Delete the 90 fitting at circle F2 and repeat steps 5 and 6 to replace it with a 6 INCH (150mm) TEE.

◀

If the new fitting does not insert exactly at the ends of the pipes, delete it and repeat step 9.

10. On the View tab of the ribbon, within the Model Viewports panel, click Named. On the Named Viewports tab of the Viewports dialog box, click Pipe Design, and then click OK. Your screen will now be divided into three viewports: plan view on the left, profile view on the top right, and 3D view on the bottom right.

11. In the plan view on the left, click the newly created tee; then click the northern plus sign grip. Snap to the center of circle H to create a new pipe. Press Esc twice to end the command and clear the selection.

12. Click the new pipe; then click Draw Parts In Profile on the ribbon. Click one of the grid lines within the Jordan Court profile view. The new pipe will now be drawn in the profile view. Notice the tee connection and the short pipe stub located down and to the left of the new pipe. This is the location where the new water line will connect to the existing water line.

13. On the ribbon, select Edit Network ➤ Profile Layout Tools.

14. Next to Add Bend, select 6 INCH (150mm) ELBOW 45 DEG. Then click Add Bend.

15. Place your cursor near the right end of the short pipe segment located just below the red circle. When the glyph appears, as shown in Figure 14.26, click the pipe. Type **CO** at the command line, and press Enter to invoke the Counterclockwise option. A new 45 bend should appear. It may look odd in profile view because of the vertical exaggeration. If you zoom into the new fitting in the 3D view, it will look more like you would expect.

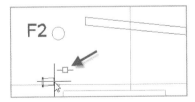

FIGURE 14.26 A glyph indicating the proper connection of a pipe to a fitting

 16. Verify that 6 INCH (150mm) DUCTILE IRON is selected as the current pipe size and click Add Pressure Pipe. When prompted for the part at the start of the range, click the newly created elbow.

17. When prompted for the part at the end of the range, click the pipe to the right of the red circle. Click Yes when asked if you want to continue.

 18. Click the newly created elbow, then snap to the center of the red circle located above the new bend.

19. Click Add Bend; then click the end of the newly created pipe, making sure that the proper glyph is showing, as per Figure 14.26. Type **CL** at the command line and press Enter to invoke the Clockwise option. Another 45° bend is created.

20. Click the pipe just to the right of the newly created bend. Click the upright triangle grip at the left end of the pipe and drag it toward the new bend. Click the newly created bend to connect the pipe to it. In the 3D view, you can now see the complete design of the connection between the existing and proposed water mains (Figure 14.27).

FIGURE 14.27 The connection of the proposed water line to the existing water line, shown in a 3D perspective

21. Press Esc to clear all selections in the drawing. In profile view, pan to the right and select the long pipe. Click Follow Surface on the Pressure Network Profile Layout tab of the ribbon.

22. Press Enter; then type **4.5 (1.5)** at the command line when prompted for depth below surface. Press Enter to complete the command. The pipe has been broken into segments so that it can maintain a constant depth below the surface.

THE ESSENTIALS AND BEYOND

In this chapter, you began by learning the role that gravity pipe network design plays in a land development project. You then studied and practiced two methods for creating new gravity networks: by object and by layout. With the networks in place, you then practiced four different editing methods to improve your pipe network design.

After learning about gravity network design, you then learned about the new pressure network design capabilities of Civil 3D 2013. You created a pressure network by layout and then edited it by using grips and by using the specialized ribbon tabs provided for editing pressure network designs in plan and profile view.

ADDITIONAL EXERCISE

Open the drawing named Pipe Networks Beyond.dwg located in the Chapter 14 class data folder. This drawing contains the pipe networks you've created to this point, along with red circles indicating additional inlet locations that are needed for the storm-water management design. Create inlets at these locations and pipes that connect them according to the following design parameters:

▶ All pipes should lead to the south inlet at Jordan Court station 17+17.34 (0+523.445).

▶ A 36" (900mm) pipe should be drawn from the south inlet at station 17+17.34 (0+523.445), through the drainage easement, to an end wall somewhere within the stormwater treatment area hatched in green.

▶ The pipes farthest upstream should be 15" (400mm) in diameter and increase gradually as the network progresses downstream.

▶ In places where the storm pipes are outside the right-of-way, manholes should be provided to bend the path of the storm pipes to keep them within the right-of-way.

▶ Draw pipes and structures in the profile views of the roads that they fall within. Structures near intersections may appear in two profile views.

(Continues)

THE ESSENTIALS AND BEYOND *(Continued)*

Visit www.sybex.com/go/civil2013essentials to download a video of the author completing this exercise. You can also download the Answers to Additional Exercises Appendix which contains even more information about completing this exercise.

CHAPTER 15

Displaying and Annotating Pipe Networks

As you have learned with other types of design that I have discussed to this point, simply designing an object or a system isn't the end of the story. Your ability to share important information about the design is as important as the design itself. After all, without the effective sharing of information, the design cannot be properly reviewed or constructed. Pipe network design is no different and relies heavily on graphical appearance and annotation to convey design information.

In this chapter, you will study the use of pipe, structure, and fitting styles to control the appearance of pipe networks in plan and profile view. You will also learn about annotating pipe networks using labels and tables. In a more general sense, you will learn how to combine all of these features to effectively communicate the intent of your design to others.

In the previous chapter, gravity and pressure networks were presented separately because they each required a unique approach for layout and design. The stylization and annotation of gravity and pressure networks are virtually the same, however. In fact, with the exception of fitting styles versus structure styles, the stylization and annotation of gravity and pressure networks can be considered the same. For this reason, most of the information in this chapter does not need to be duplicated for both types of networks as it was in the previous chapter.

▶ **Displaying pipe networks using styles**

▶ **Annotating pipe networks in plan view**

▶ **Annotating pipe networks in profile view**

▶ **Creating pipe network tables**

Displaying Pipe Networks Using Styles

Pipe and structure styles are two of the most sophisticated AutoCAD® Civil 3D® styles. They provide many options for displaying the components of your pipe network design in plan, profile, model, and even section view. It is important to have many options for displaying pipe networks, because often you have different types of systems in the same drawing that need to be differentiated graphically.

Applying Structure and Fitting Styles

Civil 3D styles provide a number of fundamental ways to display structures and fittings. In plan view, you can display a structure as an outline of its 3D form, or you can use an AutoCAD® block as a symbol representing the structure. When you use a block, you can determine its size according to the drawing scale, a fixed scale, or the actual dimensions of the part. Figure 15.1 shows a structure represented using an AutoCAD block on the left and as an outline of its 3D shape on the right.

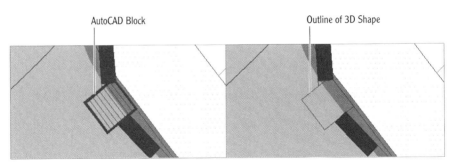

AutoCAD Block

Outline of 3D Shape

FIGURE 15.1   A structure shown as a block (left) and as an outline of a 3D shape (right)

In profile view, there are three ways to display a structure: as a solid, as a boundary, or as a block.

Solid   The structure is shown as a slice through the 3D model of the part, which means the size, shape, and dimensions are an accurate representation (Figure 15.2). Any detail within the interior of the part is visible with this option.

Boundary   An outline of the 3D model of the part is shown (Figure 15.3). This is also an accurate representation of the part but without the interior detail.

Block   A block (Figure 15.4) is inserted and sized based on one of several options. The most common option is to scale the block vertically to match the height of the part and horizontally to match the width of the part. A block can provide the desired appearance of the part, but because of the horizontal and vertical scaling, it may not be an exact dimensional match to the actual part.

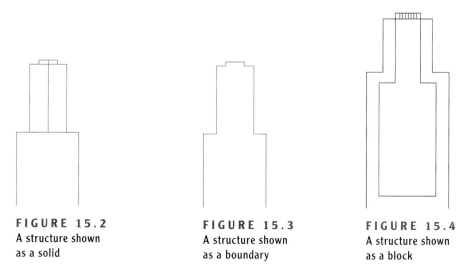

FIGURE 15.2
A structure shown
as a solid

FIGURE 15.3
A structure shown
as a boundary

FIGURE 15.4
A structure shown
as a block

For fittings, the plan view choices are Centerline, Catalog Defined Block, or User Defined Block. Centerline is the simplest choice, which represents the fitting as a single line. Catalog Defined Block is the true 3D form of the fitting shown in plan view. The User Defined Block option allows you to use any AutoCAD block to represent the fitting. In profile view, there are no options for the display of fittings; they are simply represented as an outline.

It is not likely that you, as a designer, will be responsible for configuring styles or having to choose which display configuration to use—these things are typically taken care of by a CAD manager.

However, knowing the ways in which structures and fittings can be displayed will be helpful when you're asking your CAD manager to build some styles for you.

To use styles to control the display of structures in your drawing, follow these steps:

1. Open the drawing named `Applying Structure and Fitting Styles` `.dwg` located in the `Chapter 15` class data folder. In the left view, the drawing is zoomed in to two manholes that are in close proximity to one another but do not appear to be conflicting. In the right view is a storm manhole that you'll use near the end of this exercise.

2. Click the Sanitary manhole (the one with the *S* inside the circle), and then click Structure Properties on the ribbon. This will open the Structure Properties dialog box.

3. Click the Information tab, and then select C-SSWR – Outline as the Style. Click OK. This style shows the outline of the actual 3D part, which reveals that the manhole is actually much larger than the symbol suggests.

D **is for drainage, a term that is often considered interchangeable with stormwater.**

4. Press Esc to clear the selection of the sanitary manhole. Click the storm manhole (the one with the *D* inside the circle), and then select Structure Properties on the ribbon.

5. Change the Style of this manhole to C-STRM – Outline. With both manholes shown at their actual size, there is an obvious conflict (Figure 15.5).

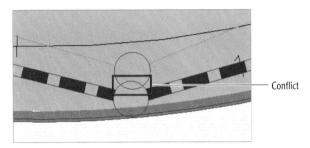

Conflict

FIGURE 15.5 A conflict between two manholes is evident when the style reflects their true size.

6. Press Esc to clear the selection. Pan northward to the beginning of Jordan Court where the new water line ties to the existing water line. Click the tee fitting and the two elbow fittings near the connection point.

7. Right-click and select Properties. Change the Style property to Water 3D. The fittings now appear in their true 3D form as a result of the style change.

8. Press Esc to clear the previous selection but keep the Properties window open. Pan northeast to the other corner of the Jordan Court – Emerson Road intersection, and select the storm manhole there.

9. In the Properties window, change the Style to C-STRM – MH Symbol Plan & Profile. As you select the new style, watch the manhole in the profile view on the right to see its shape change slightly. This is because the block is not an accurate dimensional representation of the manhole. This may be acceptable for some instances, but when you need to see the exact dimensions of a manhole, you would use a different style.

A NOTE ABOUT UNITS

Throughout this chapter, you'll notice that two values are provided for units of measurement. The first value is provided for the imperial system that is used in the United States, and the second value in parentheses is provided for the metric system that is used in many other countries. These values most often represent imperial feet and metric meters. It is important to note that generally only the numeric values are entered in the software, not terms like *feet* or *meters*. Also, you should know that the two numbers provided are not necessarily equal. In most cases, they are similar values that are rounded to work efficiently in their respective measurement systems.

IT'S NOT CALLED 3D FOR NOTHING

The true form of a Civil 3D pipe or structure is a 3D object. For example, a manhole structure is typically some form of cylinder and is often somewhat complex, including tapers, eccentric cylinders, and so on. Some of the ways in which structures can be displayed involve slicing through this shape or showing an outline of it. In the following image, the same structure is shown from a 3D perspective (left), in plan view as an outline (center), and in profile view as a slice through the part (right). By using 3D representations of structures in your drawings, you can design more accurately and ensure that your structures are not conflicting with other underground objects.

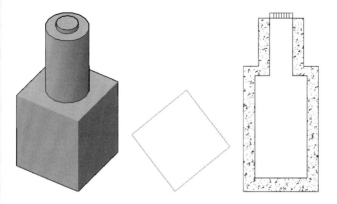

Applying Pipe Styles

A pipe object is a bit simpler than a structure object in that it is essentially the extrusion of a circle, ellipse, or rectangle. Even so, the graphical representation of a pipe is broken down into numerous parts, each of which can be stylized differently. Figure 15.6 shows a pipe and its components in profile view.

You can use pipe styles to control the various pipe components as follows:

Pipe Centerline In addition to controlling the visibility and graphical properties of the pipe centerline such as layer, color, and linetype, you can also set the width of the centerline to match the diameter of the pipe (as well as several other sizing options). The striped appearance of the storm pipes you have seen in the example drawings was achieved by setting the centerline width to the inside pipe diameter and using a dashed linetype.

Inside and Outside Pipe Walls You can use styles to control the visibility and graphical properties of the inner and outer walls.

Pipe End Line This is a line drawn across either end of the pipe. The style can determine whether this line is drawn to the outer pipe wall or inner pipe wall.

Pipe Hatch You can use a pipe style to hatch a pipe across its inside or outside diameter or in the area between the inner and outer walls. The pattern, scale, and rotation of the hatch can be specified as part of the style.

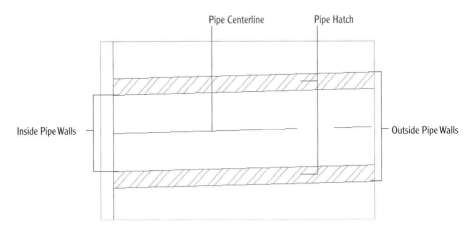

FIGURE 15.6 A pipe in profile view

Crossing Pipe You can use a pipe style to show a pipe as though it is crossing through the profile view rather than oriented parallel to it. This typically takes the form of an ellipse either because of vertical exaggeration or because the pipe crosses through at an angle. This is extremely useful for ensuring that crossing pipes do not conflict with one another. In profile view, you can control the visibility and graphical properties of the crossing pipe components such as inside walls, outside walls, and hatching.

Again, it is not likely that you will be responsible for creating the styles that configure these different display options. However, if you have a basic understanding of what is possible, you can more accurately request the specific styles you need from your CAD manager.

PROFILE VIEW OVERRIDES

The Profile View Properties dialog box has a special Pipe Networks tab that lists all of the pipes and structures in the drawing. You can display any of them in a given profile view by simply checking a box in the Draw column. You can even perform a style override so that a pipe or structure can be displayed in a given profile view using a different style than the one assigned to it in the Pipe Properties dialog box. This is especially handy when you need to show a pipe using a crossing style in one profile view and using a "normal" style in another. The following image shows the Pipe Networks tab of the Profile View Properties dialog box.

To use pipe styles to control the display of pipes in your drawing, follow these steps:

1. Open the drawing named Applying Pipe Styles.dwg located in the Chapter 15 class data folder. In this drawing, the left view is zoomed in to Logan Court where a sanitary pipe crosses a storm pipe, and the same pipes are shown in profile view on the right.

 2. In the left view, click the green pipe labeled SAN. Click Pipe Properties on the ribbon.

3. In the Pipe Properties dialog box, click the Information tab. Change the Style to C-SSWR – Double Line and click OK. The appearance of the pipe changes in the plan view. The SAN label has been turned off, and the pipe is now shown as a double line representing the inside diameter.

4. Press Esc to clear the previous selection, and then click the profile view grid in the right viewport. Click Profile View Properties on the ribbon.

5. In the Profile View Properties dialog box, click the Pipe Networks tab. Scroll down and locate the pipes listed beneath the Storm2 network. One of the pipes is set to Yes in the Draw column. Check the box in the Style Override column for this pipe.

6. In the Pick Pipe Style dialog box, select C-PROF-STRM – Crossing and click OK. Click OK once more to dismiss the Profile View Properties dialog box. You are returned to the drawing, and the storm pipe is now represented as an ellipse. The ellipse is placed at the location where the storm pipe crosses the alignment (Figure 15.7). When you view the storm and sanitary pipes this way, you can clearly see that there is a conflict and that you need to change the design.

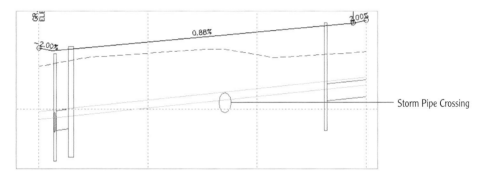

Storm Pipe Crossing

FIGURE 15.7   A storm pipe crossing shown as an ellipse indicates a conflict with a sanitary pipe.

Annotating Pipe Networks in Plan View

For a pipe system to function properly, it must be installed with a considerable amount of accuracy. For this to take place, detailed information must be conveyed to the contractor installing the pipes and structures in the field. The most common way to do this is to add text to your drawing. With stations and offsets you will provide the horizontal location of each structure, and with slopes and elevations you will dictate the depth of each pipe and the slope needed for water to flow through it properly. These values are typically expressed to the nearest hundredth of a foot or thousandth of a meter. It's amazing to even think that a trench can be excavated and a heavy concrete pipe laid within it with such accuracy, but it happens every day.

So far you have worked with functions that create pipes and structures, edit their design, and control their graphical appearance in the drawing. In this section you will learn how to annotate your design, which is arguably even more important than the design itself. The lines and symbols provide a useful picture of the design, but the stations, offsets, elevations, slopes, and so on provided by your annotations will be used to make precise measurements that locate and orient each pipe and structure in the field.

Renaming Pipes and Structures

Many pipe network designs involve a large number of pipes and structures. For this reason, it is good design practice to have a naming and/or numbering system that helps you keep track of these many components. Before labeling pipes and structures, you should spend some time renaming them according to the system you will use.

To rename pipes and structures in your drawing, follow these steps:

1. Open the drawing named Renaming Pipes and Structures.dwg located in the Chapter 15 class data folder.

2. Click the Inlet at station 5+50 (0+170) that is on the east side of Jordan Court. Right-click and select Properties.

3. In the Properties window, change the Name to **INLET-01**.

4. Press Esc to clear the selection, and then click the inlet across the street from INLET-01.

5. In the Properties window, change the Name to **INLET-02**. Press Esc to clear the selection.

6. Click the pipe between INLET-01 and INLET-02 and change its Name to **STM-01**.

7. Change the name of the pipe exiting INLET-02 to the north to **STM-02**.

8. Change the name of the manhole near station 3+50 (0+110) to **STMH-01**.

9. Continue working along the pipe network, renaming the inlets, pipes, and manholes according to this sequence.

10. When you get to the final structure, which is the endwall, name it ENDWALL-01.

11. In Prospector, expand Pipe Networks ➤ Networks ➤ Storm1. Under Storm1, click Pipes. In the item view at the bottom of Prospector, the pipe names should all be updated as shown in Figure 15.8 but may appear in a different order.

12. Under Storm1, click Structures. In the item view at the bottom of Prospector, the values listed in the Name column should match Figure 15.9.

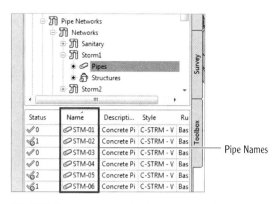

FIGURE 15.8   Revised pipe names shown in the item view of Prospector

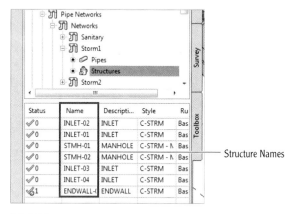

FIGURE 15.9   Revised structure names shown in the item view of Prospector

Creating Labels in Plan View

To create labels in plan view, you use the Add Labels command. You can create labels one by one or for all of the parts of the network at once. After the labels are in place, you may have to drag them to clear areas in the drawing so they can be read more easily.

To create pipe network labels for the storm pipes in your drawing, follow these steps:

1. Open the drawing named Creating Labels In Plan View.dwg located in the Chapter 15 class data folder.

2. On the Annotate tab of the ribbon, click Add Labels.

3. In the Add Labels dialog box, do the following:

    a. For Feature, select Pipe Network.

    b. For Label Type, select Entire Network Plan.

    c. For Pipe Label Style, select C-STRM – Pipe Data (One Line).

    d. For Structure Label Style, select C-STRM – Structure Data.

    e. Click Add.

4. Click any pipe or structure in the storm network near the entrance to Jordan Court. Labels are added on every pipe and structure in the network, which makes the drawing look cluttered (Figure 15.10). This will be addressed in the next exercise.

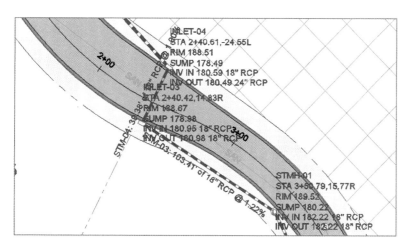

FIGURE 15.10   The initial placement of labels in the drawing is rather cluttered and will require modification.

Editing Labels in Plan View

After creating pipe network labels in your drawing, you may need to do a fair amount of editing to improve their appearance and readability. This can involve assigning different styles and/or moving the labels using their grips.

Certification
Objective

To edit the appearance and placement of pipe network labels in your drawing, complete these steps:

1. Open the drawing named Editing Labels in Plan View.dwg located in the Chapter 15 class data folder.

2. Zoom in to INLET-01, which is on the east side of Jordan Court near station 5+50 (0+170). Click the label, and then click the square grip. Drag the label to an open area in the drawing where it is not conflicting with any other text or linework.

3. Repeat step 2 for INLET-02, which is across the road from INLET-01.

4. Press Esc to clear the previous selection. Click the pipe label for STM-01 (the pipe that connects INLET-01 to INLET-02). Right-click and select Properties.

5. In the Properties window, change the value for Pipe Label Style to C-STRM – Pipe Data (Stacked).

6. With the label still selected, click the square grip and drag it to a clear location in the drawing.

7. Use the square label grip to move the STMH-01, INLET-03, and INLET-04 labels to a clear location in the drawing.

8. Change the style for the STM-04 label to C-STRM – Pipe Data (Stacked) as you did in steps 4 and 5 for the STM-01 label. Drag it to a clear location in the drawing as you did for the STM-01 label in step 6.

 9. Press Esc to clear any label selections. Click the STM-05 label, and then click Flip Label on the ribbon. This places the label on the east side of the pipe, where it is much more readable.

10. With the STM-05 label still selected, click its diamond-shaped grip and drag the label along the pipe to demonstrate the behavior of this grip.

11. Drag the remaining structure labels to clear areas within the drawing and change the label style for STM-06 to C-STRM – Pipe Data (Stacked). With all of the edits to the labels complete, the annotation of the design is much clearer and more readable, as you can see if you compare Figure 15.11 to Figure 15.10.

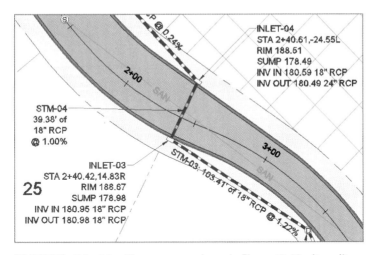

FIGURE 15.11 The same area shown in Figure 15.10 after edits have been made to the labels

Annotating Pipe Networks in Profile View

For most pipe system designs, you will also need to provide labels in profile view because this view is just as important as the plan view for illustrating the design and providing important textual and numerical information about it. Often, you will duplicate the information in plan view, enabling the contractor or the reviewer of the drawing to have the information he or she needs without having to flip back and forth between drawings.

You will not need to rename the pipes and structures for the profile view if you have already done so in plan view. This is because the plan and profile versions of the pipe network are the same objects viewed from different perspectives. In other words, renaming in plan automatically renames in profile view because the two represent a single object.

Creating Labels in Profile View

Once again, creating pipe network labels in profile view is done using the Add Labels dialog box. This time you will use either the Entire Network Profile option to label all the pipes and structures at once or the Single Part Profile option to label them one by one.

To create pipe network labels in the profile view of your drawing, complete the following steps:

1. Open the drawing named Creating Labels in Profile View.dwg located in the Chapter 15 class data folder.

2. On the Annotate tab, click Add Labels.

3. In the Add Labels dialog box, do the following:

   a. For Feature, select Pipe Network.

   b. For Label Type, select Single Part Profile.

   c. For Pipe Label Style, select C-PROF-STRM – Pipe Data.

   d. For Structure Label Style, select C-PROF-STRM – Structure Data (Above).

   e. Click Add.

   Figure 15.12 shows the Add Labels dialog box with these settings.

FIGURE 15.12 The Add Labels dialog box showing the styles selected for labeling pipes and structures in profile view

4. Click the first and last structure in the profile view. This creates labels that are oriented above these two structures. For the remaining two structures, the road profile label is in the way, so the structure labels will be placed below the structures.

5. In the Add Labels dialog box, select C-PROF-STRM – Structure Data (Below) as the Structure Label Style. Click Add.

6. Click the second and third structures. The labels are still placed above the structure, but notice that the formatting is a bit different. You will reposition these structure labels in the next exercise.

7. Click the three pipes in the profile view to place a label above each one. The drawing should now look like Figure 15.13.

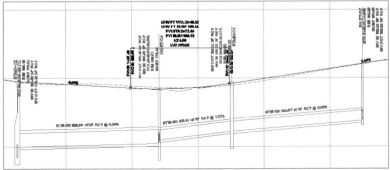

FIGURE 15.13 The initial placement of pipe network labels in profile view

Editing Labels in Profile View

Just as in plan view, you will most likely have to change the initial placement and styles of your profile view labels in order to make them easier to read. As you did before, you can assign different styles to change formatting, and you can use grips to move the labels. For some label styles you have an extra grip located at the *dimension anchor*. The dimension anchor is a floating point that can only be moved vertically. This can be quite useful since you often need to move a label up or down to improve readability while maintaining its horizontal position on the profile view. There are additional settings that enable you to position a label based on the location of a part or the profile view grid. Simply put, the dimension anchor gives you more options and more flexibility with label placement in profile view.

Certification Objective

To edit pipe network labels in the profile view of your drawing, complete these steps:

1. Open the drawing named Editing Labels in Profile View.dwg located in the Chapter 15 class data folder.

2. Click the first structure label (STMH-02), and then click the square grip at the top of the label and drag it upward to a clear area in the drawing. Note that this grip is constrained to up and down movements. This is because the grip is located at the *dimension anchor*.

3. Press Esc to clear the previous selection. Click the second structure label (INLET-04), and then click Label Properties on the ribbon.

4. In the Properties window, change Dimension Anchor Option to Below. The label flips to a downward position but is still overlapping the structure.

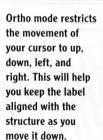

Ortho mode restricts the movement of your cursor to up, down, left, and right. This will help you keep the label aligned with the structure as you move it down.

5. Click the square grip at the top of the label. Then click the Ortho Mode button at the bottom of your screen, and move the label downward until the end of the line is at the bottom of the structure.

6. Repeat steps 3 through 5 for the third structure label (INLET-05). With the label edits you have made, the annotation of the pipe network in profile view has been greatly improved. Compare the result in Figure 15.14 with the initial placement of the labels in 15.13.

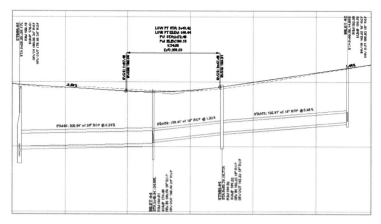

FIGURE 15.14   Pipe network labels in profile view that have been edited to improve readability

Creating Pipe Network Tables

As you have learned in previous chapters, tables are an effective way to convey information about a design. The main advantage of tables is that they organize the information in an orderly fashion, making it easy to read. The disadvantage is that the reader has two places to look for information: the main drawing for the graphical representation of the design and the table for the numerical and textual information. For this reason, tables are typically used if the main drawing would become too cluttered or difficult to read if the textual and numerical information were included in it.

In previous chapters, you created tables for parcels and alignments. One fundamental difference when working with pipe network tables is that they do not need to reference labels in the drawing. For parcels and alignments, you had to create tag labels and then create the tables by selecting those labels. For a pipe network, the table references the pipes and structures directly, so no tag labels are required. However, it is good practice to provide labels in the drawing that identify each pipe and structure so that the reader of the drawing can see how they relate to the table. In the current release of Civil 3D, tables are not available for pressure networks.

To create a pipe network table in your drawing, complete the following steps:

1. Open the drawing named Creating Pipe Network Tables.dwg located in the Chapter 15 class data folder.

 2. On the Annotate tab of the ribbon, click Add Tables ➤ Pipe Network ➤ Add Structure. This opens the Structure Table Creation dialog box.

3. For Table Style, select C-SSWR – Structure & Pipe Data.

4. Verify that By Network is selected and that Sanitary is chosen under Select Network. Click OK.

5. Pick a point in the drawing in some open space. The table will be inserted into the drawing. Zoom in and study the information shown on the table (Figure 15.15).

◀

With these settings, all of the pipes and structures in the Sanitary pipe network will be included in the table. There is also a Multiple Selection option, which enables you to hand pick the items you want represented in the table.

STRUCTURE TABLE			
STRUCTURE NAME:	DETAILS:	PIPE(S) IN:	PIPE(S) OUT
SSMH-01	JORDAN COURT STA 1+44.11, 0.00' RIM = 188.67 SUMP = 189.2		SAN-01, 8" PVC, INV OUT =185.18
SSMH-02	JORDAN COURT STA 3+79.77, 4.19'L RIM = 189.59 SUMP = 178.5	SAN-01, 8" PVC, INV IN =180.61	SAN-02, 8" PVC, INV OUT =180.61
SSMH-03	JORDAN COURT STA 6+73.31, 0.12'L RIM = 193.88 SUMP = 175.5	SAN-02, 8" PVC, INV IN =177.57	SAN-03, 8" PVC, INV OUT =177.57
SSMH-04	JORDAN COURT STA 9+39.29, 0.00' RIM = 193.22 SUMP = 173.0	SAN-03, 8" PVC, INV IN =174.97	SAN-04, 8" PVC, INV OUT =174.97
SSMH-05	JORDAN COURT STA 12+22.00, 9.72'L RIM = 182.07 SUMP = 170.0	SAN-04, 8" PVC, INV IN =172.05	SAN-05, 8" PVC, INV OUT =172.05
SSMH-06	JORDAN COURT STA 15+25.31, 0.00' RIM = 171.23 SUMP = 169.9	SAN-05, 8" PVC, INV IN =166.92	SAN-06, 8" PVC, INV OUT =166.92

FIGURE 15.15   A portion of a structure table created for a sanitary sewer pipe network

6. On the Annotate tab of the ribbon, click Add Labels.

7. In the Add Labels dialog box, do the following:

   a. For Feature, select Pipe Network.

   b. For Label Type, select Entire Network Plan.

   c. For Pipe Label Style, select C-SSWR – Name Only.

   d. For Structure Label Style, select C-SSWR – Name Only.

   e. Click Add.

8. Click any sanitary pipe or structure in the drawing. The entire network will be labeled with the name of each pipe and structure.

9. For each sanitary sewer manhole, click the label and then use the square grip to drag the label into a clear location of the drawing.

10. For each sanitary sewer pipe label, click the label and use its diamond-shaped grip to slide it to a location that is clear of other text or linework. If that is not possible, use the square grip to drag it to a clear area in the drawing. With the labels you have added, a person reading the drawing could match the name of a pipe or structure with information in the table.

THE ESSENTIALS AND BEYOND

In this chapter, you learned how to use styles to create visual distinction between different types of pipes. You also learned how to rename each pipe and structure according to a predetermined naming system and to provide annotation for each pipe and structure in a network. You now know how to use styles to control the appearance and content of the labels to meet various requirements. Finally, you learned how to use tables as an alternate way of organizing and displaying pipe network information.

ADDITIONAL EXERCISE

Open the drawing named Displaying and Annotating Pipe Networks Beyond .dwg located in the Chapter 15 class data folder. This drawing contains the stylization, labels, and tables that you created in earlier exercises in this chapter. In this exercise, use the following guidelines to stylize and label the remaining pipes and structures for the storm sewer:

▶ Apply the C-STRM – Walls in Profile style to all storm pipes in the drawing.

▶ Change all current plan view labels to C-STRM – Name Only for all storm pipes and structures.

▶ Label the remaining storm pipes and structures using the C-STRM – Name Only styles.

▶ Rename the storm pipes and structures to continue the naming and numbering system that you've used so far.

▶ Create a table for each storm sewer pipe network in the drawing. Use the C-STRM – Structure & Pipe Data table style.

Visit www.sybex.com/go/civil2013essentials to download a video of the author completing this exercise. You can also download the Answers to Additional Exercises Appendix which contains even more information about completing this exercise.

CHAPTER 16

Designing New Terrain

With the completion of the pipe network designs, the design of the road is nearly finished. It is now time to move on to the next area of the design, which is the shaping of the land, or *grading*, of the adjacent areas. In Chapter 9, you designed a 3D model of the road in the form of a corridor. This model will serve as a basis for much of the adjacent design that will take place, such as the shaping of individual lots and grading within the stormwater management area.

Each of these areas has unique design objectives. The individual lots will be shaped so that homes can be built on them without requiring significant earthmoving. The stormwater management area will require a pond to serve as a means of collecting and treating the stormwater runoff. These designs will serve as opportunities for you to study the two primary grading tools: *feature lines* and *grading objects*.

▶ **Understanding grading**

▶ **Understanding feature lines**

▶ **Creating feature lines**

▶ **Editing feature lines**

▶ **Understanding grading objects**

▶ **Creating grading objects**

▶ **Editing grading objects**

Understanding Grading

Grading is the term that is most often used to describe the shaping of the land as a construction or design activity. From a design perspective, it is usually considered different than corridor design, which is also a form of terrain shaping but most often used for long, uniform, linear designs such as roads, channels, and so on. The term *grading* is typically used to describe shaping the land in small areas or modeling features that are not long and uniform.

The final product of a grading design will be a surface—the same type of object that you used to model the existing terrain in Chapter 4. As you may recall, to create a surface representing existing ground (EG) elevations, you use breaklines drawn along linear terrain features such as curb lines, ditch lines, and so on. You can use AutoCAD® Civil 3D® software tools to make these breaklines from data collected in the field by surveyors. To create a design surface, you draw breaklines along curbs and ditch lines that are *going* to be built in the field. The process is fundamentally the same as creating an EG surface except that, in this case, the linear features are part of your design. For example, in Figure 16.1 you see the grading design for a pond represented by the red and blue contours. Civil 3D tools were used to draw the edges of this pond according to the required design specifications such as size, shape, depth, and so on. The objects representing the edges were then used to build a pond surface.

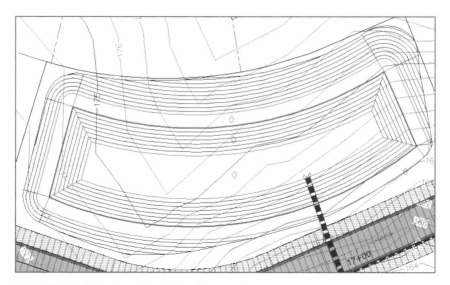

FIGURE 16.1   A grading design for a pond

Understanding Feature Lines

In Chapter 4, you used survey figures to serve as breaklines in the EG surface. For a design surface, you will use *feature lines* for most of your breaklines. Survey figures and feature lines are fundamentally similar: they are three-dimensional linear objects that can be named, stylized, and shown in Prospector. The primary difference is that you design feature lines, whereas survey figures are driven by data collected in the field.

Understanding Sites

When working with feature lines, you have to consider the use of *sites*. Feature lines in the same site are "aware" of one another and will try to interact if the opportunity presents itself. For example, if one feature line crosses over another feature line in the same site, one of the feature lines will bend so that the two share the same elevation at the intersection point. The point where they intersect is called a *split point*. In cases where this interaction needs to be prevented, you can simply place each feature line in its own site. Figure 16.2 shows two crossing feature lines in plan view (left) and 3D view (right). Because these two feature lines are in the same site, a split point is created, causing the red feature line to bend so that it can match the green feature line.

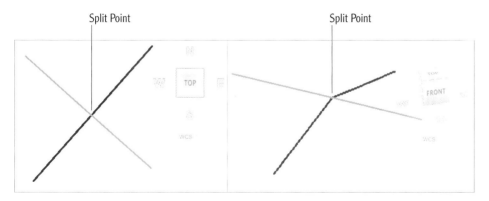

F I G U R E 1 6 . 2   Two crossing feature lines that occupy the same site

Understanding Feature Line Geometry

Feature lines have two types of points that define their geometry: *PIs* and *elevation points*. A PI is represented by a square grip and can be modified in all three dimensions. An elevation point is represented by a circle grip and has a more constrained editing behavior. Figure 16.3 shows both types of grips on the same feature line. The elevation of an elevation point can be edited, but its location in plan view must slide along the feature line geometry determined by the PIs. This constrained behavior is actually quite handy, because you can create many elevation points on a simple plan view shape such as a rectangle.

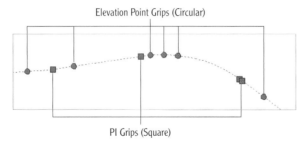

FIGURE 16.3 A plan view of PI and elevation point grips on a feature line

Creating Feature Lines

Certification
Objective

Civil 3D provides a comprehensive set of tools for creating feature lines. They can be drawn "from scratch," by converting an AutoCAD® polyline, or by extracting them from more complex Civil 3D objects such as corridors or profiles. When drawing a feature line from scratch, you must provide the elevations of each PI. For all other methods, the elevations are obtained from the object you have selected.

To use feature lines in your drawing to begin designing some lot grading, follow these steps:

1. Open the drawing named Creating Feature Lines.dwg located in the Chapter 16 class data folder. This drawing is zoomed in to lot 25 and is split into two viewports. The one on the left is a plan view, and the one on the right is a 3D view. You'll also notice that the corridor layer has been thawed to reveal the road corridor.

2. On the Home tab of the ribbon, click Feature Line ➤ Create Feature Line From Corridor. You will be prompted on the command line to select a corridor feature line.

3. Click the edge of the corridor that aligns with the front of lot 25. The Create Feature Line From Corridor dialog box opens.

4. Verify that Site is set to Lot Grading. For Style, select Lot Grading - ROW, and then click OK. The new feature line will be displayed as a thick red line.

5. Press Esc to end the previous command. On the Home tab of the ribbon, click Feature Line ➤ Create Feature Line. The Create Feature Lines dialog box opens.

6. For Style, select Lot Grading, and then click OK. You are prompted to specify the start point.

Note the Create Dynamic Link To Corridor option. If the corridor is modified, this feature line will respond to match the new design.

7. Use the Center object snap to select the center of the red circle at the north corner of lot 25.

8. When you're prompted to specify an elevation, press Enter. You will then be prompted to specify the next point.

Although 0.000 is listed as the elevation, feature line interaction will match this feature line to the corridor feature line at this location.

9. Use the Endpoint object snap to pick the west corner of lot 25. You will be prompted to specify the elevation.

10. At the command line, type **SU** and press Enter to invoke the SUrface option. The Select Surface dialog box will open.

11. Verify that EG is selected and click OK. The default elevation on the command line becomes 190.059 (57.930), which is the elevation of the EG surface at the corner of the lot.

12. Press Enter to accept the elevation. You are prompted to specify the next point.

13. At the command line, type **A** and press Enter to invoke the Arc option. You are prompted to specify the arc endpoint.

14. At the command line, type **S** and press Enter to invoke the Secondpnt option. You are prompted to specify the second point.

15. Use the Nearest object snap to select a point along the back line of lot 25. You are then prompted to select the endpoint of the arc.

16. Use the Endpoint object snap to select the south corner of lot 25. You are then prompted to specify the elevation.

17. At the command line, type **SU** and press Enter to invoke the SUrface option. The elevation at the command line becomes 190.456 (58.027).

18. Press Enter to accept the elevation. You are prompted to specify an arc endpoint.

19. At the command line, type **L** and press Enter to invoke the Line option. You are prompted to specify the next point.

20. Use the Center object snap to pick the circle at the east corner of lot 25.

21. When prompted to specify the elevation, press Enter.

22. Press Esc to end the command. You have drawn a feature line that matches the edge of the corridor at the front of the lot and EG elevations at the back lot corners.

 23. On the Home tab of the ribbon, click Feature Line ➢ Create Feature Lines From Objects. You are prompted to select an object.

24. Click the rectangle at the center of lot 25 and press Enter. The Create Feature Lines dialog box opens.

25. Check the box next to Style and select Lot Grading. Click OK. The feature line is created but is located at elevation zero. If you zoom out in the 3D viewport on the right, you will see the blue rectangle at the location of the lot label and parcel lines.

A Note about Units

Throughout this chapter, you'll notice that two values are provided for units of measurement. The first value is provided for the imperial system that is used in the United States, and the second value in parentheses is provided for the metric system that is used in many other countries. These values most often represent imperial feet and metric meters. It is important to note that generally only the numeric values are entered in the software, not terms like *feet* or *meters*. Also, you should know that the two numbers provided are not necessarily equal. In most cases, they are similar values that are rounded to work efficiently in their respective measurement systems.

Editing Feature Lines

Civil 3D provides an extensive set of tools for editing feature lines. The tools are divided into two categories represented by two panels on the Feature Line ribbon tab: Edit Geometry and Edit Elevations (Figure 16.4).

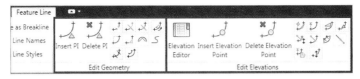

FIGURE 16.4 The Edit Geometry and Edit Elevations panels of the Feature Line ribbon tab

Using Edit Geometry Commands

The feature line geometry editing commands provided by Civil 3D are as follows:

Insert PI   Use this command to insert a new PI at a point you specify. A PI can be edited in all three dimensions.

Delete PI   Use this command to remove PIs from the feature line.

Break   Use this command to break one feature line into two feature lines. You can do this by creating a gap between the two feature lines, or you can have them meet end to end.

Trim   Use this command to shorten a feature line by making it end precisely at another object.

Join   Use this command to join two or more feature lines to make one feature line. If there is a gap between the two feature lines, it must lie within a certain tolerance or they will not be joined.

Reverse   Use this command to change the direction of the feature line. This swaps the beginning and ending points as well as reverses the direction of stationing. This can affect editing and labeling.

Edit Curve   Use this command to change the radius of a feature line curve.

Fillet   Use this command to add a feature line curve where there is currently a PI. The command includes options to set the radius of the curve and to create multiple fillets at once.

Fit Curve   Use this command to replace a series of line segments with an arc. This helps to simplify the feature line by replacing multiple points with an arc. This command differs from the Smooth command because you can control where curves are created. Also, the curves that it creates are static, meaning that they do not change when adjacent geometry changes.

Smooth   Use this command to replace PIs with curves. This command is different from the Fit Curve command because it creates curves for the entire feature line and the curves are dynamic, meaning they remain tangent as the feature line is modified.

Weed   Use this command to simplify a feature line by reducing the number of vertices. The command includes several options for determining which vertices to remove.

Stepped Offset   This command creates a new feature line that is parallel to another. The command includes several options for determining the elevations of the new feature line.

To practice using geometry editing commands to make changes in your drawing, complete these steps:

1. Open the drawing named Editing Feature Line Geometry.dwg located in the Chapter 16 class data folder. In this drawing, two more feature lines have been added for lot 26. You'll begin by adding more PIs and a curve to the back of lot 26.

2. Click the green feature line. If the Edit Geometry panel is not visible, click Edit Geometry on the ribbon.

3. Click Insert PI. When you're prompted to specify a point, use the Center object snap to select the center of the blue circle. You will be prompted to specify an elevation.

4. On the command line, type **S** and press Enter to invoke the Surface option. The Select Surface dialog box will open.

5. Verify that EG is selected and click OK.

6. Press Enter to accept the elevation shown on the command line. You will be prompted to specify the next point.

7. Use the Center object snap to select the center of the red circle. You will be prompted to specify an elevation.

8. On the command line, type **S** and press Enter to invoke the Surface option. Press Enter again to accept the surface elevation. Additional PIs have been added, but you still need to address the missing curve.

9. Press Esc twice to clear the previous command. Click the green feature line, and then click Fit Curve on the ribbon. You are prompted to specify a point.

10. At the command line, type **P** and press Enter to invoke the Points option. You are prompted to specify the start point.

11. Use the Center object snap to select the center of the blue circle.

12. Use the Center object snap to select the center of the red circle. Press Esc twice to end the command and clear the selection. A curve is added to match the geometry of the back lot line. Next you will break the feature line for lot 25 and join it to the feature line for lot 26.

13. Click any feature line in the drawing, and then click Break on the ribbon. You are prompted to select an object to break.

14. Click the blue perimeter feature line for lot 25. You are prompted to specify a second break point.

15. Type **F** and press Enter to invoke the First point option.

16. Use the Endpoint object snap to select the back corner where lots 25 and 26 meet. You are prompted to select the second break point.

17. Repeat the previous step to select the same point again. Press Esc twice to end the command and clear the selection. The drawing does not appear different, but the blue feature line has been broken into two feature lines.

18. Click the blue feature line at the back of lot 25, and then click Join on the ribbon.

19. Click the green feature line. The green changes to blue, indicating that the feature lines are joined to create a single feature line (Figure 16.5).

> ◀
>
> By choosing the same location for the first and second point, you break the feature line without creating a gap.

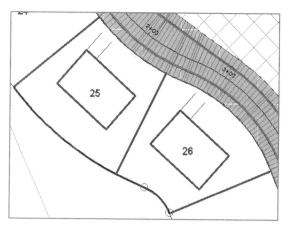

FIGURE 16.5 The result of editing the feature lines in this exercise

Using Edit Elevation Commands

The feature line elevation editing commands provided by Civil 3D are as follows:

Elevation Editor   Use this command to open the Grading Elevation Editor tab in Panorama. From here, you can perform a number of edits while viewing all of the feature line data at once.

Insert Elevation Point   Use this command to create one or more elevation points on a feature line.

Delete Elevation Point   Use this command to simplify a feature line by removing elevation points from it.

Quick Elevation Edit   Use this command to interactively edit the elevations and slopes of a feature line. The command uses tooltips to show you elevations, slopes, and slope directions.

Edit Elevations   Use this command to edit individual points and segments on the command line.

Set Grade/Slope Between Points   Use this command to set a constant grade through multiple points. You do this by specifying a start point and an endpoint, and the command calculates the elevations of any points in between.

Insert High/Low Elevation Point   Use this command to have Civil 3D calculate a high or low point on a feature line. You do this by selecting two points and specifying the slope that should be projected from each point. Civil 3D will then calculate the intersection of the two slopes and create a point at the correct location and elevation. This command is especially useful for setting high and low points along curb lines to control drainage.

Raise/Lower By Reference   Use this command to adjust all of the elevations of a feature line simultaneously by specifying a reference point and an elevation difference.

Set Elevation By Reference   Use this command to calculate the elevations of individual points on a feature line by specifying a reference point and elevation difference for each point.

Adjacent Elevations By Reference   Use this command to project the elevations from one feature line to another while providing an elevation difference, if desired. This command is especially useful for parallel feature lines such as curb lines or wall lines.

Grade Extension By Reference   Use this command to calculate the elevation of a point on a feature line by extending the grade of another feature line.

Elevations From Surface   Use this command to project a feature line onto a surface. This command has the option to create elevation points at locations where the feature line crosses triangle edges in the surface. When this option is used, the feature line becomes an exact match to the terrain represented by the surface.

Raise/Lower   Use this command to edit all of the elevations of a feature line simultaneously by providing an elevation difference.

To use the elevation editing commands to modify feature lines in your drawing, follow these steps:

1. Open the drawing named `Editing Feature Line Elevations.dwg` located in the `Chapter 16` class data folder.

2. Click any feature line in the drawing. If the Edit Elevations panel is not visible, click Edit Elevations on the ribbon.

3. Click Quick Elevation Edit. Place your cursor over the north corner of lot 25. The elevation on the tooltip should read 189.297′ (57.695m).

4. Place your cursor at each corner of lot 25 and take note of the elevations. The highest elevation is the south corner, which is at 190.456′ (58.027m). The goal is to make sure that water flows away from the building pad (the blue rectangle). To do this, you will place the building pad at an elevation slightly higher than the highest lot corner.

YOUR PAD OR MINE?

For land development projects that involve buildings, it is common for the contractor to prepare a flat area where the building will be placed. This is often referred to as the *building pad*. In a residential development such as the example in this book, a building pad is often prepared for each lot to accommodate the home that will be built.

---

5. Press Esc twice to end the current command and clear the feature line selection. Click the building pad feature line of lot 25.

6. On the ribbon, click Raise/Lower By Reference. You will be prompted to specify a reference point.

7. Invoke the Endpoint object snap and place your cursor on the south corner of lot 25, but do not click the mouse.

8. Look at the coordinate readout in the lower-left corner of your screen. If the third value in the coordinate readout is 0.0000, press the Tab key. Keep pressing the Tab key until the value reads 190.4564 (58.027), as shown in Figure 16.6. The Tab key allows you to toggle between the parcel geometry, which is at elevation zero, and the feature lines, which are at true design elevations.

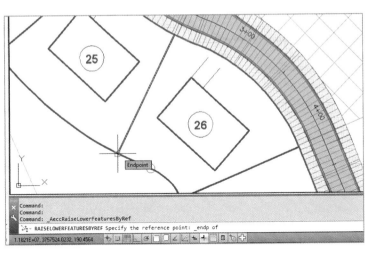

FIGURE 16.6 Using the Tab key and coordinate readout to select the correct elevation

9. With the proper value shown in the coordinate readout, click the point to snap to it. You will be prompted to specify a point on the building pad feature line.

10. Click the south corner of the building pad feature line. When you're prompted to specify the grade, type 2 and press Enter. This places the building pad at an elevation that creates a 2 percent downward slope from the south corner of the building pad to the south corner of the lot. All other slopes will be steeper because the other lot corners are lower than the south corner.

11. Press Esc to clear the previous selection. Click the feature line that represents the rear of the lots, and then click Elevations From Surface on the ribbon. The Set Elevations From Surface dialog box opens.

Notice that there are only five square grips along the rear lot line. We'll take a look at this again after the next few steps.

12. Verify that EG is selected and that the box next to Insert Intermediate Grade Break Points is checked. Click OK.

13. At the command line, type **P** and then press Enter to invoke the Partial option.

14. Select the feature line representing the rear of the lots. You will be prompted to specify the start point.

15. Click the west corner of lot 25, and then click the south corner of lot 26 to specify the endpoint. A series of green circle markers will appear on the feature line.

16. Press Enter to complete the command. There are now a number of circular grips visible on the feature line (Figure 16.7). These represent additional elevation points that were required for the feature line to match the surface precisely.

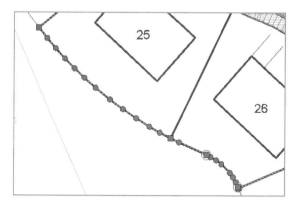

FIGURE 16.7 Circular grips mark elevation points added to match the feature line to the surface.

Understanding Grading Objects

At times you will want Civil 3D to calculate the location, shape, and elevations of feature lines rather than designing them yourself. Examples of this situation would be projecting a slope through a certain distance or elevation or finding the intersection of a slope with a surface. For these cases, Civil 3D provides the *grading object*. Figure 16.8 shows a pond design composed of several grading objects, each one using a different set of parameters to calculate an edge that defines the shape of the pond.

A grading object is a collection of feature lines whose geometry, location, and elevation are calculated by Civil 3D based on design parameters you have applied to a feature line. That's quite a daunting definition, so here's a look at it broken down into several parts:

▶ A grading object is a *collection* of feature lines (and other things not important to name at this time), so it behaves as one object. The feature lines in this collection have many of the same characteristics as individual feature lines, as well as some unique characteristics that relate to being part of a grading object.

▶ Everything about a grading object is calculated by Civil 3D. Very similar to the way that Civil 3D calculates a corridor, grading objects cannot be edited directly, but they respond automatically when their design parameters are edited. This is a little different from an individual feature line, which you can grip edit at will.

▶ The design parameters are assigned to a feature line by you. To create a grading object, you start by picking a feature line in the drawing. The design parameters you provide such as slope, distance, elevation, and so on are projected from this feature line to create the resulting grading object. A feature line that serves as the basis for a grading object is called a *baseline*.

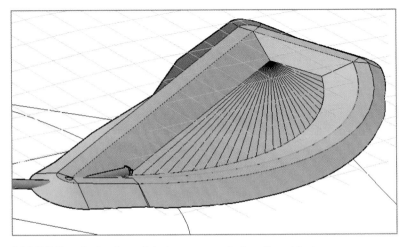

FIGURE 16.8 A pond design composed of grading objects

Understanding Grading Criteria

The design parameters that you apply to a grading object can require multiple pieces of information. For this reason, Civil 3D utilizes a system of *grading criteria*, which enables you to refer to a set of instructions by name rather than having to re-specify them for each grading design. For example, you might have criteria with the name Curb, which instruct Civil 3D to project upward at a very steep slope for a very short distance. Similar criteria with names like Pond Embankment, Ditch Slope, and so on might be created alongside your Curb criteria. You can organize your named grading criteria even further by grouping them into *grading criteria sets*. For example, you might have one criteria set for pond grading, another for parking lots, another for athletic fields, and so on. Figure 16.9 shows grading criteria that would be used to create the inside slope of a pond.

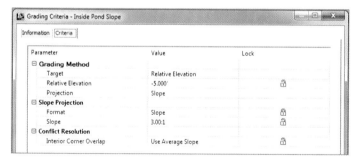

FIGURE 16.9   An example of grading criteria typically used for the inside slope of a pond

Understanding Grading Groups

A *grading group* is a named collection of grading objects that enables you to perform certain important functions with multiple grading objects simultaneously. For example, you can create a surface from a grading group or calculate cut and fill values by comparing a grading group to a surface in the drawing.

Understanding Grading Objects and Sites

Like feature lines, grading objects must exist within a Civil 3D site. When two or more grading objects occupy the same site, there is potential for them to interact. There is also the potential for grading objects to interact with other feature lines in the same site. This interaction can benefit some designs, but there are cases where this interaction will cause the design to be incorrect. Therefore, it is important to proactively manage sites while you're working with grading objects and feature lines.

Creating Grading Objects

You begin creating a grading object by launching the Grading Creation Tools command. This opens the Grading Creation Tools toolbar (Figure 16.10), which is similar to the Alignment Layout Tools and the Pipe Network Layout Tools toolbars that you used in previous chapters. Like those toolbars, the Grading Creation Tools toolbar provides the commands to configure your design, create new design objects, and edit those objects.

Certification
Objective

FIGURE 16.10   The Grading Creation Tools toolbar

To create grading objects in your drawing, complete the following steps:

1. Open the drawing named `Creating Grading Objects.dwg` located in the Chapter 16 class data folder. The drawing is zoomed in to the proposed location of a stormwater detention pond. You will use grading objects to build a model of the pond, starting with the green feature line that represents the top inside edge of the pond.

I THOUGHT DETENTION WAS A BAD THING

The pond that you design in this exercise is referred to as a *detention pond*. Its function is to slow down the release of stormwater to the same rate that existed prior to development. When it rains, runoff is collected by the inlets and conveyed to the pond through underground pipes. The pond outlet is restricted to reduce the flow of water. This causes the water to back up, hence the need for a pond to *detain* it. After the storm is over, the water will stay in the pond for a bit until it empties out.

What's the reason for all this? Before replacing grass, soil, and forest with pavement, runoff water was released from this area of land at a relatively slow rate. Now, less of the water is being absorbed, and it is traveling much faster along the pavement and concrete that carry it. This increase in flow and velocity causes erosion damage and must be mitigated. A common way to accomplish this mitigation is by including a pond in your design.

2. On the Home tab of the ribbon, click Grading ➤ Grading Creation Tools. The Grading Creation Tools toolbar will open.

3. Click Set The Grading Group. The Site dialog box will open.

4. Select Pond and click OK. The Create Grading Group dialog box will open.

5. Type **Pond** in the Name field. Verify that Automatic Surface Creation is turned on, and then click OK. The Create Surface dialog box opens.

6. Click OK to dismiss the Create Surface dialog box.

7. Expand the criteria list and choose Grade To Relative Elevation, as shown in Figure 16.11.

8. Expand the list of creation commands and click Create Grading, as shown in Figure 16.12. You will be prompted to select a feature.

FIGURE 16.11   Selecting grading criteria on the Grading Creation Tools toolbar

FIGURE 16.12   Selecting the Create Grading command

9. Click the green feature line. When you're prompted to select the grading side, click a point inside the feature line.

10. Press Enter to apply the grading to the entire length. You are prompted for the relative elevation value.

11. Type -7 (-2.13) and press Enter. When you're prompted for format, press Enter to accept the default of Slope.

12. When you're prompted for slope, type 3 and press Enter to apply a slope of 3:1. After a pause, a new grading object is created that represents the inside slope of the pond. A surface is also created and is displayed as red and blue contours in plan view.

13. Expand the list of creation tools and select Create Infill. Click a point near the center of the pond. The 3D view now shows that the pond has a bottom.

14. Select the Grade To Distance criteria.

15. Expand the list of creation tools and select Create Grading. When you're prompted to select a feature, click the same green feature line that you picked in step 9.

16. When prompted for the grading side, pick a point outside the pond. Press Enter to apply the grading to the entire length.

17. Press Enter to accept the default distance of 10.000′ (3.000m). When you're prompted for format, type G to invoke the Grade option, and press Enter.

The infill created in step 13 is a special type of grading object that simply fills a void in a grading group. It does not provide additional elevation points; instead, it enables the grading group surface to extend across an open area. An infill can be placed in any closed area created by one or more feature lines that occupy the same site.

18. Press Enter to accept the default grade of 2 percent. A new grading object is created that represents the berm of the pond.

19. On the Grading Creation Tools toolbar, click Set The Target Surface. In the Select Surface dialog box, select EG and click OK.

20. Select the Grade To Surface criteria. Expand the list of creation tools and select Create Grading.

21. Click the outside edge of the grading object created in step 18. Press Enter at all prompts to accept the default values. This creates a 3:1 daylight slope that intersects with the EG surface. This also completes the surface for the pond as indicated by the red and blue contours (Figure 16.13).

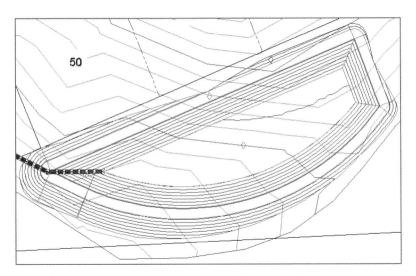

FIGURE 16.13   Contours representing the pond design

Editing Grading Objects

Because of the dynamic nature of grading objects, any edits to a feature line that serves as a grading object baseline will automatically trigger an update of the grading object. This makes most grading object editing fairly easy. In addition, there are two tools that you can use to edit the criteria that were used to create the grading object: Grading Editor and Edit Grading. The Grading Editor command opens Panorama, enabling you to edit the criteria in a table format. The Edit Grading command is a command-line interface.

To edit grading objects in your drawing, follow these steps:

1. Open the drawing named Editing Grading Objects.dwg located in the Chapter 16 class data folder.

2. Click the green feature line that represents the inside edge of the pond berm. Click the grip at the northeast corner, and then use the Center object snap to select the center of the red circle to the east. The grading object will recalculate based on the new shape of its baseline. The grading group surface will also update, enabling the contours to match the new shape as well.

3. With the feature line still selected, click Raise/Lower on the Edit Geometry panel of the ribbon. You will be prompted to specify an elevation difference.

If the Edit Elevations panel is not visible, click Edit Elevations on the ribbon.

4. Type -1 (-0.3) and press Enter to lower the feature line by 1′ (0.3 m). The entire grading group and associated surface will update. Now the bottom of the pond is too low and will need to be raised.

5. Press Esc to clear the selection of the feature line. On the Modify tab of the ribbon, click Grading.

6. Click Grading Editor, and then click a point within the inside embankment of the pond. The edges of the grading object are highlighted to help you make your selection.

7. On the Grading Editor tab of Panorama, type -6 (-1.83) for Relative Elevation and press Enter. The grading group is updated and the pond bottom has been raised by 1′ (0.3 m).

8. On the Grading tab of the ribbon, click Edit Grading. Click a point within the area representing the top of the berm.

9. When you're prompted to specify a distance, type 12 (3.6) and press Enter.

10. Press Enter twice to accept the default Format of Grade and the default Grade of 2 percent. Press Enter a third time to end the command. The grading group and surface update to accommodate the wider berm. The pond model now reflects the wider berm along with the shape and elevation changes made in earlier steps (Figure 16.14).

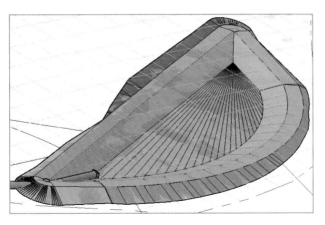

FIGURE 16.14 The pond model after several edits

THE ESSENTIALS AND BEYOND

In this chapter, you learned how to use Civil 3D to shape the land. You saw how you can use feature lines to draw new breaklines to represent the edges of landforms such as curbs, ditches, and embankment edges. You should now have an understanding of the tools that are used to create these feature lines and also to modify them.

For cases where you need Civil 3D to calculate the locations and elevations of new break-lines, you learned how to use grading objects to create complex grading models, such as the pond that you built and modified in the last two exercises. You have learned how the dynamic nature of grading objects enables you to make edits and generate surfaces with minimal time and effort.

Use the following additional exercise to apply what you have learned to several similar designs.

ADDITIONAL EXERCISE

Open the drawing named Grading Beyond.dwg located in the Chapter 16 class data folder. This drawing contains an alternate layout for the detention pond in a different location. Complete the following tasks:

1. Create a pond design similar to the one you created in the last two exercises. A feature line has been provided between lots 62 and 66, which represents the top inside edge of the pond.

2. Continue grading lots 27, 28, and 29 in the same manner that you graded lots 25 and 26.

3. Create a surface from the feature lines that are used to define the grading for lots 25–29.

Visit www.sybex.com/go/civil2013essentials to download a video of the author completing this exercise. You can also download the Answers to Additional Exercises Appendix which contains even more information about completing this exercise.

CHAPTER 17

Analyzing, Displaying, and Annotating Surfaces

In Chapter 16, you experienced a few examples of designing new terrain in the form of lot grading and pond design. With more time, you would have completed the shaping of all the lots, resulting in a grading design for the entire project. With all of the major grading design components complete (roads, lots, and pond in this example), it is now time to combine them into one complete design. Once you have done this, you can analyze the design to ensure that it meets several additional design and construction requirements. This analysis may result in the need for an adjustment to the design, at which time you begin an iterative process: design, analyze, adjust, design, analyze, adjust, and so on. You will repeat this cycle until the design is the best that time and resources permit. Once the design is optimized, you can then provide annotation that provides the necessary information for the contractor to build your design of the new shape of the land.

▶ **Combining design surfaces**

▶ **Analyzing design surfaces**

▶ **Calculating earthwork volumes**

▶ **Labeling design surfaces**

Combining Design Surfaces

In Chapter 16, if you completed the additional exercise under "The Essentials and Beyond," you created a new surface that represents the grading of individual lots. Had you continued working on this for a few hours, you would have eventually finished all of the lots, creating a surface that covered nearly the entire project. You also created a pond design that resulted in a surface of its own. In Chapter 9, you created a corridor surface to represent the model of the roads. This approach of designing the shape of the terrain in parts is common and recommended. For even the most talented designer, it is difficult to design all aspects of a project at once. It is easier, and often more efficient, to divide the design into "mini-designs" such as the road, lots, and pond that you experienced for yourself.

Once the parts are in place, it is then time to combine them into one "master" surface. To accomplish this, you use a simple but very powerful capability of AutoCAD® Civil 3D® surfaces: *pasting*. Just as you are able to paste a paragraph of text into a document, you are also able to paste one surface into another. The similarities between surfaces and documents end there, however. For example, when you paste one surface into another, the pasted version is a "live" copy of the original, meaning that if the original is modified, the pasted version is modified also. To find the command to paste surfaces, right-click Edits within a surface in Prospector or choose the Surfaces ribbon tab (Figure 17.1).

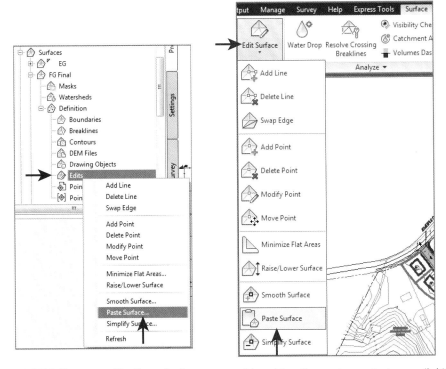

FIGURE 17.1   The Paste Surface command found in a Prospector context menu (left) and the Surface ribbon tab (right)

When working with multiple pasted surfaces, you can leverage the order in which they are pasted to achieve a desired result. The way this works is that when two overlapping surfaces are pasted, the second one will overwrite the first in the area where they overlap. The order in which surfaces are pasted can be controlled on the Definition tab of the Surface Properties dialog box (Figure 17.2). Here the order of operations can be rearranged, not just for pasting surfaces but for other operations as well.

Arrow Buttons

Order of Operations

F I G U R E 1 7 . 2   The order of operations can be changed using the arrow buttons. This can affect the result of pasting multiple surfaces together.

To see for yourself how to combine design surfaces, follow these steps:

1. Open the drawing named Combining Surfaces.dwg located in the Chapter 17 class data folder. In this drawing, all of the lot grading design is complete, as shown by the blue, red, and green feature lines. There is also a small area between lots 73 and 76 where a grading group was used to calculate daylighting.

2. In Prospector, expand Surfaces and note the surfaces that are listed there. Right-click Surfaces and select Create Surface. This opens the Create Surface dialog box.

3. Enter **FG Final** in the Name field and select Contours 1' and 5' (Design) (Contours 0.5m and 2.5m (Design)) as the Style. Click OK. The new FG Final surface will be listed in Prospector.

4. In Prospector, expand Surfaces ➢ FG Final ➢ Definition. Right-click Edits and select Paste Surface. The Select Surface To Paste dialog box opens.

5. Select Lots – Exterior, and then click OK. Contours representing the grading for exterior lots appear in the drawing. Zoom in to the interior lot area and note the haphazard contours extending across the road and through this area.

Make sure your background color is set to white before completing the exercises in this chapter.

All of the surfaces except EG have a style of _No Display assigned to them. That is why there are no design contours shown in the drawing.

6. Click one of the red or blue contours to select the surface, and then click Edit Surface ➤ Paste Surface on the ribbon.

7. Select Road FG and click OK. Within the road areas, the contours you saw in step 5 are replaced with contours that accurately represent the road elevations. The interior lot area has no contours because this area has a hide boundary applied to it within the Road FG surface.

8. Repeat steps 6 and 7, this time selecting the Pond surface. Contours now appear in the area of the pond.

9. Repeat steps 6 and 7, this time selecting the Lots – Interior surface. Contours are now shown for the interior lot grading, but the pond area has been overwritten with inaccurate contours. You'll fix this in the next few steps by changing the order in which the surfaces are pasted.

10. Click one of the red or blue contours and select Surface Properties on the ribbon. The Surface Properties dialog box opens.

11. On the Definition tab, click Add Surface Lots – Interior and then click the up-arrow icon (Figure 17.3). This moves the Lots – Interior surface above the Pond surface in the paste order.

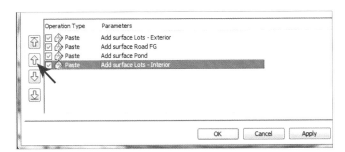

FIGURE 17.3 Clicking the up arrow will change the order of operations so that the Lots - Interior surface is pasted before the Pond surface.

12. Click OK, and then click Rebuild The Surface. The lot grading contours and the correct pond contours are now shown. This is an example of the importance of managing the order of pasted surfaces to achieve the desired result.

13. Repeat steps 6 and 7, this time selecting the Lot Daylight surface. Contours are now shown in the area between lots 73 and 76, and all design grading for the project is now represented as one surface (Figure 17.4).

FIGURE 17.4 Grading for the entire project is represented by one surface.

A NOTE ABOUT UNITS

Throughout this chapter, you'll notice that two values are provided for units of measurement. The first value is provided for the imperial system that is used in the United States, and the second value in parentheses is provided for the metric system that is used in many other countries. These values most often represent imperial feet and metric meters. It is important to note that generally only the numeric values are entered in the software, not terms like *feet* or *meters*. Also, you should know that the two numbers provided are not necessarily equal. In most cases, they are similar values that are rounded to work efficiently in their respective measurement systems.

MODULAR DESIGN

In the preceding exercise, you saw five design surfaces listed within Prospector, each representing its own mini-design. The origin of these surfaces is as follows:

Lots Exterior   This surface is created from the feature lines used to grade all of the lots except those enclosed between Jordan Court, Madison Lane, and Logan Court. The feature lines were added to the Lots Exterior surface as breaklines. A polyline was drawn along the back edges of the lots and added to the surface as an outer boundary. The surface was allowed to triangulate across the road and interior lot areas. The following image shows the Lots Exterior surface in 3D.

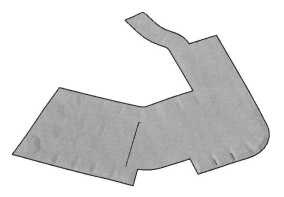

Lots Interior   This surface is created from the feature lines used to grade all of the lots enclosed between Jordan Court, Madison Lane, and Logan Court. The feature lines were added to the surface as breaklines. A polyline was drawn along the front edges of the lots and added to the surface as an outer boundary. The surface was allowed to triangulate across the pond area. The following image shows the Lots Interior surface in 3D.

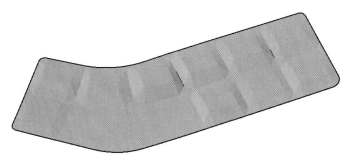

MODULAR DESIGN *(Continued)*

Pond This surface is created from the grading group used to design the pond south of lots 69 and 70. The following image shows the Pond surface in 3D.

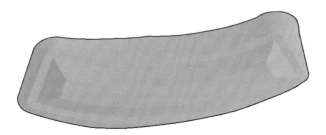

Road FG This surface is created from the road corridor. The following image shows the Road FG surface in 3D view.

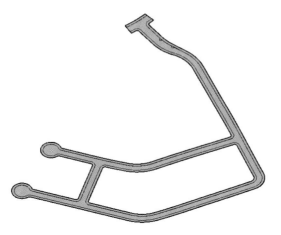

Lot Daylight This surface is created from a grading group used to design the daylighting between lots 73 and 76. It is shown in the following graphic in red along with the Road FG surface and Lot Exterior surface in tan.

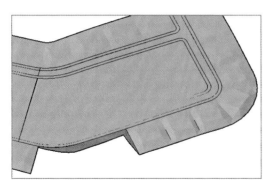

(Continues)

MODULAR DESIGN   *(Continued)*

In the preceding exercise, you combined all of these surfaces to create a single finished ground surface as shown in 3D view in the following image.

Analyzing Design Surfaces

There is much more that you can do with a Civil 3D surface than just display contours. Unfortunately, I cannot discuss them all in a single chapter, let alone a section within a chapter, but I will cover several of the most commonly used surface analysis features available within Civil 3D. I've grouped these features into three categories: surface analysis, hydrology tools, and quick profiles.

Using Surface Analysis

A watershed is a discrete area of land that directs the flow of runoff to a specific point or area.

In the context of this category, *surface analysis* refers to the functions that appear on the Analysis tab of the Surface Properties dialog box. Here you can perform detailed analyses relating to elevations, slopes, contours, and watersheds (Figure 17.5). The results of an analysis are shown graphically within the drawing, and depending on the type of analysis, can appear as shaded areas, arrows, contours lines, or even 3D areas—all color-coded for the identification of different ranges of data. In addition, you can create a legend for an analysis to help convey the meaning of each color.

Performing an analysis can be thought of as a two-step process. The first step is to create the analysis ranges on the Surface Properties dialog box. This step does not produce anything visible in the drawing, but it creates the data that will be used to generate graphical output. To create something visible in the drawing you must perform the second step, which is to assign a style to the surface that displays the components of that analysis. For example, to display the slope arrows for a surface, you must first create the slope ranges and then apply a surface style within which the slope arrow display is turned on.

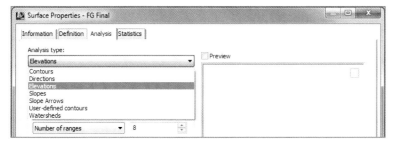

FIGURE 17.5 The types of analysis available on the Analysis tab of the Surface Properties dialog box

To perform a slope analysis of the design grading for the example project, follow these steps:

1. Open the drawing named Analyzing Surfaces.dwg located in the Chapter 17 class data folder. This drawing contains the FG Final surface that you created in the previous exercise.

2. Click one of the red or blue contours in the drawing, and then click Surface Properties on the ribbon. The Surface Properties dialog box opens.

3. On the Analysis tab, select Slopes as the Analysis Type.

4. Under Ranges, enter a value of 4 in the Number field.

5. Click the Run Analysis icon (downward-pointing arrow). Four ranges are listed within the Range Details section of the dialog box.

6. Edit the slope ranges as follows:

ID	Minimum Slope	Maximum Slope	Colors
1	0.0000%	2.0000%	2
2	2.0000%	10.0000%	3
3	10.0000%	34.0000%	30
4	34.0000%	1158.7766%	1

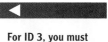

For ID 3, you must enter the Maximum Slope first and then the Minimum Slope.

7. Click the Information tab and change the Style to Slope Banding (2D). Click OK and then press Esc to clear the selection of the surface. As shown in Figure 17.6, the drawing displays colored areas indicating excessively flat slopes (0%–2%) in yellow, moderate slopes (2%–10%) in green, steep slopes (10%–34%) in orange, and excessively steep slopes (>34%) in red. The red areas are of particular concern, because they represent slopes that are not stable with the type of soil found on this site.

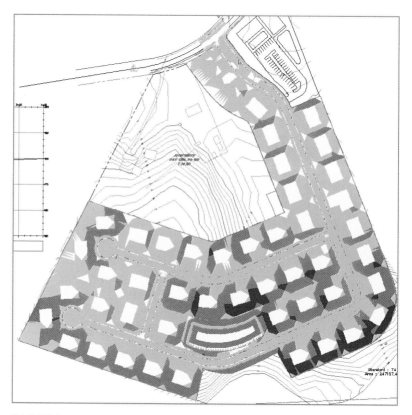

FIGURE 17.6 Colored areas indicate different slope ranges within the FG Final surface.

8. Click one of the colored areas to select the surface, and then right-click and select Display Order ➢ Send To Back. This allows the feature lines and other drawing graphics to be displayed on top of the colored shading rather than hidden beneath it.

MORE ABOUT SLOPES

Slopes are a significant aspect of land development design. For every project, certain slope ranges are targeted for specific purposes, and the ranges can vary from project to project. For our project, we're interested in knowing where there are excessively flat areas (yellow, 0%–2%), because there could be potential drainage problems in these areas. Yellow areas on building pads are OK, because there will be a building there, but yellow areas on the road could represent drainage problems. Green areas (2%–10%) represent slopes that can be traveled across safely by foot or with a vehicle. We would want the entire road surface to be green as well as enough area between a building pad and the street to install a driveway. Orange areas (10%–34%) represent places where traveling could not take place, but the slopes are still stable and safe from collapse. In this project, we would expect the pond embankments and the backs of some of the lots to be orange. Orange areas on the road or entire front yards that are orange would not be acceptable. Finally, red areas represent slopes that are too steep for the soil to support. These areas would be subject to collapse and would be considered dangerous. Red areas must be removed.

9. Press Esc to clear the previous selection. Click the blue rectangular feature line at the center of lot 70. On the Edit Elevations panel of the ribbon, click Raise/Lower.

If the Edit Elevations panel is not visible, click Edit Elevations.

10. When you are prompted on the command line to specify an elevation difference, type -5 (-1.524) and press Enter. After a pause, the surface rebuilds and the red area within lot 70 is removed. The front yard is still green, which means it is within the slope range to install a driveway (Figure 17.7).

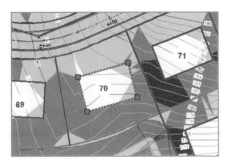

FIGURE 17.7 Lot 70 after the building pad was adjusted downward to eliminate the steep slope

Using Hydrology Tools

Civil 3D provides two very useful tools to help you analyze the drainage performance of your surface: Water Drop and Catchment. The Water Drop tool shows you the theoretical path of a drop of rain as it flows downhill from a location that you specify. By analyzing this path, you can determine the direction of flow and find low spots where water will stop flowing and begin to accumulate. A catchment shows you the area that drains to a point that you specify. This is helpful for stormwater management design such as determining how large an inlet opening needs to be based on the size of the area contributing runoff to it.

To use the hydrology tools to analyze the design surface for the example project, follow these steps:

1. Open the drawing named Using Hydrology Tools.dwg located in the Chapter 17 class data folder. In this drawing, the feature line layers have been turned off. Also, a new surface named EG-FG Composite has been provided. This surface was made by creating a new surface and pasting EG and FG Final into it. The purpose of this surface is to enable the analysis of the entire project as though it has already been built.

2. Click the Analyze tab of the ribbon, and then click Flow Paths ➢ Water Drop. You are prompted to select a surface.

3. Press Enter to indicate that you would like to select the surface from a list. The Select A Surface dialog box opens.

4. Click EG-FG Composite, and then click OK. The Water Drop dialog box opens.

5. Click OK to close the Water Drop dialog box. Click a point within lot 29 near the road. A blue water drop path is drawn from lot 29, runs down the curb line, and then stops at the inlet near station 2+50 (0+080).

6. With the Select point: prompt still active, click a point near the southeast corner of lot 23. This water drop path travels toward the west along the curb line of Madison Lane. It ends at the inlet near station 7+25 (0+220) on Madison Lane.

7. Press Esc to clear the current command. On the Analyze tab of the ribbon, click Catchments ➢ Create Catchment From Surface. You are prompted to specify a discharge point.

8. Use the Center object snap to choose the center of the red circle at the end of the second water drop path you created. The Create Catchment From Surface dialog box opens.

9. Select EG-FG Composite for Surface and click OK. A blue outline indicates the shape of the catchment area that drains to the inlet at the location you selected.

Using a Quick Profile

In Chapter 7, you learned how to create surface profiles using alignments and surfaces. You also learned that a profile is a useful tool that enables you to slice through your design and view it from a different perspective. Well, what if you could create a profile from a whole list of entities that are readily available in your drawing? You can, and the command that does it is called Quick Profile.

The Quick Profile command creates a temporary profile along the path of a line, arc, polyline, parcel line, feature line, survey figure, or a selected series of points. Once you have selected the object to represent the path, you are presented with a dialog box that enables you to select any surface in the drawing that you would like to display in the temporary profile view. If you have selected a 3D object such as a 3D polyline or feature line, you will also be given the option to represent that object as a profile.

If you modify the object you used to define the path of the profile, the quick profile view will update automatically. This is a great tool for viewing slices of your design at many different locations very efficiently. Quick profiles are intended to be temporary and will disappear whenever you save the drawing.

To create a quick profile in your drawing, follow these steps:

1. Open the drawing named Using a Quick Profile.dwg located in the Chapter 17 class data folder. In this drawing, there is a heavy red polyline that crosses through the entire project at the location of the pond.

2. Click the Analyze tab of the ribbon, and then click Quick Profile.

3. When you are prompted to select an object, click the heavy red polyline that crosses through the pond. The Create Quick Profiles dialog box will open.

4. Uncheck the box next to Select All Surfaces; then check the boxes next to EG and FG Final. Select Design Profile as the Profile Style for FG Final.

5. Click OK, and then click a point in an open area of the drawing. A new profile view shows existing ground in red and proposed ground in black. As you study the profile, you should be able to identify the shape of the road in two locations and the shape of the pond in between (Figure 17.8).

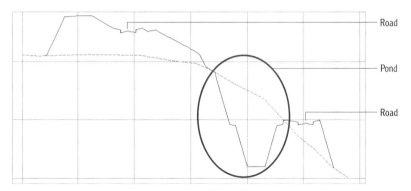

FIGURE 17.8 Several prominent design features can be noted within the quick profile.

6. Click the red polyline to show its grips, and then click one of the grips and move it to a new location. Notice the change to the quick profile. Use the red polyline and the quick profile to study the design of the project at several different locations.

7. Press Esc to clear the selection of the red polyline. Zoom in to the interior lots and identify the green feature line that forms the back sides of lots 68–70.

8. Click Quick Profile on the ribbon. When you're prompted to select an object, click the green feature line described in the previous step. The Create Quick Profiles dialog box opens.

9. Check the box next to EG.

10. Make sure that the Draw 3D Entity Profile option is checked, and then select Design Profile as the 3D Entity Profile Style.

11. Click OK, and then click an open area in the drawing. A new profile view is created that shows existing ground in red and a profile of the feature line in black. Notice how the feature line matches existing ground except for a certain length at either end where it ties into the finished ground elevations (Figure 17.9).

▶

The 3D Entity options were not available the first time you used the Quick Profile command because the red polyline you selected was a 2D object.

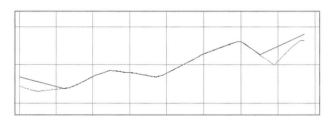

FIGURE 17.9 A quick profile view showing a feature line and a surface profile

Calculating Earthwork Volumes

Moving earth is one of the most expensive construction activities in a land development project. For this reason, there are two important questions that you will need to answer about nearly every grading design that you do.

▶ How much earth must be moved?

▶ How much earth must be brought into or transported away from the project site?

As a designer or engineer, one of your most important tasks is to answer these questions with the smallest values possible. The less soil that is required to be moved for a project, the more money you have saved the client and/or owner. Transporting soil to or from the site is also a very costly construction activity and therefore one that you should also minimize.

Understanding Earthwork Volumes

When talking about earthmoving, you will often use the terms *cut* and *fill*. Cut is soil material that is removed from the ground, and fill is soil material that is added to it. When an excavator takes a scoop of soil out of the ground, that soil is called cut. When that scoop is carried to another location on the site and dumped, it becomes fill. Grading the site is nothing more than a complex series of scoops and dumps: cuts and fills. At the end of the project, all of the scoops added together represent the cut value and all of the dumps added together represent the fill value. If these values are equal, then no soil needs to be transported to or from the site, thus reducing the cost of construction (not to mention the environmental impact). When cut and fill are equal, the condition is referred to as a *balanced* site. As a designer, you should strive to balance the earthwork of your designs whenever possible.

Using the Volumes Dashboard

Although there are several methods that can be used to calculate earthwork volumes in Civil 3D, I will only cover one of them in this book in detail: the *Volumes Dashboard*. The Volumes Dashboard command is found on the Analyze tab of the ribbon. Clicking this opens Panorama, which displays the Volumes Dashboard tab. Here you can add or create one or more TIN volume surfaces, and the cut and fill results are shown. You can also create *bounded volumes*, which are smaller areas within a volume surface that might represent individual lots or project phases. You can even generate detailed reports that are displayed within a browser or imported into the drawing, as shown in Figure 17.10.

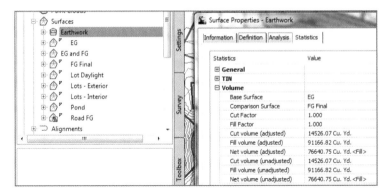

FIGURE 17.10   A TIN volume surface named Earthwork shown in Prospector and its volume results shown in the Surface Properties dialog box

WHAT'S A TIN VOLUME SURFACE?

As you may recall from Chapter 3, the acronym TIN stands for *Triangular Irregular Network*, which is a method of creating surfaces by drawing lines between 3D points to form triangles. A TIN surface is any surface that is created using this method. When you create a TIN *volume* surface, Civil 3D superimposes one TIN surface over another and creates a point at each location where the triangle edges cross. New triangles are then created by connecting the calculated points. The resulting surface has the same distinctive triangular shapes, but instead of elevations, the values it represents are differences in elevation between the two surfaces. These differences in elevation are referred to as *cut* when they are negative and *fill* when they are positive.

OTHER VOLUME METHODS

Civil 3D provides three additional methods for calculating cut and fill: the TIN Volume Surface, the Grading Volume Tools, and Quantity Takeoff Criteria.

TIN Volume Surface   You can create a TIN Volume Surface without using the Volumes Dashboard by simply using the Create Surface command and choosing TIN Volume Surface as the type. You can view the volume results for the surface by opening Surface Properties and clicking the Statistics tab.

Grading Volume Tools   You use the Grading Volume Tools with Grading Groups that have been assigned a volume base surface. Not only can the Grading Volume Tools report cut and fill, but they can also be used to adjust the design and even balance the design automatically.

OTHER VOLUME METHODS *(Continued)*

Quantity Takeoff Criteria   You use Quantity Takeoff Criteria to generate section-by-section volume calculations based on a sample line group. This method is nearly always associated with a corridor model for a transportation design project.

To use the Volumes Dashboard to calculate cut and fill for the example project, follow these steps:

1. Open the drawing named `Calculating Volumes.dwg` located in the Chapter 17 class data folder.

2. Click the Analyze tab of the ribbon, and then click Volumes Dashboard.

3. On the Volumes Dashboard tab of Panorama, click Create New Volume Surface.

4. In the Create Volume Surface dialog box, do the following:

   a. For Name, enter **Earthwork**.

   b. For Style, select _No Display.

   c. For Base Surface, select EG.

   d. For Comparison Surface, select FG Final.

   e. Click OK.

5. The cut and fill results are shown in Panorama. Here you see that the Cut Volume is a much smaller value than the Fill Volume. The project is not balanced, and the requirement for extra fill means that soil will have to be delivered to the project site. The design should be adjusted to bring it closer to balance. This can be accomplished by lowering the profiles and building pad feature lines to create more cut while eliminating the need for fill.

6. Click Earthwork, and then click Add Bounded Volume. When prompted to select Bounding Object, click the parcel area label of lot 1.

7. Repeat the previous step for lots 2 and 3. Click the plus sign next to Earthwork to expand the information below it. Note the individual cut and fill results that are shown for lots 1, 2, and 3.

8. Rename Earthwork.1 to **Lot 1**, Earthwork.2 to **Lot 2**, and Earthwork.3 to **Lot 3**. Check the boxes next to Lots 1, 2, and 3 and then click

Checking the boxes tells the Volume Dashboard to include information for these items in the report.

Generate Cut/Fill Report. Your browser should open, displaying a detailed cut-and-fill report for the overall earthwork as well as the three individual lots.

Labeling Design Surfaces

As you have done with every other type of design in this book, you need to annotate your surface design. Like all annotation, the information you convey here is almost as important as the design itself, particularly with regard to grading.

From a strictly documentation standpoint, the primary final product of a grading design is a set of design contours. By themselves, the contours are not very useful for construction, but once they are labeled, they begin to show the contractor exactly how to shape the land to meet its desired function. In some areas, contours alone do not provide enough detail and must be supplemented with labels that call out specific elevations and slopes. Labels that refer to the elevation of a single point on a drawing are often referred to as *spot elevations* or *spot grades*.

Although it was some time ago, you already learned how to create contour, spot, and slope labels in Chapter 4. You will apply those skills once again, but this time you'll label proposed elevations rather than existing elevations.

To use surface labeling to annotate your design, follow these steps:

1. Open the drawing named `Labeling Design Surfaces.dwg` located in the `Chapter 17` class data folder. The drawing is zoomed in to the first few lots at the beginning of Jordan Court. You will be adding labels in this area to provide information about contour elevations, slopes, and spot elevations.

2. Click the Annotate tab of the ribbon, and then click Add Labels.

3. In the Add Labels dialog box, do the following:

   a. For Feature, select Surface.

   b. For Label Type, select Contour – Multiple.

   c. Click Add.

4. When you're prompted to select a surface, click one of the red or blue contours in the drawing. You are then prompted to specify the first point.

5. Pick two points that draw a line through the contours in the front yard of lot 2 (Figure 17.11).

6. In the Add Labels dialog box, change Label Type to Contour – Single. Click Add.

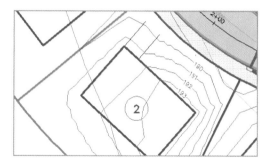

FIGURE 17.11 Contour labels in the front yard of lot 2

7. When you're prompted to select a surface, click one of the red or blue contours in the drawing. You are then prompted to select a contour line.

8. Click several contours on the Jordan Court road surface.

9. In the Add Labels dialog box, change the Label Type to Slope. Click Add. You are prompted to select a surface.

10. Click one of the red or blue contours in the drawing to select the surface. You are prompted to choose between the One-Point and Two-Point labeling options.

11. Press Enter to select the One-Point option. Pick a point near the center of the front yard for lot 2. The slope label indicates that the grade here is greater than the allowable 10%. This is something you will address at the end of this exercise.

12. In the Add Labels dialog box, change the Label Type to Spot Elevation.

13. Click Add, and select a red or blue contour when you're prompted to select a surface.

14. Using an Endpoint object snap, select the four corners of the lot 2 building pad. This will place a spot elevation label at each corner.

15. Press Esc to clear the previous command. Click the blue building pad feature line for lot 2. On the Edit Elevations panel of the ribbon, click Raise/Lower.

If the Edit Elevations panel is not visible, click Edit Elevations.

16. When you're prompted to specify the elevation difference, type -2 (**-0.691**) and press Enter. After a pause while the software rebuilds the surface, the contour labels, slope label, and spot elevation labels all update to reflect the change (Figure 17.12). The slope in the front yard of lot 2 is now less than the maximum of 10%.

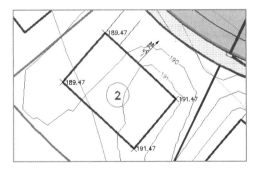

FIGURE 17.12   The labels update, indicating
that the maximum slope requirement is now met for lot 2.

THE NEW WAY TO BUILD

Although contours are the most common final product of a design surface, there are other ways that your grading design can be used and one in particular that is becoming more popular every day: a *machine model*. Contractors are now able to use GPS-guided excavation machines that can synchronize their operation with a computer-generated model representing the design of a project. Where does this model come from? You guessed it: Civil 3D and other programs like it. Although the contractor often has your model checked and reworked before uploading it to a machine in the field, it all starts with your grading design in Civil 3D. A well-defined, accurate, finished ground surface translates directly to a well-built, well-functioning project.

THE ESSENTIALS AND BEYOND

In this chapter, you combined several individual grading designs to create one master surface for the project. You then analyzed the slopes to locate problem areas and even corrected one of them. Next, you calculated earthwork volumes for the project and identified the need for design adjustments based on the findings. Finally, you used several types of annotation to convey information about your design and reveal a design flaw, which you addressed. All of these tools and skills are important in performing grading design for a project, and you will find yourself using them many times in projects to come.

Complete the additional exercise to apply some of these tools and skills to further refine the design for the example project.

THE ESSENTIALS AND BEYOND (Continued)

ADDITIONAL EXERCISE

Open the drawing named Grading Analysis and Labeling Beyond.dwg located in the Chapter 17 class data folder. This drawing contains the grading design as it should be at the end of the last exercise. Continue refining the design in the following ways:

▶ Adjust the road profiles and rebuild the corridor to improve the balance of cut and fill.

▶ Change the surface style so that you can see the slope ranges again. Adjust building pads to eliminate red areas and provide ample green areas in the front yards for driveway installation.

▶ Create slope labels for each lot to show the slope of the front yard.

▶ After adjusting the corridor, you will need to adjust the building pads to account for the change in road elevation. Use the slope analysis and labels to help you adjust your design.

Visit www.sybex.com/go/civil2013essentials to download a video of the author completing this exercise. You can also download the Answers to Additional Exercises Appendix which contains even more information about completing this exercise.

CHAPTER 18

From Design to Construction

You have now completed all of the major design tasks in the example project. It's now time to prepare for construction by documenting your design, determining material quantities, and estimating construction costs. In this chapter, you will learn how to use your design model to perform these tasks.

▶ **Calculating quantities**

▶ **Creating individual sheets**

▶ **Creating multiple sheets using Plan Production**

Calculating Quantities

Throughout the land development process—whether it's during the conceptual phase, design phase, or construction phase—there will be much attention focused on cost. As a designer, you will constantly receive inquiries about the cost to build certain parts of the project or even the entire project. A fundamental piece of information that you'll need in order to do a cost estimate is the *quantity* of each item or material. There are several powerful AutoCAD® Civil 3D® software tools that can extract quantity information from your design. In fact, you have already experienced one of them in Chapter 17 when you calculated cut and fill volumes for your grading design. In this chapter, you will study two more methods: using the QTO Manager and using section volumes.

Calculating Quantities Using QTO Manager

QTO Manager is an all-purpose utility for compiling information about quantities in your design. (QTO stands for quantity takeoff.) When you click QTO Manager on the Analyze ribbon tab, Panorama will open, displaying a new tab titled QTO Manager (Figure 18.1). The main feature of this tab is the *pay item* list. Each pay item in the list can be assigned to any number of objects in the drawing. QTO Manager works with nearly any type of Civil 3D or AutoCAD® software entity.

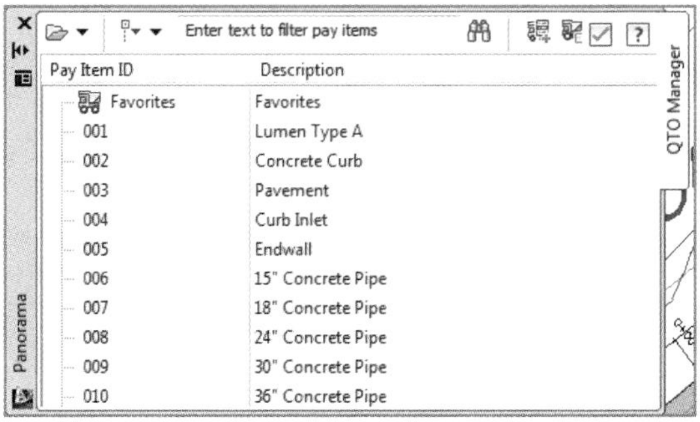

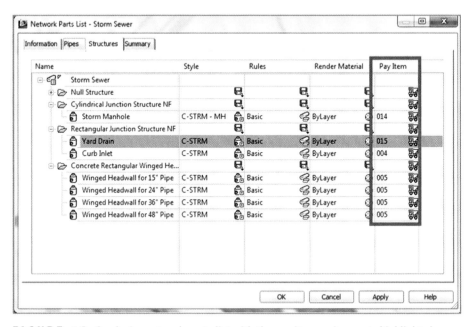

FIGURE 18.1   The QTO Manager tab of Panorama

You may have already noticed that certain Civil 3D objects have a Pay Item property that is already integrated into the properties of the object. For example, a pipe network parts list has a Pay Item column where you can associate a pipe or structure with one of the same pay items that QTO Manager uses (Figure 18.2).

FIGURE 18.2   A pipe network parts list with the pay item assignments highlighted

Also, the code set styles you used in Chapters 10 and 11 to control the display and labeling of corridor sections can also be used to assign pay items to a corridor (Figure 18.3).

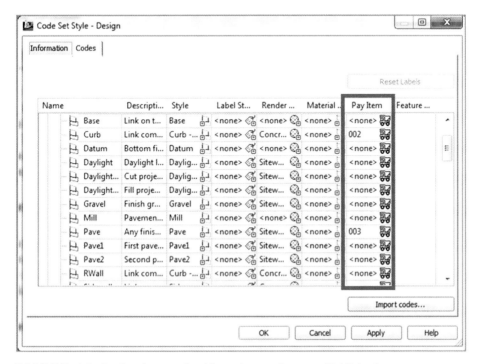

FIGURE 18.3 A code set style with pay item assignments highlighted

Once you have assigned pay items to objects in your drawing, you can execute the Takeoff command, which will gather up all of the quantities and present them to you in a report.

To calculate lighting, pavement, curb, and storm network quantities for your design, complete the following steps:

1. Open the drawing named Calculating Quantities Using QTO.dwg located in the Chapter 18 class data folder. The drawing is zoomed in to the recreation area, where you can see the proposed parking lot. There are several symbols representing light poles located around the perimeter of the parking lot. The paved area has been hatched with a dot pattern.

2. Click the Analyze tab of the ribbon, and then click QTO Manager. Panorama will open, displaying the QTO Manager tab.

3. Right-click Lumen Type A, and then click Assign Pay Item, as shown in Figure 18.4.

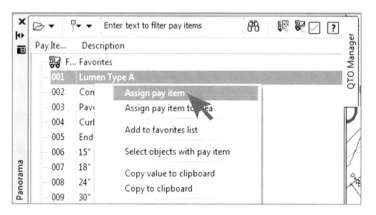

FIGURE 18.4 Assigning a pay item to an object in the drawing

If you look at the command line, you'll see that Pay item 001 assigned to object was reported each time you clicked a light pole.

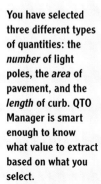

You have selected three different types of quantities: the *number* of light poles, the *area* of pavement, and the *length* of curb. QTO Manager is smart enough to know what value to extract based on what you select.

4. Click the six light pole symbols and press Enter. There is no apparent change to the drawing, but the association between the pay item and the blocks has been established.

5. On the QTO Manager tab of Panorama, right-click Pavement and select Assign Pay Item To Area.

6. At the command line, type **O** and press Enter to invoke the Select Object option. Click the hatch representing the paved area, and then press Enter. The command line should report that pay item 003 was assigned to an area.

7. Right-click Concrete Curb and select Assign Pay Item. Zoom in to the parking lot and select the two blue polylines representing the face of the curb: one for the perimeter of the parking lot and the other outlining the island in the center.

8. Press Enter. Right-click Lumen Type A and click Select Objects With Pay Item. Verify that all six light pole symbols are selected, as shown in Figure 18.5.

This pay item was already assigned within the file before you opened it.

9. Repeat step 8 for 18″ (450mm) Concrete Pipe. Zoom out and note the locations where 18″ (450mm) concrete pipe has been utilized in the design.

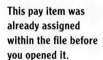

10. On the Analyze tab of the ribbon, click Takeoff. The Compute Quantity Takeoff dialog box opens.

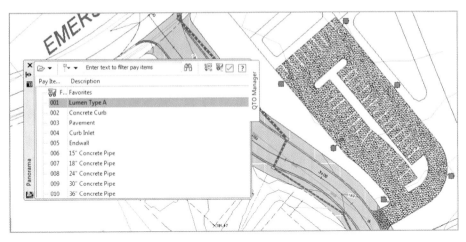

FIGURE 18.5 Light poles are selected through QTO Manager.

IMAGINE THE POSSIBILITIES

Imagine associating all of the key components of your design with pay items in QTO Manager. You now have a spatial relationship between a material list and your project. This becomes especially useful during construction. For example, a contractor could use this to determine where to stage different sizes of pipes until it is time to install them. If an item is unavailable, the contractor could determine which areas of the project are impacted. These are just two examples of the usefulness of the QTO feature even before a report is generated.

11. Verify that Report Type is set to Summary and uncheck the Report Selected Pay Items Only box. Click Compute.

12. In the Quantity Takeoff Report dialog box, select Summary (HTML) .xsl from the drop-down list at the lower-left corner. A summary report is displayed that includes the pay items you assigned as well as those that had already been assigned to the storm pipe network (Figure 18.6).

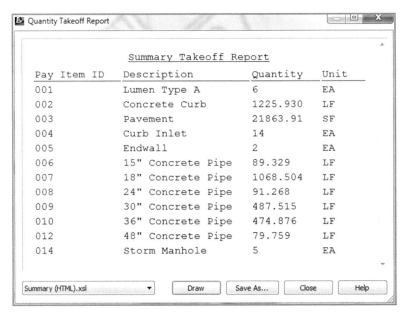

FIGURE 18.6 A summary takeoff report

A NOTE ABOUT UNITS

Throughout this chapter, you'll notice that two values are provided for units of measurement. The first value is provided for the imperial system that is used in the United States, and the second value in parentheses is provided for the metric system that is used in many other countries. These values most often represent imperial feet and metric meters. It is important to note that generally only the numeric values are entered in the software, not terms like feet or meters. Also, you should know that the two numbers provided are not necessarily equal. In most cases, they are similar values that are rounded to work efficiently in their respective measurement systems.

Calculating Quantities Using Sectional Volumes

Certification Objective

As discussed earlier, QTO Manager is an all-purpose tool that responds to many types of AutoCAD and Civil 3D objects. Sectional volumes, on the other hand, have a very specific application: they apply only to corridor sections created from a sample line group.

To calculate sectional volumes, you first need *quantity takeoff criteria*, which is a generalized list of the quantities you want to measure. For example, quantity takeoff criteria for road materials would typically include asphalt, base, subbase, and curb (Figure 18.7).

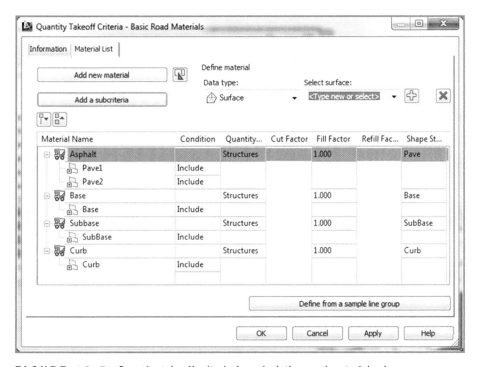

FIGURE 18.7 Quantity takeoff criteria for calculating road material volumes

The quantity takeoff criteria you define can be stored in your company template for use on future projects. With quantity takeoff criteria in place, you can launch the Compute Materials command and match the actual objects sampled by your sample lines with the generic material names of the quantity takeoff criteria. Civil 3D then samples these shapes throughout the sample line group and adds their sections to the others that have been sampled. Figure 18.8 shows the additional sections listed in Prospector after running the Compute Materials command.

Finally, you choose a method to output the calculations, which will result in either an external report or a table within the drawing. In the case of earthwork calculations, there is a third output method: a mass haul diagram.

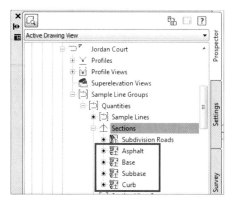

FIGURE 18.8 Sections created by the
Compute Materials command are highlighted in Prospector.

WHAT IS A MASS HAUL DIAGRAM?

A mass haul diagram is a graphical representation of the earthmoving activities for a linear project such as a road. This diagram helps a contractor analyze and plan how earth that is excavated from one part of the project will be moved to other parts of the project. The image shown here is an example of a mass haul diagram.

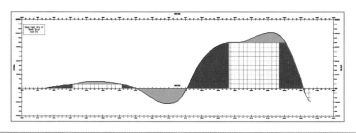

To calculate material quantities for Jordan Court, complete these steps:

1. Open the drawing named `Calculating Quantities Using Sections
   .dwg` located in the `Chapter 18` class data folder. This drawing contains the Subdivision Roads corridor and a sample line group named Quantities. You will use this sample line group to calculate road material quantities for Jordan Court.

2. Click the Analyze ribbon tab, and then click Compute Materials. The Select A Sample Line Group dialog box opens.

3. Click OK to accept the default alignment and sample line group. The Compute Materials – Quantities dialog box opens.

In this drawing, Quantities is the only sample line group that was created for the Jordan Court alignment.

4. Select Basic Road Materials from the drop-down list under Quantity Takeoff Criteria.

5. Click Map Objects With Same Name. The Object Name column will be populated with named shapes from the corridor (Figure 18.9).

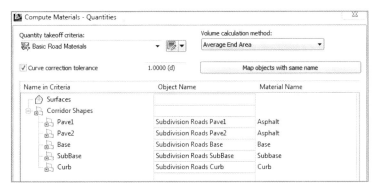

FIGURE 18.9   Corridor shapes assigned to materials

6. Click OK. After a pause, the Command: prompt returns to the command line. The computations have been completed, but there is no visible change to the drawing.

7. On the Analyze ribbon tab, click Volume Report. The Report Quantities dialog box opens.

8. Click the folder icon for Select A Style Sheet. Click Select Material.xsl and then click Open.

During the pause, Civil 3D samples four sections for each sample line, one for each material.

9. Click OK to dismiss the Report Quantities dialog box. Your browser will open and may display a warning dialog about running scripts. Click Yes to continue. The report will be displayed in your browser, showing the area, volume, and cumulative volume for each material at the location of each sample line.

10. Scroll to the bottom of the report and view the values in the Cum. Vol. column. These are the total quantities of the four different materials that will be required to build Jordan Court (Figure 18.10).

Station: 23+97.711				
	Asphalt	7.70	10.32	377.44
	Base	13.81	19.26	755.70
	Subbase	40.68	62.06	2766.07
	Curb	5.24	7.19	265.86

FIGURE 18.10   Material quantities for Jordan Court

Creating Individual Sheets

One of the most important tasks you will perform as a designer is the effective documentation of your design. Regardless of how accurate and well designed your models may be, most of the construction that takes place will be based on paper drawings. As the preparer of these drawings, you are responsible for ensuring that your design documentation contains all the essential information and is displayed in a way that's suitable for construction. Fortunately, Civil 3D has tools that will automatically extract the information you need and expedite this process.

Although creating individual sheets is more of a basic AutoCAD task, it is a good place to start because it gets you thinking about the process of documenting your design. It also enables you to familiarize yourself with the Civil 3D label properties that make sheet creation easier. For example, Civil 3D will automatically resize labels based on the drawing scale or viewport scale as well as orient labels to a specific view.

To create an Overall Plan sheet, follow these steps:

1. Open the drawing named `Creating Individual Sheets.dwg` located in the `Chapter 18` class data folder.

2. If you do not see the Model and Layout1 tabs at the bottom of your screen, right-click the Model icon and select Display Layout And Model Tabs, as shown in Figure 18.11.

FIGURE 18.11   Displaying layout and model tabs

3. Right-click the Layout1 tab and select From Template. The Select Template From File dialog box opens.

▶

"From Template" means to create a new layout by selecting a template drawing (.dwt).

4. Browse to the `Chapter 18` class data folder. Click `Civil 3D (Imperial) Plan Only.dwt` (`Civil 3D (Metric) Plan Only.dwt`), and then click Open. The Insert Layout(s) dialog box opens.

5. Click ARCH E Plan Only 50 Scale (ISO A0 Plan Only 1 To 750), and then click OK.

6. Click the ARCH E Plan Only 50 Scale (ISO A0 Plan Only 1 To 750) layout tab to make it active. Then double-click it and change the name to **Overall Plan.** You can now see the newly created layout that is currently an empty title block.

7. Double-click in the center of the layout to activate the viewport.

8. At the command line, type **ZE** and press Enter to perform a Zoom – Extents. The drawing objects will now come into view.

9. Pan and zoom within the viewport so that the plan view of the project fills the viewport. Note the size of the lot labels, which appear to be much too large for the current display scale.

Make sure to keep the viewport activated for the next few steps.

10. Change the viewport scale to 1″ = 50′ (1:750) by selecting it from the menu at the bottom of your screen, as shown in Figure 18.12. The viewport scale changes slightly and all of the labels resize according to the newly selected scale.

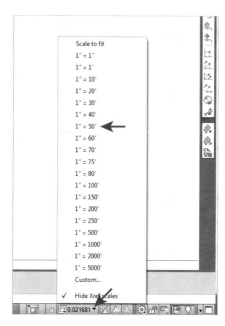

FIGURE 18.12 Changing the scale of the viewport

11. On the Home tab of the ribbon, click Layer Properties. The Layer Properties Manager window opens.

12. Under Filters, click All. Then right-click one of the layer names in the Name column and click Select All on the context menu, as shown in Figure 18.13.

13. Scroll right and click any icon in the VP Freeze column. This will freeze all layers in the current viewport.

14. Under Filters, click Overall Plan. Right-click one of the layer names in the Name column, and then click Select All.

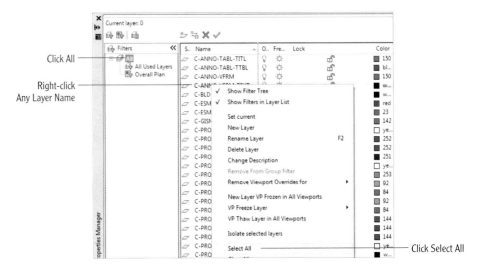

Click All

Right-click
Any Layer Name

Click Select All

FIGURE 18.13   Selecting all layers in the Layer Properties dialog box

15. Click any icon in the VP Freeze column, and then close the Layer
Properties Manager window. This thaws the selected layers in the
current viewport. You now have a layout that shows a simplified
overall plan for the project (Figure 18.14). This type of plan is usually
placed in the front of a plan set to serve as a low-detail, comprehensive view of the project.

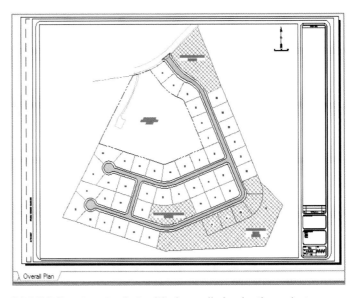

FIGURE 18.14   A simplified overall plan for the project

Creating Multiple Sheets Using Plan Production

Certification
Objective

For certain types of projects, you may need to create multiple sheets that are similar in format and in the type of information that they show. A classic example of this is the plan and profile sheet used for linear projects such as roads or pipelines. This type of drawing is typically smaller scale, so it requires multiple sheets to cover the whole project. Each drawing in the series is the same except that it shows a different part of the site. Civil 3D provides *Plan Production* tools, which are used for creating multiple sheets in a series. Using Plan Production involves two primary steps: creating view frames and creating sheets.

Creating View Frames

A view frame is a rectangle that represents the area that Plan Production is supposed to show in the plan view of a given sheet. Because a view frame is a Civil 3D object, you can assign a style to it and label it. View frames are accompanied by match lines that identify where two sheets meet. Match lines are also Civil 3D objects, capable of being stylized and labeled.

The Create View Frames command launches a wizard that steps you through the process of creating view frames. The size and scale of the view frames originate from a drawing template that you specify. The default settings of the wizard will create evenly spaced view frames that cover the entire alignment and are oriented to it. Once the view frames have been created, you can move and rotate them to the desired configuration.

To begin setting up plan and profile sheets for Jordan Court by creating view frames, follow these steps:

1. Open the drawing named Creating View Frames.dwg located in the Chapter 18 class data folder.

2. Click the Output ribbon tab, and then click Create View Frames. The first dialog box of the wizard, Create View Frames – Alignment, is displayed.

3. Select Jordan Court as the alignment and click Next. The Create View Frames – Sheets dialog box opens.

4. Click the ellipsis for Template For Plan And Profile Sheet. The Select Layout As Sheet Template dialog box opens.

Notice that you can apply a user-specified station range for cases where you do not want sheets created for an entire alignment.

⬚ 5. Click the ellipsis for Drawing Template File Name. This opens the Select Layout As Sheet Template dialog box.

6. Browse to the Chapter 18 class data folder and select Civil 3D (Imperial) Plan and Profile.dwt (Civil 3D (Metric) Plan and Profile.dwt). Click Open.

7. Select ARCH E Plan And Profile 20 Scale (ISO A0 Plan And Profile 1 To 250) and click OK. You are returned to the Create View Frames – Sheets dialog box.

It's All About the Template

In steps 6 and 7 of this exercise, you chose a template as part of the process of creating view frames. This template is very important because it sets the size and scale of the view frame and provides the title block and other important components of the final sheets. If you want to use Plan Production in your office, ask your CAD manager to set up a series of Plan Production templates for you.

8. Click Next. Examine the settings in the Create View Frames – View Frame Group dialog box. Click Next without making any changes.

9. Examine the settings in the Create View Frames – Match Lines dialog box. Click Next without making any changes.

▶ 10. Examine the settings in the Create View Frames – Profile Views dialog box. Click Create View Frames without making any changes. Four view frames are created in the drawing along the Jordan Court alignment, as shown in Figure 18.15.

It may seem strange to select a profile view and band set so early in the process, but these choices factor into how the profile view will fit within the view frame.

11. Click one of the view frames, and then click the diamond-shaped grip that appears at the center of the view frame. Move your cursor along the alignment and observe how the view frame maintains its orientation to the alignment as it moves.

12. Test out the function of the square grip and the circular grip. Notice that the square grip moves the view frame in any direction without changing its rotation. The circular grip rotates the view frame about its center point. When you begin the next exercise, the view frames will have been repositioned for you to get the best sheet configuration possible. These grips were used to reposition the view frames.

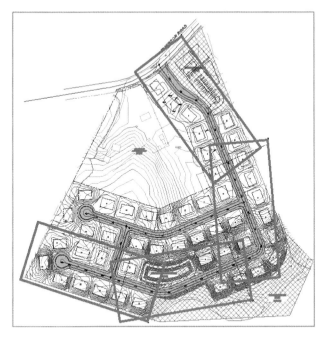

FIGURE 18.15   Four view frames created along the Jordan Court alignment

Creating Sheets

Once the view frames are in place, you can then use the Create Sheets command to automatically generate layouts that display what is contained within the view frames. In the case of plan and profile sheets, the Create Sheets command will also create a profile view for each view frame that corresponds to the station range shown in plan view. Each plan and profile view will then be arranged in a single sheet, providing two views of the same design area. This plan and profile sheet configuration is a very common way of documenting the design of linear features such as roads, railroads, and pipelines.

To create plan and profile sheets based on the view frames in your drawing, follow these steps:

1. Open the drawing named Creating Sheets.dwg located in the Chapter 18 class data folder.

2. Click the Output tab of the ribbon, and then click Create Sheets. This will open the first dialog box in the Create Sheets Wizard: Create Sheets – View Frame Group And Layouts.

3. Verify that the All Layouts In Current Drawing option is selected under Layout Creation, and that North is selected under Choose The North Arrow Block to Align in Layouts. Click Next.

Sheet Placement and Storage

When you're using the Create Sheets command, there are three options for the final destination of the sheets that you create. The option used in this exercise is to simply create the new sheets as additional layout tabs in the current drawing. You could also create a new drawing and place all of the new layout tabs there. In this case, your current drawing would be XREFed to provide the graphical information for the plan view. An XREF, or *external reference*, is AutoCAD's way of showing one drawing within another. For the profile view, the alignment, profile, and pipe network (if applicable) would be data referenced into the resulting file and used to create a new set of profile views. Data references, as you learned in Chapter 2, are Civil 3D's way of showing one drawing's design data within another. Yet another option is to create multiple new drawing files with a set number of layouts in each drawing. If your goal is to improve the performance of each individual sheet, then this option is the best choice. If your goal is simplicity and accessibility, then the option used for the exercise is the best choice.

4. Examine the settings in the Create Sheets – Sheet Set dialog box. Notice that the Create Sheets command integrates with the AutoCAD Sheet Set Manager function. This added benefit enables you to store and manage the resulting sheets in an AutoCAD sheet set if desired.

5. Click Next. This will advance the wizard to the Create Sheets – Profile Views dialog box.

6. Under Other Profile View Options, click the Choose Settings option. Then click Profile View Wizard. The Create Multiple Profile Views – Profile Height dialog box opens. This is the first in a series of dialog boxes contained within the Create Multiple Profile Views Wizard.

This option will cause the profile to show in the middle of the profile view, roughly halfway between the top and bottom of the grid.

7. Change the Profile View Datum By option to Mean Elevation. Click Next to advance to the Create Multiple Profile Views – Profile Display Options dialog box.

8. Scroll to the right until you see the Labels column. For the Jordan Court FGCL profile, select the Curves-Grades-Breaks label set. For the EG – Surface (11) profile, select the _No Labels label set (Figure 18.16).

Create Multiple Profile Views - Profile Display Options

General

Specify profile display options:

Name	Style	Ov...	Labels	Alignment	Station Start
Jordan C...	Design Pr...	☐	Curves-Grades-Bre...	Jordan C...	0+00.00'
EG - Surf...	Existing ...	☐	No Labels	Jordan C...	0+00.00'

Station Range

Profile View Height

▷ Profile Display Options

Pipe Network Display

Data Bands

FIGURE 18.16 Assigning label sets to the profiles

9. Click Finish to return to the Create Sheets – Profile Views dialog box.

10. Click Create Sheets. A warning dialog box will open, informing you that you must save the drawing to continue. Click OK.

11. When you're prompted for the profile view origin, pick a point in the open area to the north of the site. Four new profile views will be created along with four new layout tabs. Also, the Sheet Set Manager window will open, displaying the names of four sheets (Figure 18.17).

12. Click the first new layout tab. Note how the layout has been automatically configured to show the plan in the top view and the corresponding profile in the bottom view (Figure 18.18).

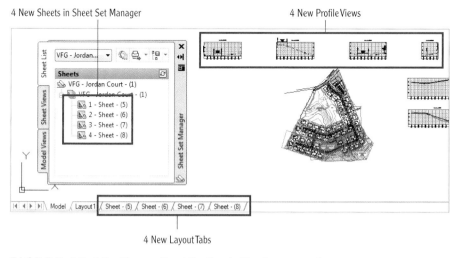

4 New Sheets in Sheet Set Manager

4 New Profile Views

4 New Layout Tabs

FIGURE 18.17 The results of the Create Sheets command

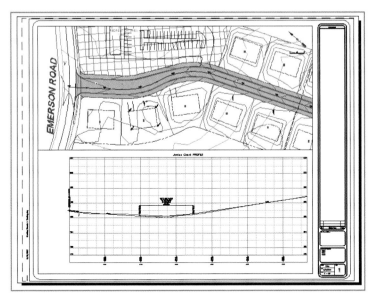

FIGURE 18.18 A plan and profile sheet resulting from the Create Sheets command

13. Click the remaining layout tabs to review the sheets that have been configured. Notice how all the lot labels read upright, regardless of their orientation of the plan view. This is a function of the area label style used to label the lot numbers. Also notice that the north arrow in each sheet has been rotated automatically to reflect the correct north orientation. This is because of a feature within the Create Sheets command.

THE ESSENTIALS AND BEYOND

In this chapter, you learned how to utilize your design to gather and convey important information about how the project will be built and what it will cost. One might argue that a design is only as good as the information it is able to convey. As you learned in this chapter, the models you create in Civil 3D must provide adequate and accurate information to be taken into the field and constructed using real materials such as soil, asphalt, and concrete. In this final chapter, you explored some of the ways in which the electronic version of the project becomes the real-world version.

In the additional exercise, you will employ your knowledge of the quantity analysis and sheet production functions that you studied in this chapter to convey even more information about the example design.

THE ESSENTIALS AND BEYOND *(Continued)*

ADDITIONAL EXERCISE

Open the drawing named Sheets and Quantities Beyond.dwg located in the Chapter 18 class data folder. This drawing contains an alternate layout for the detention pond in a different location. Complete the following tasks to generate information about the design and create documentation of the design.

▶ Use QTO Manager to assign the Chain Link Fence pay item to the fence around the pond and on the north side of the conservation area. Run a report to determine the length of the fence.

▶ Compute materials for the corridor along the Madison Lane alignment and create a material volume report to determine the volume of asphalt, base, subbase, and curb.

▶ Create view frames and plan and profile sheets for Madison Lane.

Visit www.sybex.com/go/civil2013essentials to download a video of the author completing this exercise. You can also download the Answers to Additional Exercises Appendix which contains even more information about completing this exercise.

AutoCAD Civil 3D 2013 Certification

Autodesk certifications are industry-recognized credentials that can help you succeed in your design career, providing benefits to both you and your employer. Getting certified is a reliable validation of skills and knowledge, and it can lead to accelerated professional development, improved productivity, and enhanced credibility.

This Autodesk Official Training Guide can be an effective component of your exam preparation. Autodesk highly recommends (and we agree!) that you schedule regular time to prepare, review the most current exam preparation roadmap available at www.autodesk.com/certification, use Autodesk Official Training Guides, take a class at an Authorized Training Center (find ATCs near you here: www.autodesk.com/atc), and use a variety of resources to prepare for your certification—including plenty of actual hands-on experience.

To help you focus your studies on the skills you'll need for these exams, the following tables show objectives that could potentially appear on an exam and in what chapter you can find information on that topic—and when you go to that chapter, you'll find certification icons like the one in the margin here.

Certification Objective

Table A.1 is for the Autodesk Certified Professional Exam and lists the section, exam objectives, and chapter where the information is found. The sections and exam objectives listed in the table are from the Autodesk Certification Exam Guide.

These Autodesk exam objectives were accurate at press time; please refer to www.autodesk.com/certification for the most current exam roadmap and objectives.

Good luck preparing for your certification!

TABLE A.1 Certified Professional Exam sections and objectives

Topic	Learning Objective	Chapter
User Interface	Navigate the user interface	1
	Use the functions on the Prospector Tab	1
	Use functions on the Settings Tab	1
Styles	Create and use object styles	2,4,6,8,11,13,15,17
	Create and use label styles	2,4,6,8,11,13,15,17
Lines & Curves	Use the line and curve commands	1
	Use the Transparent command	1
Points	Create points using the Point Creation command	3
	Create points by importing point data	3
	Use point groups to control the display of points	3
Surfaces	Create and edit surfaces	4,16
	Use styles and settings to display surface information	4,16
	Create a surface by assembling fundamental data	4,16
	Use styles to analyze surface display results	4,16
Parcels	Create parcels using parcel layout tools	12
	Design a parcel layout	12
	Select parcel styles to change the display of parcels	13
	Select styles to annotate parcels	13
	Create alignments	5
Alignments	Design a geometric layout	5

(Continues)

TABLE A.1 *(Continued)*

Topic	Learning Objective	Chapter
Profiles & Profile Views	Create a surface profile	7
	Design a profile	7
	Create a layout profile	7
	Create a profile view style	8
	Create a profile view	8
Corridors	Design and create a corridor	9
	Derive information and data from a corridor	18
	Design and create an intersection	9
Sections & Section Views	Create and analyze sections and section views	10
Pipe Networks	Design and create a pipe network	14
Grading	Design and create a grading model	16
	Create a grading model feature line	16
Managing and Sharing Data	Use data shortcuts to share/manage data	2
	Create a data sharing setup	2
Plan Production	Generate a sheet set using plan production	18
	Create a sheet set	18
Survey	Use description keys to control the display of points created from survey data	3
	Use figure prefixes to control the display of linework generated from survey data	3
	Create a topographic/boundary drawing from field data	3

INDEX

Note to the Reader: Throughout this index **boldfaced** page numbers indicate primary discussions of a topic. *Italicized* page numbers indicate illustrations.